Kenya: From Colonization
to Independence, 1888–1970

KENYA

From Colonization to
Independence, 1888–1970

R. Mugo Gatheru

McFarland & Company, Inc., Publishers
Jefferson, North Carolina, and London

LIBRARY OF CONGRESS ONLINE CATALOG DATA

Gatheru, R. Mugo, 1925–
    Kenya : from colonization to Independence, 1888–1970 /
R. Mugo Gatheru.
        p.   cm.
    Includes bibliographical references and index.

    ISBN 0-7864-2199-1 (softcover : 50# alkaline paper)

    1. Kenya—History.   I. Title.
    DT433.557 .G37   2005
    967.62—dc22   2005010601

British Library cataloguing data are available

*On the front cover: top ©2005 ImageState; bottom Jomo Kenyatta,
first African prime minister of Kenya, 1963*

Manufactured in the United States of America

McFarland & Company, Inc., Publishers
    Box 611, Jefferson, North Carolina 28640
        www.mcfarlandpub.com

Acknowledgments

A deep gratitude is owed to Mr. Charles Fisk of Flushing, New York, an Englishman (now deceased) who traded with the Kenyan people as far back as 1902 and who later emigrated to the United States of America. He was one of the Europeans that Sir Harry Johnstone, then Commissioner for the Uganda Protectorate, referred to as "white freebooters." I am indebted to Mr. Fisk for much background information about the European and Asian traders of those days.

I must pay special tribute to those authors whose books I have quoted by way of illustration or emphasis. In particular, I thank Professor Margery Perham and Mary Bull, who edited *The Diaries of Lord Lugard*, Volume 1 (London, 1959), and George Bennett, former senior lecturer in commonwealth history at the University of Oxford, whose book, *Kenya—A Political History: The Colonial Period*, has been extremely helpful to me.

I am very thankful to Professor Donald Rothchild of the University of California at Davis for his suggestions, and for reading the first draft of this manuscript.

I am also grateful to the late Mzee Kenyatta, who offered me a job as an assistant editor of *Sauti Ya-Mwafrika* (*The African Voice*) from 1947 to 1949—a position which gave me an opportunity to experience the adversities that faced the Kenya African Union's leaders and the organization itself. In addition, I should pay my gratitude to the late Hon. Mr. E. W. Mathu, who introduced me to Mzee Kenyatta in 1947 and also acted as treasurer for my travel fund before I left Kenya for the United States by way of India.

In the course of my sabbatical leave in 1977, I was reunited with the late Dr. Gikonyo Kiano, previously Minister of Labor in the Kenyan government, who was my classmate in the elementary school at Kahuti in Fort Hall (now Muranga) in 1938, and who read the rough draft of this manuscript and made important suggestions, especially details relating to the Lancaster Round-Table Conference in 1960 and also to deliberations in which he participated, as well as information about the eventual collapse of the East African Community.

I should thank the staffs of the University of Nairobi Library; the McMillan Memorial Library; the Institute of African Studies; and the Headmaster of Martin Luther Primary School in Makandara, Nairobi, Mr. Permenas Kamau Muguimi, who not only gave me many details about the "Muthirigu," emotional nationalistic songs sung from 1929 through the 1930s by Kikuyu Christians, but also provided information on the Kikuyu Karinga Independent Churches and Schools, the Kikuyu Independent Churches and Schools, and the difference between the two organizations.

I am also very thankful to Mr. Evanson Gicuhi Wa Ngiabi, Assistant Registrar of the University of Nairobi, for his generosity and hospitality in letting me use his home in Nairobi as a base of operations while doing my research work.

Special thanks go also to Peter Kamau Gachwe, Secretary representing Fort Hall (now Muranga) at the Mau Mau Central War Council before Operation Anvil in 1954. He related to me that important weapons, especially guns, were obtained in Nairobi and then sent to the fighting forces in the forests and that Ndondora, a few miles from Nairobi, was the real center of transition. His details corroborated the account of the incident at Naivasha on May 12, 1950, regarding the name "Mau Mau."

Finally, I should thank my wife, Dolores, for taking very good care of our three small children while I was away doing research work in Kenya.

Contents

Preface

Kenya is independent, but we have yet to weigh the rights and wrongs of that independence.

Is Kenya to be condemned for the massacre at Lari of British loyalists by Kikuyu freedom fighters? If so, then the history of Great Britain before and after the "Hola Camp Massacre," a similar massacre of Kikuyu by loyalist guards at a detention camp during the Emergency, stands for nothing. Politicians and generals have the awful responsibility of deciding by which methods to achieve what each nation believes to be its legitimate ends. The reckoning must wait until later. To take an innocent life is difficult to justify at any time, but although the morality of the Hiroshima bomb is debated still, there is less argument on the validity of the Allied cause.

Perhaps we are too close to those grim days in Kenya for a final verdict, but it would be desirable to replace recrimination with understanding. To this end, we must analyze the historical causes of Mau Mau and delve further into the colonial history of the country. That history, for better or worse, explains the forging of Kenya from 1888 to 1970.

The object of this volume, therefore, is to deal effectively with the molding of the present-day Kenya. The book may perhaps offend some people, but it is a small man who cannot face the truth. Propaganda is certainly not the motive for its writing. The aim is not to stir up the ashes of discord, any more than historians of two world wars seek to revive hatred of Germany. However, insidious neo-colonialism still exists in the world, and with it one cause of war, at least, which is avoidable.

1

It will not be necessary to deal with the entire range of the early histories of the Chinese, Indian, Persian, and Portuguese contacts with the East Coast of Africa, and the word "Indian" is sometimes used in this book as a noun or adjective in reference to the Hindus, Goans, Pakistanis and Punjabis in Kenya. This book will also deal briefly with the problem of "multi-racial society" which was highlighted by Sir Philip Mitchel, the Governor of Kenya from 1944 to 1952, as a result of Arab, Indian, and European presences in the country.

There are few parts of the world where so marked a variety of climate is concentrated in an area as small as that of Kenya, which is only about twice the size of the United Kingdom. Although the line of the Equator passes almost through the center of the country, there is an eternally snow-capped mountain, Kenya, from which the country takes its name, almost directly below it. There are great highlands in the interior which are cool by day and chilly at night. It is a very beautiful country.

The shortest land route from the coast to the shores of Lake Victoria, Nyanza—about six hundred miles—is still the original line of the Kenya-Uganda Railway, constructed by the British Government between 1895 and 1901 to open up the country and provide rapid access to the Uganda Protectorate.

Within a few hours' travel from the palm-fringed beaches of the Indian Ocean at Mombasa, the hills of the uplands are covered with evergreen forests, and blackberry bushes are plentiful in the open spaces. About 360 miles from the coast, the traveler may stand on the forest-clad heights of the Kikuyu Escarpment, 7,800 feet above sea level, and see the great Rift Valley, about 2,000 feet below. A few miles to the northwest, an extinct volcano thrusts itself upward from the depths of the valley, its black mass as forbidding as Vesuvius itself. In other directions, apart from a few scattered hills, the bottom of the valley is almost treeless and appears fairly level until, in the far distance, it reaches the range of hills which form its western limit.

The railway makes its way gradually down the eastern wall of the valley for about a hundred miles, passing several small lakes—once the haunt of vast herds of hippopotami—until the traveler emerges at the range of hills known as the Mau Escarpment, crowned with dense forest, where occasionally there is heavy hoar frost in the early morning.

It was against this background that the drama of Mau Mau was enacted—and the tragedy is that it would never have occurred if the actors in the drama had been able to settle their differences in other ways.

After the Emergency in Kenya was declared in the autumn of 1952, the British, European, and American public heard much about Mau Mau.

Throughout 1953 and 1954, the press and radio carried stories of Mau Mau atrocities and government attempts to stamp out the terrorists. In 1955, the newspapers began to report that the British armed forces were getting things under control. Films were made about Mau Mau, such as *Simba* and *Something of Value*. Several novels and other books on the subject appeared. Some of these, in the opinion of this author, did contribute to an understanding of the reasons why Mau Mau arose in Kenya.

At the time of the uprising, many felt mistakenly that the emergence of Mau Mau implied that large sections of Kikuyu had "reverted" to savagery. Others assumed that the Kikuyu were trying to slaughter all the white people in Kenya. And yet during the anxious years, according to official statistics, only ninety white people were killed by Mau Mau, compared with over 2,000 Africans.

Then, too, some books declared that Mau Mau was a kind of religion which Africans had adopted because they were opposed to Christianity. In actual fact, such accusations were misleading. Although Mau Mau was a reaction against a particular form of European settler domination, it was not in essence a racial movement. The Kenyan Revolution—for such it was—cannot be explained so simply, any more than the American Revolution can be explained in terms of the Boston Tea Party. The true explanation will, it is hoped, emerge from this book.

First, as has already been said, the history of Mau Mau is part of the history of Kenya. As historians, we hope that our physical, if not mental, detachment from the Kenyan people during those critical years enables us to synthesize events more accurately even than those who participated in them—a burning man does not always judge the intensity of the fire!

It will be noted that the word "whites" has been used in the book. The word "natives" referred to Kenyan Africans from the time of the Imperial British East Africa Company until 1947, when Mr. Eliud Wambu Mathu, the first nominated African member in the history of the Kenya Legislative Council, in 1945 introduced a motion which, in effect, repealed all references to Black Kenyans as "natives" instead of "Africans." The word "natives" as then used had political, racial, economic, and social connotations. The employment in this book of the word "whites" has no derogatory intention. This should be made immediately clear, for otherwise the use of the term might impart an unintentionally nationalistic flavor, even a touch of xenophobia, to that which follows.

R. Mugo Gatheru
Rancho Cordova, California
USA

Introduction

The opening up of the African continent to direct European influence during the nineteenth century was probably the most important series of events in Africa's history. New currents of thought as well as technical skills were introduced, and Africa was drawn into the mainstream of world history. Out of all the changes and tensions have emerged the new independent states of Africa.

It could be argued that if Africa had been left alone to develop, sooner or later she would probably have assimilated Western influence in a manner wholly of her own making. As far as the geographical map is concerned, Africa would have been very different today. To use one example, Great Britain created the political unit known as Nigeria and thereafter divided the country into three regional units under a federation. "God did not create Nigeria, the British did," declared Sir Ahmadu Bello.[1]

There was unfortunately one fatal mistake in the nineteenth century Europeans' attitude toward Africa. The belief in "darkest Africa" and the primitive nature of all African life might have encouraged the wave of altruistic feeling of men like David Livingstone, but at the same time it encouraged those, like Leopold II of the Belgians, who felt no qualms about exploiting people who appeared to Europeans to be inferior beings. The element of racism generated in this way remains today a serious and difficult problem, but also led to the paternalism of British administration and the assimilation of the French policy, resulting in the policy of restraint and conservatism practiced by the European powers during the period between the two World Wars. Faced with this lack of improvement or activity, those

Africans who benefited from Western education became angry and resentful, and the seeds of African nationalism were sown.

European contact with Africa had at first been mainly destructive. The increase in the demand for slaves for the American plantations had been growing since the sixteenth century, and the Europeans in West Africa and the Arabs in East Africa both encouraged cruel intertribal wars in their search for slaves. Down the coast of Africa went the Portuguese in their attempt to introduce Christianity to the Congolese, but this attempt foundered as they took to slaving and the decimation of the native population. At the tip of Africa the Boers trekked north from the original refreshing station at the Cape to clash with the well organized Bantus. However, the interior of the continent did not yet mean much to the new colonizers.

The first half of the nineteenth century was a period of increasing penetration of the interior of Africa by Europeans. Great Britain determined to end the slave trade and substitute legitimate trade, and the interest of geographical societies concerning the exploration of the great watershed in Central Africa led to increasing penetration of the continent.

Difficult climate, disease, and the danger of being attacked reinforced the idea that Africa was primitive and backward. Of the great kingdoms of the Sudan, Ethiopia, and Zimbabwe, and other great empires on the African continent the Europeans knew very little. This was true of the Congo kingdom also, though it had been roughly explored by the Portuguese in times past. The Europeans had an indication of the strength and organization of these centers of development, but knew little about their culture. The close links these kingdoms had with slavery did not impress European missionaries and traders, who were conscious of the barbarities of the Arab and European slavers and determined to wipe out the slave trade. Of the ancient and important links between East Africa and the rest of the Indian Ocean they knew next to nothing.[2]

To most of these European traders, explorers, and missionaries conditions on the African continent were a source of strong feelings centered around the "white man's burden." It stimulated the introduction of Western trade, the Christian faith, and European techniques. These would counteract disease, poverty and early death, it was believed.

It was not until the 1920s and 1930s that anthropology began to study the African tribes at first hand and to determine that tribal life was complex, with systems of land holdings, values, world views and kinship organizations. The British made use of the indigenous African leaders for local government, mostly out of necessity. This system of indirect rule will be investigated in the book.

Late in the 19th century the so-called "scramble for Africa" took place.

The complications that arose from the Franco-Prussian war of 1870–71 led the great European powers to use Africa as a safety valve.[3] Rivalries which might have generated another war in Europe were channeled into what seemed to be a less dangerous struggle for African colonies. The Belgians under Leopold II, Great Britain, France, and Germany were finally forced to hold a conference, the Berlin Conference of 1884–85.

The motives of these European countries were mixed, but the institution of slavery was to be outlawed for all time, and trade stimulated. One must also call attention to the philanthropic element even though abuses, in particular those of Leopold II, did exist. But the large scale attempt that was successful in ending the slave trade brought with it the hope of a new Africa.

The Imperial Government preferred to work through a chartered agent in its development of Kenya even though Great Britain was involved in Egypt and was not yet ready to interface openly in the affairs of East Africa. Hence, the Imperial British East Africa Company was chartered in 1888, its operational base at Mombasa, the old Arab town for which, together with Zanzibar's ten mile strip of territory along the Coast, the Company paid the Sultan an annual rent of £11,000. This area, by itself, did not look too promising for commercial trade and so there appeared to be only one solution: to strike out for Uganda, "the pearl of Africa" as the explorer Speke had named it.[4]

There was also a German expedition to Uganda under the explorer Carl Peters, and the British competed with him in trying to obtain a treaty with the Kabaka Mwanga. This proved to be pointless since in Europe at the same time the Anglo-German agreement of July 1890 provided that Uganda would be under the British sphere and reaffirmed the boundaries between Kenya, Uganda, and Tanganyika.

The Imperial Company was faced with the problem of developing the 700 mile route from Mombasa to Uganda, which lay through scrub desert and then over the steep slopes of the Kenya Highlands. The Company saw the solution in the building of a railway though it hadn't enough financial backing. Civil war broke out in Uganda in which the Company was involved under the direction of Captain Lugard. The complications and expense of Uganda were too much for the Company and it tried to withdraw. In Great Britain there raged a public controversy over what was to be done with Uganda and ultimately a Protectorate was proclaimed in June 1894.

The following year, in June of 1895, a British Protectorate was proclaimed over Kenya and the British government assumed control over the British East Africa Protectorate, paying rent to the Sultan of Zanzibar for the coastal strip and charging the cost to the Protectorate.

The British government expected that the Imperial British East Africa Company would act on its behalf in Uganda, despite the fact that the company had inadequate funds to work with. Only the threat of withdrawing the company's agents to the coast brought the government to recognize its responsibilities.

In order to maintain control over the strategically important headwaters of the Nile and to fulfill obligations concerning the ending of the trade in slaves which had been discussed in the Brussels Conference in 1889–90, Lord Salisbury's government discussed the possibility of constructing a railway from the coast to Lake Victoria. In the face of strong opposition from anti-imperialists, the first survey was conducted in 1891. The factor that made the railway inevitable was the decision to listen to the advice of its commissioner, Sir Gerald Portal, and declare a Protectorate over Uganda.

Work began on the railway at Mombasa in 1896 and was completed in 1901. The greater part of the construction had been carried out by Indians brought to East Africa for that purpose. Thirty two thousand workmen were brought to Africa and over six thousand decided to remain there. Some took up market gardening and artisan occupations. They proved themselves able traders and were instrumental in developing trade along the railway as small merchants. They were able to encourage the use of money where there had been only barter. They played an important part in establishing the economy of the country on a working basis.

In his report, Sir Gerald Portal recommended that the Imperial British East Africa Company should lose its charter since it had, in his opinion, failed to fulfill its responsibilities. The British government offered the company £250,000 to surrender its charter. The company accepted the proposal and the East Africa Protectorate was created on July 1, 1895.

To the British government, the East Africa Protectorate appeared to be unimportant economically or strategically.[5] British activities were centered in Zanzibar and Uganda, and it was believed that security lay in keeping control of the adjacent areas to protect the Nile Valley and Uganda. The Protectorate was to be administered from Zanzibar by career diplomats. The first Commissioner was also the Consul General in Zanzibar.

This system of dual responsibility had other implications in the administrative area. Great Britain held to the fiction that the new Protectorate would practically control its internal affairs. The British officials would be consuls supervising local administration. This arrangement, though commonly operative between sovereign states and Great Britain, deteriorated to the point where such a pretense could not be countenanced. The government decreed that responsibility for Zanzibar should be transferred from the Foreign Office to the Colonial Office and the Consul General was replaced by a Resident.[6]

This consular theory of administration was not as meaningful as it could have been in East Africa.[7] There was no definite system of administration from the Imperial British East Africa Company, which was mismanaged and near bankruptcy. There simply was not any adequate form of government when the Foreign Office took over in 1895.

The establishment of British overrule in the Protectorate was not achieved without overcoming a series of rebellions among many of the tribes in the area opposed to outside rule. However, the major concern of the Foreign Office between 1895 and 1901 was the construction of the Uganda railway. For strategic and economic reasons it was desirable for the line to be quickly completed and this, in turn, meant that the tribes on either side of the railway had to be pacified.

In time, the British administration insisted that the means be found to keep the railway moving, and it was then that the dreaded Hut Tax was instituted over the Africans and a call issued for white settlers to establish themselves in the Highlands area.

The immediate problem was that most of the African people in the Protectorate had never accepted European rule; therefore, it became necessary to organize military expeditions against those tribes who were against the government. Indeed, from 1900 to 1908 several expeditions were sent to persuade the Africans to accept the colonial government. Force was used in the majority of cases to establish British rule.[8]

The Africans themselves were not united and it was this divisiveness which helped the British to overtake the tribal elders and leaders. Wherever it was possible the British found tribal leaders who were willing, as local government, to act as liaison between the African people and the colonial government.

1

People of Kenya

Kenya is basically an African country. However, because of various historical circumstances which will be explained later in this book, Kenya has also been the home of immigrant Europeans, Asians, and Arabs. Each group stemmed from and tended to adhere to a different cultural and social pattern, with contact between them being restricted largely to the realm of economic activity. This was especially true of the Asian community in Kenya.

As a British colony, a form of "economic-political stratification" was promoted and instituted. This meant that the Europeans enjoyed top priority as far as economic, political and social privileges were concerned. The Asians and Arabs were second, while the Kenyan African majority were third.

In the industries, in the civil services, and on the farms, the Europeans held the key positions, although some educated Africans were to be found here and there, perhaps as "tokens," holding some limited important positions. The Africans did not, however, get equal pay for equal work. The Report of the East Africa Commission in 1953–1955 said:

> There is far less chance for the African in the public service to
> rise to the higher appointments in Kenya than in the other two
> territories (Tanganyika and Uganda).... Because Europeans are
> more available in large numbers than in the other territories they
> get higher paid appointments without due consideration of the
> paramount need of making increased provision for the promotion
> of Africans. In practice, officers are graded by race rather than by
> responsibility....[1]

After the first years of European settlement, the Africans' desire to see whether or not they could attain an equal footing with the other races in Kenya was very great. Africans realized that many of their old tribal economic, social, and political institutions were at least open to question, and were attracted by the ideas of western technology and by the western political arrangements. Indeed, as is explained later, as the result of intercultural relations between the Africans and the Europeans the Africans accepted much of the western pattern of social values. There was not, however, a total adoption of western values and institutions, but rather a synthesis of the old tribal ways and European culture. This is perhaps what contemporary sociologists and anthropologists call "transculturation." This is usually a gradual process, giving the weaker entity the opportunity to assimilate and make use of the new material.

In this new colonial set up, the Africans were not regarded as equal participant actors in the political, economic, and cultural processes, but as the observers or outsiders. The Africans found themselves competing with Europeans and Asians who were much better equipped economically, politically, and educationally for the new society. Facilities to assist Africans to advance and catch up with the Europeans and Asians in the economic life were insufficient.

The Asian Indians in Kenya

The chief importance of the Indian presence in Kenya goes back to the time of the Kenya-Uganda Railway. The railway was constructed in 1896–1901 with the aid of 32,000 Indian "coolies," as they were called, mostly recruited in the Punjab. There were also a number of "higher-grade" Indian employees, many of whom were highly educated and spoke quaint, biblical English. In addition to the Indians there were numerous European subordinates, mostly of Indian birth, or "home-bred" Britons with Indian experience. These were supplemented by a few Anglo-Indians. The higher executive positions were limited to Britons appointed by the British Government.

The construction of the railway was not of course the first Indian contact with East Africa. Indians had traveled along the coast of East Africa for centuries during the pre–European period, but until completion of the Kenya-Uganda Railway in 1901, there had been no significant settlement. Then some of the Indian railroad workers decided to stay in Kenya.

As has been stated, between 1896 and 1903, 32,000 "coolies" were imported. Indians who were repatriated to India because of their strike against working conditions on the railroad (and also because of their anti-British behaviors) numbered 16,312, while 2,493 Indians died from poor working conditions. Indians to the number of 6,454 were disabled in the process of building the railroad, so it looks as if only 6,741 Indians decided to stay in Kenya—about 20 percent, or a fifth of the original number of 32,000 Indian "coolies."[2]

In spite of the small number of Indians remaining in Kenya, a very high birth rate, in addition to later Indian immigration, rapidly increased their numbers.

Like the Africans, the Indians were not allowed to buy land in the Kenya Highlands, the best and most beautiful of the farmlands. The Indians were disliked by the white settlers, mainly because their frugal manner of living and characteristic shrewdness made them keen competitors. However, in the early days of the East African Protectorate, the Indian traders were a distinct convenience to the white man.

Various criticisms have been leveled against the Indians in East Africa, chiefly that they had no interest in African advancement. Instead, they concentrated on spreading their control of commerce and trade throughout East Africa, even taking over from African traders in rural areas and, where possible, taking their profits and contributing nothing in return. They built their own schools and hospitals and excluded Africans from them.

The traditional Indian answer to such criticism was that they (the Indians) did not control Kenya politically or economically and therefore they themselves were also victims of colonial administration. It is true, however, that a number of Indian businessmen did appear to promote their self-interests and, in the process, advanced self-aggrandizement and selfishness.

In this book, it would be equally unfair to put a blanket of blame on all Indians alike. As will be said later in the volume, there were some businessmen, professionals, journalists, printing press owners and civic leaders in the Indian community who aided and abetted the very few Africans who were trying to organize their people and air their grievances.

The Indians were vehemently against the white settlers of the Kenya Highlands. Indeed, the Indians acted as a big barrier, stopping or helping to stop Kenya from becoming another Southern Rhodesia. It was Indian leaders who promoted the concept of trade union movement in East Africa, Kenya included. The Indians also promoted the idea of international trade connection, even though it was limited to India. In addition, they contributed some limited technical skills.

It would be unfair to suggest that the majority of the Indians in East

Africa, and Kenya in particular, had a desire to see an establishment or extension of Greater Indian Empire or colonization of Kenya by the Indians.

Mr. A. M. Jeevanjee, who was the first to represent the Indian community in the Kenya Legislative Council in 1909, is reported to have written in 1910 that:

> I would go so far as to advocate the annexation of the African territory (meaning Kenya) to the Indian Empire, with Provincial Government under the Indian Viceroy. Let it be opened to us, and in a very few years it will be a second India.[3]

Could this have been possible? The Indian government in India was under British control. The Secretary of State for India in Great Britain—who was also a member of the cabinet—was a Briton. The Indian National Congress in India did not exist until 1885. As a matter of fact the idea of forming a party as an educational group was initiated in 1883 by an Englishman who had retired from civil service, Allan Hume. Hence, the formation of the Indian National Congress in 1885.

The Indian National Congress under G. K. Gokhale and Surandranath Benerjea was not a political mass movement for all of India. It was dominated by a few Indian intellectuals, whose demands of the British were moderate. It did not become truly a mass movement until Gandhi returned to India in 1915 from South Africa and took over the leadership of the Indian National Congress in 1920. The Indians in India proper were under very strong British control. How could they have supported the idea of the Indian colonization of Kenya?

The Indian Community in Kenya appeared to have been inhibited by a latent fear of the overpowering European settlers' political, social and economic domination. Thus, the Indians seemed to have been scared of investing financial capital in the country—which in turn could be useful for the country's development. They were ambivalent.

The Indian ambivalence and insecurity in Kenya continued notwithstanding the Duke of Devonshire's declaration of 1923 about the African "paramountcy." European settlers' political, economic and social dominance continued unabated for the next twenty nine years—specifically, until 1952.

Arabs in Kenya

Arab influence on the east coast of Africa and, in particular Kenya, has been considerable, disproportionate to the actual numbers who lived there. Excellent and uninhibited traders for centuries, they established strategic trading centers at Mombasa and especially in Zanzibar, so famous for its spices and slaves that all the most famous European explorers mounted their expeditions to eastern and central Africa in the 19th century. But for many years before Burton and Livingstone, while the white man's map of Africa was still blank, Arab caravans had been traveling to and fro across the enormous continent seeking slaves, ivory and other merchandises.

The city of Zanzibar lies on the island of the same name and has been an Arab and Indian trading center throughout its known history. The Sultan of Zanzibar considered the coast region for several miles north and south as part of his dominion. His sovereignty was recognized even by the Britons when they arrived. The people of this coastal strip are the Swahili, today a racial mixture of the Arabs and the African population. The lasting influence of the Arabs can be found in the widespread use of Swahili as the trade language of an enormous area of East Africa.

Swahili is now widely spoken in Kenya proper, Tanganyika (now Tanzania), Uganda (although not all people in Uganda are fluent in Swahili), and to a certain extent in Burundi, Rwanda, Zaire, Mozambique, Malawi and Northern Rhodesia (now Zambia). In addition, large numbers of Africans were converted to Islam. This process continues today, as the Islamic faith appears to have a more natural attraction for some Africans than the beliefs of Christianity.

After Kenya was declared a Crown Colony of Great Britain, the Arabs, like the Indians, were allowed to move into the interior and establish their businesses. Commercially, they were unable to match the Indians but, through religion and the Swahili language, their influence on East Africa has been incomparably greater.

2

The Birth of Mistrust

Some believe that the first event in the series which led up to the Mau Mau rebellion occurred before Britain annexed East Africa, when the first settlers made their appearance in the highlands of Kenya, the author citing the relatively orderly progress of other African dependencies to self-order.[1] Others point to several key events, including the establishment of the first mission station in 1891 and the appearance of the first Indian trader as well as bitter struggles between the Kikuyu and various European caravans along with the arrival of the first British settlers.[2]

Some of the European caravans referred to by Oliver and Mathew were those led by a German explorer named G. A. Fisher and a Hungarian traveler, Count Samuel Teleki. The Kikuyu found it difficult to forget and forgive their deeds. These two men had decided to go across the Kikuyu country by force of arms. They managed it, massacring numerous Kikuyu in the process.

Ironically, however, George Delf in his book *Jomo Kenyatta* quotes Teleki as follows:

> Count Teleki, who passed through Kikuyuland in 1887 with an expedition ... found them (the Kikuyu) "shy and timid," despite the countless tales he had heard of the fierceness and hostility of the natives. He wrote of the charming landscape and added, "As far as the eye could reach stretched well-cultivated, undulating pasture-lands, which were a revelation to us." He went on to describe the appearance of the Kikuyu. "The lively, restless temperament of the Kikuyu is far more indicative of their relationship to the great

Bantu stock than their physical appearance, which resembles that of the Masai. Though seldom above medium height, they are well built, muscular, and strong. Their characters vary much." The Count thoughtfully observed that the tribe was destined to play an important part in the future of East Africa.[3]

When Captain (later Lord) Lugard entered the Kikuyu country, the Kikuyu were at first distrustful because of their previous unhappy experience. A Kikuyu leader of high repute named Waiyaki, son of Hinga, however, appears to have been impressed by Lugard. Equally, Lugard was impressed by Waiyaki, the Kikuyu country, and the Kikuyu in general.

At this time Lugard was on his exploratory journey to Uganda. While on this journey he was also establishing what he called "stockades" or "station posts" for the use of the Imperial British East Africa Company.

On hearing his intentions, Waiyaki—in consultation with the other Kikuyu leaders, elders and Ago (medicine men)—invited Lugard to set up a station, the first of its kind, at Dagoretti, in October 1890.

The Kikuyu, however, did not want to take Lugard's sincerity for granted. They therefore arranged for a ceremonial oath between Lugard and the Kikuyu, led by Waiyaki. The "shamanistic words" used while this oath was being administered were to the effect that Lugard and his people would not interfere with the Kikuyu land or any other property. It was administered according to the Kikuyu tradition, both parties banging their weapons together as though they were having a mock fight.

As always, this oath was taken very seriously by the Kikuyu. Subsequent to it, a treaty between Lugard and the Kikuyu was signed on October 11, 1890. These two occasions must have been very exciting to all parties concerned and, if our modern television cameras were to be focused on them today, we would have witnessed colorful events indeed!

Writing about the oath and the treaty in his diary as edited by Professor Perham, Lugard says:

> 11th [November 1890]. Today we settled up with Eiyeki [Waiyaki], and gave him a handsome present for the ground. Altogether to various chiefs, headsmen, etc., everything included, and deducting the value of 5 sheep brought, I estimate we have given the local value of 14 goats for presents, land, etc. I think this very fair on both sides. I now presented him with a flag, and explained its use. I also made a treaty, but as I do not believe in the printed treaty forms of the Company by which a man gives all his land and rights of rule to the Company in exchange for their "Govt. and Protection," I made out my own treaty form. This Company's treaty is an utter fraud. No man if he understood would sign it and to say that

A cartoon from *Punch*, a British magazine, depicting the traditional Kikuyu oath between Waiyaki, the Kikuyu leader, and Captain Lugard in 1890.

a savage chief has been told that he cedes all rights to the Company in exchange for nothing is an obvious untruth. If he had been told that the Company will protect him against his enemies, and share in his wars as an ally, he has been told a lie, for the Company has no idea of doing any such thing and no force to do it with, if they wished. So I said that he bound himself to supply us with food, to demand no Hongo, to do no harm or damage to our settlement, and be our friend and ally, and we promised not to harm or molest him and his people.... All this I put as being understood by the ceremony of bloodbrotherhood, an idea he can grasp, while the idea of a compact by having certain marks on paper he could not possibly understand.[4]

So the two men were now blood-brothers and, in consequence, their two countries were to live in peace, harmony and mutual respect. This high idealistic spirit, as the record shows, did not last long.

When Lugard left Dagoretti station in the care of Wilson (one of his companions), porters from the station started looting, raping and mishandling the Kikuyu. In turn, the Kikuyu acted swiftly. They were thoroughly incensed by the acts of "Lugard's men," though Lugard himself would hardly have ordered them to commit such excesses. Bitter fighting erupted, culminating in the Kikuyu burning the station and forcing Wilson and his men out of Dagoretti.

Some of his men returned to Mombasa and others retreated to Fort Smith. Those who retreated to Fort Smith were heavily reinforced, and on August 16, 1892, Wilson's men invaded the Kikuyu country from there. It appears to have been a well organized "blitz." On his part, however, Waiyaki and his army were well organized. The two forces fought bitterly.

Unfortunately for Waiyaki, he was captured on August 17, 1892, and taken to Kibwenzi, his hands chained together. This was a great fall for such a famous warrior and able Kikuyu leader, and of course a great shock to the Kikuyu people.

As Waiyaki was being taken into captivity, it is said that he kept on shouting back to his people while he was being pushed forward as a prisoner of war by the guards. He kept on saying, as he turned his head back:

> I am being taken away by force. I do not know whether I shall
> return to you. In the event of my never returning, please do not
> give up the fight or an inch of our "ng'undu" [land]. Continue the
> fight like good "njamba" [warriors]. We may be defeated physically,
> but our spirit is a winning spirit. Keep up the good fight. I wish
> you well.

To the militarily defeated Kikuyu force and the Kikuyu people in general, these words by Waiyaki were taken as a deathbed wish. The whole affair was a nightmare to them. The betrayal was a permanent shock which has not been completely forgotten to this day. Captain Lugard had taken their traditional oath that neither he nor his people would interfere with the Kikuyu people and their property. They had agreed to administer this oath to him, an honor rarely granted to anyone outside the tribe. The sacrifice was a terrible omen.

It should be remembered that the Kikuyu had no written record. Tribal history was therefore transmitted from generation to generation by means of legends and proverbs. In this way, Waiyaki's famous words were recalled afresh sixty years later—that is, in 1952 when the Mau Mau political and military songs were sung. For example, one famous song in memory of Waiyaki's words:

> Andu aitu Waiyaki Niakuire-eeee!
> Na agitutigira kirumi-iii', ati
> Ng'undu icio ciitu tutikendie-eee!
> Naithui tutikaineana-aaaa!

Meaning:

> Our people, Waiyaki died
> He left a death-bed wish about our lands
> He said never sell them
> We shall never give them away.

What followed? Deep-rooted suspicion and mistrust among the Kikuyu already existed and this was confirmed when the British themselves created a new chief, Kinyanjui son of Gathirimu, in place of Waiyaki, because he (Kinyanjui) was considered more "moderate" and amenable to British influence than Waiyaki had been.

With a few notable exceptions (and with respect), European commentators have tended to misjudge African reaction in this early period of Kenya's colonial history. Professor Roland Oliver of the University of London and Gervase Mathew are no doubt correct in writing of the earliest contacts that:

> The African response to the European annexations varied widely. Most of the tribes cannot have been aware of its real meaning; the stack of treaty forms collected in the Foreign Office files in London represented, to the chiefs and elders who agreeably inscribed them with their X-marks, considerably less than the familiar ceremony of blood-brotherhood to dreaded conquerors. To some Africans they were, perhaps, at first no more than a new source of decorative beads or cotton clothes; to others, more sophisticated, they were allies or enemies in the struggle for power dominance over other tribes.[5]

However, it was not long before the Africans took proper measure of the situation. The warring tribes were inevitably crushed by superior British arms but the lessons were learnt and not forgotten. The Africans were helpless until leaders arose equipped to fight the British on their own terms—in 1919–1922, Harry Thuku, Jesse Kariuki, George Kirongothi Ndegwa and Joseph Kang'ethe; W. K. Mengo and Ezekiel Apindi in 1922–1928; and then Jomo Kenyatta, W. W. Awori, E. W. Mathu, B. A. Ohanga, Mbiyu Koinange, Oginga Odinga, Tom Mboya, James Gichuru, J. D. Otiende, Moi, Towett, Muliro and others in 1929–1963.

In the meantime much had been taken from the Africans, but the ground was laid in those early years for the struggle which, although postponed, was certain from the beginning. It reached a climax in the 1950s, fought for much the same reasons as Waiyaki, Mangeka, Koitalel, Gero, Wanji Madori and others had fought in the 1890s and 1900s, and it was won. Certainly, it was a tragic misunderstanding, but you prey on your enemies, not on those you would have as your friends.

Britain's original interest in East Africa was influenced by highly creditable motives: the nineteenth century explorers who entered Central Africa from the East Coast—some of them missionaries of the type of David Livingstone—were often philanthropic idealists whose reports of the horrors of the slave trade resulted in a widespread agitation in Great Britain for its suppression.

The organizers of this commerce in human flesh and blood were professional Arab slave traders, their raw material the inland tribes of East Africa and their chief market, where many traders had their headquarters, was the island of Zanzibar. The slaves bought in Zanzibar were dispersed by Arab dhows to their new owners in various parts of the Indian Ocean and the Persian Gulf.

To stamp out this infamous traffic and to meet insistent public demand for action, Great Britain maintained a travel patrol on the East Coast for many years at considerable expense to the British taxpayer. However, Britain made no serious attempt to control the mainland until Germany showed an interest in doing so. The inevitable result was an agreement in 1886 between the two Powers on their respective "spheres of influence" in East Africa.

The first official move inland was made by the Imperial British East Africa Company, organized in 1888 under Royal Charter to administer an area which extended from the coast to beyond the western shores of Lake Victoria, Nyanza.

Unfortunately, and perhaps inevitably, the Company was a commercial failure, and in 1894 and 1895 the British government assumed direct control of the territories it had attempted to administer. The western portion then became the Uganda Protectorate and the eastern area the British East Africa Protectorate under Sir Arthur Hardinge. Originally, the western boundary of the East Africa Protectorate was Naivasha, about 390 miles inland, but in the early part of this century it was extended to the shores of Lake Victoria 200 miles further on.

The geography of the route of the Kenya-Uganda Railway—roughly following the old caravan road to Lake Victoria—was well known, as was that of the coastal region. However, the north and south of the railway's progress contained large tracts of country which were almost entirely unexplored. When the railway finally reached Nyanza in November 1901, the white population of what now comprises Kenya was only a few hundred persons, the great majority being employees of the railway and the British East Africa and Uganda Protectorates. The rest were missionaries, representatives of

European importing and exporting concerns, a small number of would-be farmers and prospectors and six or seven men who lived by trading with the Africans. The Protectorate officials regarded these traders with such suspicion and distrust that the late Sir Harry Johnstone, then Commissioner for the Uganda Protectorate, is said to have described them as "white free-booters."

After the Kenya-Uganda Railway was completed, there was a pause to consider what use it might have. The locomotives and rolling stock which had transported the construction materials were lying idle and there was no other freight in prospect. Passenger service was restricted to one train a week in each direction, and it was clear that a radical plan was necessary to avoid a large operating deficit.

In this crisis, the British Government followed the opinion given by its legal advisors two years previously that the establishment of a protectorate would enable it to assert sovereign rights over land, *subject to the recognition of any private rights then existing.*[6]

This opinion—even though it purported to respect existing African rights to land with Protectorate—was in conflict with earlier British policy. The question of the right to lands not in actual African ownership or occupancy had been raised in the then–British Bechuanaland Protectorate in 1885 and 1895, and on both occasions the British government had decided that because its position as the protecting power was not one of absolute sovereignty, title to such lands must be held to be vested in the local African chiefs.[7]

This conclusion was logical in that under British law the populations of Protectorates were classified as aliens, and, thus handicapped, have been denied some of the elementary rights of British subjects, including access to the local courts of justice. The 1899 opinion provided, however, a legal sanction for the establishment in 1902 of a scheme of selling, leasing, and presenting free grants of land in the Highlands of Kenya, the choicest parts of the entire country.

There are several schools of thought today with regard to the necessity and justice of European settlement in Kenya. Some felt that European settlement was necessary in order to prevent the Indians from settling in Kenya, others that it was necessary to save the Kenya-Uganda Railway, and in the case of Dr. Livingstone particularly, that European settlement was necessary to foster the spread of Christianity among the people of Kenya.[8]

Whatever Livingstone's motives may have been, Lord Altrincham was certainly correct in citing him as the "chief founder" of British colonization in East and Central Africa.[9]

A passage from *The Life of Livingstone*, published in 1929 by the Rev. Dr. R. J. Campbell, and quoted by Lord Altrincham, reads:

In December, 1850, pressing his kindred to emigrate, he says he believes the cause of Christ will be better advanced by emigration than by missionaries. This conviction deepened with him as time went on, and we meet it repeatedly in his utterances, public and private, written and oral. In the opening chapter of the *Missionary Travels* he gives emphatic expression to it in the challenging statement that the promotion of commerce would do more good than the missionary with the Bible under his arm; and so sure was he of his ground in so saying that out of the profits of this, his first and most widely circulated book, he offered two thousand pounds toward the cost of equipping and sending out selected British families to colonize the shores of Lake Nyasa if the Government would support the proposal. He was before his time in his belief in the psychological benefit of a good social example, and his foresight has been amply vindicated by the planting and growth of flourishing English and Scottish communities in this part of Africa.[10]

The need for European settlement in Kenya has been stressed variously indeed. In connection with the railway, Marsh and Kingsnorth write:

> The difficulties began with the need for European settlers, if the railway was to pay. The British taxpayer had invested millions in building a railway on which every train ran at a loss. This could not go on forever: somehow the railway must be made to pay for itself. Yet the Africans would never be able to supply enough traffic without assistance. Sir Charles Eliot, the new Commissioner for the East Africa Protectorate, thought the answer was to attract European settlers. If settlers were to be attracted, it was necessary to place the alienation of land on a sound basis. With this object the East Africa (lands) Order in Council was issued in 1901 and defined Crown land as "all public lands which for the time being are subject to the control of His Majesty by virtue of any treaty, convention or agreement, and all lands which have been or may hereafter be acquired by His Majesty under the Lands Acquisition Act." The order in council then went on to arrange for disposition of such lands, but, as Mr. M. F. Hill in his book, *The Permanent Way*, rightly points out, it was unfortunate that the order did not make it sufficiently clear what was meant by "public lands."[11]

3

Mistrust Flourishes

The next phase in Kenya's drama began with Sir Charles Eliot, who succeeded Sir Arthur Hardinge as Commissioner for the British East Africa Protectorate from 1901 to 1904. Large scale European settlement now began in earnest.

Earlier on, we saw how the Imperial British East African Company tried to administer the territory until, amongst other things, the Company's financial difficulties persuaded the British Government to take direct control in 1895. In fact, it was not the Government but the Company which first encouraged serious European settlement, though on a smaller scale than would later occur. Indeed, the Company had drawn up terms for settlement. On this, writes W. M. Ross, the Company offered:

> for "country lots," on lease not exceeding twenty-one years, but renewable, no fixed rent being specified. For grazing leases, not more than 20,000 acres could be had in one block, and the annual rent was one half anna (i.e. ½d.) an acre. On agricultural land, leases of not more than 2,000 acres might be had at a rent of ½ anna an acre for the first five years.... Homesteads were of 100 acres at a rent of 4 annas an acre for the first years, during which occupation was compulsory.[1]

The above regulations were issued in July 1894. After Kenya's administration was transferred from the Company to the Foreign Office, they were maintained, though amended in 1897 to provide that:

> A certificate will not be granted in respect of any land which at the time of the commencement of these regulations is cultivated or

regularly used by any native or native tribe, but may be granted
if the Commissioner, after such inquiry as he may think fit, is
satisfied that such land is no longer so cultivated or regularly used,
and that the grant of a certificate would not be prejudicial to native
interests.[2]

The land regulations of 1894 and 1897 did not last long. In 1902
another regulation under the heading "The East Africa Order in Council
(1902)" was issued. How did it come about? Professor George Bennett of
Oxford University in his book *Kenya: A Political History*, reminds us that:

> In 1899 the Crown lawyers eventually advised that in native states
> which had no indigenous government of their own, the Crown's
> sovereign authority extended by virtue of the Protectorate status,
> over all lands subject only to an obligation to respect existing
> valid private titles. There followed from this the East Africa
> (Land Acquisition) Order in Council of 1901 which authorized the
> Commissioner to sell, grant, lease or otherwise dispose of land.
> Specific terms for this were laid down in the Crown Lands Ordi-
> nance of 1902, though the Commissioner was further limited in
> his discretion by instructions to refer grants above a certain size to
> the Foreign Office for their approval.[3]

Sir Charles Eliot felt that as the 1902 Ordinance contained the restriction on the Commissioner rather than being passed to avoid it, large numbers of European settlers could not be encouraged unless some revisions
were made in this Ordinance so as to soften the effect of the restriction.
Sir Charles put pressure to bear on the Foreign Office, and so it happened
that the Ordinance of 1902 was revised, whereupon the restriction was soft-
ened. Sir Charles Eliot could be regarded as the father founder of the
"White Highlands." He is reported to have said, "You cannot invite people to dinner and then lock the dining-room door."[4] Thereafter European
settlers started entering the country in far greater numbers than ever before.

The Foreign Office wanted settlers, and that included Indians as well
as Europeans. There was also a suggestion from Joseph Chamberlain, a
Colonial Secretary who visited the Protectorate in 1902, that persecuted
Jews from Eastern Europe should be encouraged to settle in the Protectorate. The Foreign Office, not keen on this idea, was itself at odds with
the Commissioner, Sir Charles Eliot, who strongly opposed Indian settlement (or indeed any settlement except European) in what were to be known
as "White Highlands." Sir Charles' land policy, which was followed with
little modification by successive administrations, consolidated many of the
grievances which were to plague Kenya for the following 60 years.

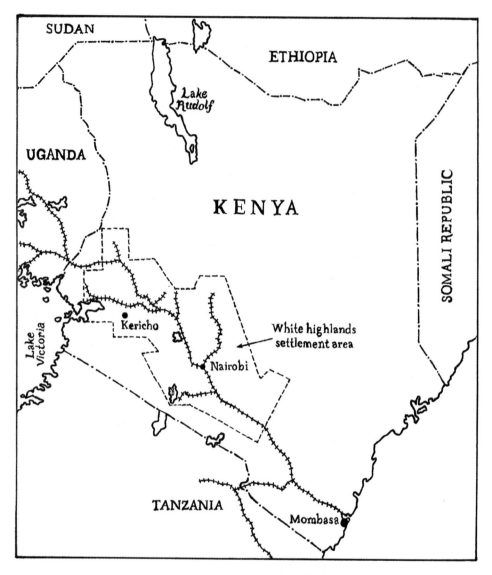

A map showing the most fertile area of Kenya, formerly known as the "White Highlands."

Broadly, however, the Foreign Office wanted rapid economic expansion and was prepared for settlers of all kinds. But it was the Commissioner who had the real control.

By 1903 settlers were arriving from South Africa, New Zealand, Australia, Europe and even from Canada. It was at this time that Delamere acquired 100,000 acres of land in the "White Highlands." Of Delamere and Sir Charles, it was said that "white settlement in East Africa is largely the creation of these two men." Colonial Kenya was almost set in the mold.

At this time, no thought was given to the paper signed by Waiyaki and Captain Lugard on October 11, 1890, guaranteeing their land to the Kikuyu and the Kenyan Africans generally. Indeed, according to the Foreign Office (2/569: Eliot to Lansdowne: 28 January 1902), Eliot had a strong detestation of the Africans. As more and more settlers arrived, their influence spread throughout the Protectorate. Having settled, they organized, and Delamere became their acknowledged leader. An organization calling itself "Colonists' Association" had been launched in 1902. At first, it was not very active but on his arrival in 1903, Delamere provided political direction.

The Association became very active and not only demanded the exclusive European occupation of the Kenya Highlands, but also adopted an anti–Semitic flavor. This was in reaction to Joseph Chamberlain's suggestion that Eastern European Jews might be invited to the Protectorate. Delamere went so far as to write a pamphlet in which he scoffed at the idea.

Sir Charles' paramount interest in the settlers eventually became an embarrassment to the Foreign Office. His determination to take land for settlement away from the nomadic Masai led to his resignation in 1904 and he published his political treatise, "The East Africa Protectorate," the following year. However, although Sir Charles lost the battle, as will appear, it was the Masai who lost the war. Sir Charles' rule was short but it did much to consolidate the gains of the settlers and the losing position of the Africans.

In 1904, Sir Donald Stewart replaced Sir Charles Eliot as Commissioner for the East Africa Protectorate. Sir Donald found many unsolved problems, not least of them the disposal of land. At first, he worked with advice from the permanent officials he inherited from his predecessor. Of these officials, it was Hobley, who had also acted as an official counsel during the time of Sir Charles Eliot, who became his chief adviser on land. Other inherited officials included Ainsworth, Hope, Horne, Bagge, and Jackson. Jackson testified in a memorandum that it was largely due to Hobley that the Masai were told to move from their "best and favorite grazing grounds."

Before the coming of the white man, the Masai were pastoral, largely nomadic people, who grazed their cattle, sheep, and goats over a vast area. Their fierce aggressiveness closed the most direct route from the coast to Lake Victoria and Nyanza to the earlier explorers until 1883, when Joseph Thomson made his way through their country. The Lake had been recorded by Speke twenty-five years before, but he had traveled from the coast by a route far to the south and then had headed north.

Describing the most warlike people in East Africa, the Report of the Kenya Land Commission, 1934, quotes Sir Charles Eliot:

> From at least 1850 to the early eighties the Masai were formidable power in East Africa. They successfully asserted themselves against the Arab slave-traders, took tribute from all that passed through their territory, and treated other races, whether African or not, with the greatest arrogance.

The area in which the Masai herded their animals was the Great Rift Valley, north and south of Naivasha, where there are several lakes. Above the Eastern wall of the Valley the Masai shared the pastoral Kinangop Plateau with vast herds of antelope, zebra, and gnu—almost every variety of Kenya wild life.

The first baton of white settlers had hardly set foot in the Protectorate before many of the newcomers cast covetous eyes on the lands of the Masai, and Section 642 of the Report of the Kenya Land Commission, 1934, relates:

> During 1903, applications were received from Europeans for land in the Rift Valley and elsewhere in places where the Masai grazed their flocks and herds and the question arose how far such applications could be granted.

A solution was soon found and, inevitably, it consisted of the eviction of the Masai from lands they and their ancestors had held from time immemorial and their removal to two reserves, one a strip of land to the south of the Kenya and Uganda Railway along the northern boundary of what is now Tanzania, and the other considerably to the north in a district known as Laikipia. After the application of considerable pressure, the Masai consented to the new arrangement, which was incorporated in a written agreement, dated August 10, 1904, and executed by the Masai chiefs and numerous white officials. Among the latter was Sir Donald Stewart, the Commissioner of the Protectorate and the principal and duly authorized representative of the British government. The agreement contained a clause declaring:

> The settlement now arrived at shall be enduring to so long as the Masai as a race shall exist, and that Europeans or other settlers shall not be allowed to take up land in the settlements (the new reserves).[5]

Professor Martin L. Kilson of Harvard University, writing in the *Journal of Negro History*, explains the effect of the agreement as follows:

> [B]etween the late spring of 1903 and the later winter of 1904, some 220,000 acres of African land were alienated and leased to 342 Europeans. Moreover, thousands of acres were granted to commercial concerns and private individuals. For instance, the East Africa Syndicate, which was founded in 1903, received 320,000 acres, the Grogan Forest Concessions obtained 200,000 acres; and Uplands of East Africa Syndicate received 350,000 acres.[5]

It should be remembered here that Lord Delamere owned 100,000 acres, while his contemporary Lord Francis Scott owned 350,000. Sir Donald now appointed a Committee to advise him on land. Its members were: two judges, the Crown Advocate and a certain Frank Watkins who represented the Planters' and Farmers' Association. Lord Delamere became its chairman when the presiding judge was transferred to Zanzibar. There was of course no African or Asian representation.

In 1905, two important things happened. Sir Donald died and was succeeded by Sir James Hayes Sadler, and the East Africa Protectorate was transferred from the Foreign Office to the Colonial Office.

Were these changes to benefit the Africans? Were they now to be heard? According to Foreign Office 2/913 Lansdowne to Stewart, January 14, 1905, the answer was yes. Lansdowne felt that the native (Africans) were carrying a heavier tax burden than the Europeans or Asians; and he requested Sir Donald to put the matter right.

But what about land, the cardinal problem in Kenya since the Lugard-Waiyaki oath in 1890? In 1905, according to Professor R. L. Buell, in his book *The Native Problem in Africa*, the Delamere Land Board declared that:

> It did not believe that the government should recognize any native rights in the land, inasmuch as the agricultural natives lay claim to no more than a right of occupation. The government was the owner of all land not held under title, whether occupied or not....[6]

This declaration was to have a great influence on land policy during the following ten years.

As to the issue of taxation, which Lansdowne had raised with Sir Donald, the Africans were taxed, but not the other races. The settlers replied to all attempts with the familiar Anglo-Saxon words, "no taxation without representation." They argued that there should be a Legislative Council in which they would be represented if they were to pay taxes. This argument was considered moderate by the Colonial Office, though it was still uneasy about some of the recent developments in Kisii, Nandi, Kikuyu country and Masai-land. As it was shown later, both Africans and Europeans were taxed but in different ways.

If there was no taxation without representation, then all races should have been represented. Sir James Hayes Sadler, appointed following Sir Donald's death, agreed with the idea of a Legislative Council. In this period, the settlers' Planters' and Farmers' Association acquired another form and assumed the name of "Colonists' Association."

Kenya was not the most important concern of the very busy Colonial Office, and, provided the settlers kept their demands within reason, they received a favorable hearing. All the same, it is worth recording that while on a visit to the Protectorate in 1906, the then Under-Secretary of State, Winston Churchill, was reported by the *East African Standard* to have expressed surprise that the Protectorate was to be granted a Legislative Council with such a small number of European settlers.

The same lack of coordination between the Colonial Administration in Kenya and the Colonial Office in London on the policy to be adopted toward the settlers can be illustrated by a far more important development in 1906. Settlers were reasonably well assured of land but there was an acute shortage of labor. This problem was solved in 1906 by the popularly known "Masters and Servants Ordinance."

It was largely based on the South African pattern (hardly surprising, considering the number of settlers who had emigrated from South Africa to Kenya). What was the effect of this Ordinance?

Professor George Bennett of Oxford University, explains:

> In 1906—to the alarm of the Colonial Office—a Masters and Servants Ordinance was promulgated based on the law of the Transvaal, allowing both payment in kind and imprisonment of laborers for breach of contract. In 1907, following a suggestion of the Land Committee, a Secretary for Native Affairs was appointed, his department being "specifically instituted to deal with the labour supply." However, the result was not to the Colonists' satisfaction. A. C. (Later Sir Claud) Hollis, this new Secretary, revealed widespread abuses in labour recruitment. A Government circular was sent out, prohibiting chiefs from compelling labour to go out, regulations to control recruitment were issued while officers explained to natives that they need not work unless they wished to do so. The labour supply diminished and the settler protests mounted.[7]

To explain further, the chief characteristic of the European agricultural enterprise in Africa was its dependence on an easy supply of cheap

African labor, rather than on machinery. In the early days of white settlement in Kenya, an easy supply of cheap African labor seemed available because the Africans already lived in what they regarded as tolerable comfort achieved with the minimum of effort. However, there was no inducement to work permanently for strangers, an idea anyway alien to African society.

The African economy was such that each household was almost self-sufficient. The agricultural tribes raised their own crops and kept a few cattle, sheep and goats. The pastoral people, nomadic when the pasture failed, depended entirely upon their livestock. Huts were constructed with materials which cost nothing, and about the only articles that had to be obtained by barter were iron objects such as spearheads, arrowheads, swords, ax heads and hoe blades. Even these were of local origin, for the African blacksmith smelted iron ore in small charcoal furnaces and fashioned the metal into the implements of war and peace. The trade goods distributed by buyers of African products or services were not essential to African life and were usually heavy brass, iron and copper wire, beads, cotton sheeting and colored cloths. All were used for personal adornment, including the textiles which merely replaced the customary African clothing—usually animal skins.

The settlers were thus confronted by an African population tolerably well satisfied and lacking the incentive to earn money for non-essentials. Even if some of the men were induced to work, they soon tired of the discipline and monotony, and desertions were frequent. However, the experienced British government had a remedy. A need for cash was created. In 1901, a small annual hut tax had been imposed on the Africans of the British East Africa Protectorate in a rather limited area—about 5 percent—under effective Government control. Two years later the tax was increased by one half, and in succeeding years the rates were still further stepped up and poll taxes were also imposed. Payment of taxes had generally to be made in cash, which most Africans could only obtain by working for the white settlers.

Failure to pay was punished with the utmost severity. The Government would eject the occupants of a hut on which the impact remained unpaid, consign the head of the household to hard labor in a concentration camp, and if the default continued sometimes burnt the hut to the ground. As late as 1936, a Commission established by the Legislative Council reported these abuses continuing. Evidence was given of physical ill-treatment, illegal arrest, seizure of stock and the arrest of women as bait to their husbands to pay the taxes.

Professor Bennett reports that "the Colonial Office was alarmed by the ordinance of 1906," but unfortunately not sufficiently to retake control and direction. Why was this so? Professor Donald Rothchild of the University of California at Davis writes:

> European privilege in Kenya followed naturally from the British government's decision to use white settlers for developmental purposes. These immigrants could press administration for concession on land, labor, taxes, education, segregation, and whatever else they desired.[8]

4

Death Wish Exploited

The first Legislative Council was set up in 1907 under the colonial administration of Sir James Hayes Sadler. We have seen that from Sir Arthur Hardinge to Sir Donald Stewart, the Protectorate was governed by a Commissioner. It was during the period of Sir James Hayes Sadler in 1906 that the title "Commissioner" was dropped, to be succeeded by the title "Governor."

The Legislature consisted of six members, all white, who were "officials" (civil servants), under the control of the Governor, who himself had a vote as presiding officer and also a deciding vote. The other two members were "unofficials," who at first were appointed by the Governor from men outside his administration. The "official majority" (six members and the Governor) were responsible for the passage of all legislation.

The Indians fought hard to be represented in the Legislative Council and Sir James agreed that they had a reasonable case. The settlers were furious but Sir James stood firm and in 1909 an Indian named A. M. Jeevanjee was nominated to represent the Indian community. Thus the Indians, against intense opposition, broke the all-white monopoly of the Legislative Council. For apart from a measure preventing Indians, like the Africans, from acquiring agricultural land in areas set aside for white settlement, the most serious cause of friction had been the prevention by the whites of Indian representation in the Legislative Council.

What about the Africans? They had not one single individual to represent them—not even a nominated chief or a missionary. The African

33

interests were left in the hands of the European officials of the Legislative Council.

In common with his predecessors, Sir James made little contribution to African advancement, although regulations to control labor recruitment were issued during his term of office. Eventually, the Colonial Office decided a much tougher Governor was needed to deal with the situation and the man they chose was Sir Percy Girouard.

Sir Percy took office in 1909. Unfortunately for both the Colonial Office and the Africans, he became openly pro-settler, having already come under settler influence in South Africa. His contribution to the settlers' cause was a further removal of the Masai from Laikipia.

By 1911 the holdings of the white settlers had expanded to such an extent that grazing grounds in Laikipia were as necessary to their welfare as those from which the Masai had been removed only seven years before. There was an apparently serious obstacle to further encroachment—the written solemn pledge of a direct representative of the British Government. But when Lenana, supreme Chief of the Masai, died on March 7, 1911, it was alleged that he expressed a dying wish that the "tribe," split by the two reserves, should again be reunited. If true, this was singularly fortunate for the settlers!

A meeting of the Masai chiefs was called by the Government, at which Lenana's alleged death-bed wish was thoroughly exploited. The result was another agreement by which the Laikipia Masai agreed to move into the southern reserve. Subsequently, Masikondi and Legalishu, the principal chiefs of the Laikipia Masai, inspecting the southern reserve, objected to moving there on the grounds that the grazing facilities were insufficient for their animals.

On May 8, 1912, the Secretary of the Colonies in London directed that the Laikipia Masai be ordered to move south forthwith. Later that month some of the Masai chiefs obtained a temporary injunction in the High Court of the Protectorate to prevent the Government evicting them in defiance of the 1904 agreement. However, the government ignored the injunction and moved the last of the Masai south nine months before the case came before the High Court. The court's ruling on the Masai complaint was something of a curiosity:

> The Court held that the agreement was not a contract but a treaty, and that treaties entered into by foreign subjects (the technical status which the Masai then had as residents of a protectorate) were not cognizable in the municipal courts.[1]

The effect of this decision was therefore that the Africans could be deprived of their lands by the exercise of sovereign rights claimed by their "protector," the British Government, but were deprived of any remedy in the local courts because they were "foreigners."

Lord Hailey comments:

> The correctness of the decision is debatable; the Masai were given leave to appeal to the Privy Council, but could not afford to pursue it.[2]

The southern reserve was enlarged to accommodate its new occupants and, although parts of it were arid and waterless and others infested by tsetse fly, it served its purpose so unexpectedly well that the Kenya Land Commission considered the Masai to "have been treated in an unduly generous manner as regards land."

This observation was prompted by the fact that "the Masai are probably the most wealthy tribe in Africa, both in the matter of land and the stock which they are able to keep on it." The Commission felt strongly that something should be done to correct this unusual situation and suggested hopefully (the Masai Reserve being of little value to the whites), "Nobody wishes to deprive the Masai of their land, but justification might arise for requiring them to lease unused portions of it to other 'tribes,' or to individual Africans."

In the Colonial Office, however, the Africans had one hope, though perhaps they did not realize this. This hope was the Secretary of State, Lewis Harcourt. Although Sir Percy was an outspoken settlers' apologist, and appeared to have been dominated by Delamere's influence particularly, Harcourt was a shrewd man who weighed matters carefully. Sir Percy may have tricked him on the Masai issue, but it was this issue which forced Sir Percy's resignation before the end of the year.

Sir Percy was succeeded by Sir Henry Belfield in 1912. On assuming his duties, Sir Henry was faced with the perennial problem of labor.

The Protectorate, which later was to be known as the "Land Commissions and Royal Commissions," witnessed yet another Commission in 1912 and 1913. This one dealt with the acute problem of labor and for the first time included some missionary members. Its report was depressing, finding that labor conditions under which Africans were still being recruited, as well as their working conditions, were deplorable.

At this time, various events appeared to befog this important issue. Among them was the danger of imminent war with the Germans in both Europe and East Africa. Another was the settlers' fierce clamor for elective representation in the Legislative Council. The British Government's control of the Legislative Council was a constant grievance of the settlers, who called for "responsible government," meaning Legislative Council controlled by locally elected Europeans and not by the Governor's official and unofficial nominees. This demand was the keystone of settler politics thereafter.

As a first step toward "responsible government," Delamere's supporters rallied behind him in a convention of Associations which met in the middle of 1913. He insisted that the Europeans should be allowed to elect their members and that the Asians (known then as Asiatics) and natives should be represented by government officials. A petition was drawn up and handed to Sir Percy, the Governor, to be forwarded to the Colonial Office.

The Governor was sympathetic to the settlers' petition, and accordingly forwarded it to the Colonial Office, where it was received unfavorably by "somewhat pro–African" Harcourt who had replaced Crewe earlier on.

It was not long, however, before the settlers obtained what they wanted in spite of Harcourt. The 1914–1918 war had given the settlers an undue importance strategically and in 1919 they were allowed eleven elected members on the Legislative Council. At the same time the Indians were allowed two elected members. Indian representation was increased to five in 1923 after pressure from the settlers. However, the Africans (98 percent of the population) were allowed no votes and no members. They were used throughout merely as a negotiating weapon by the Europeans in their struggle with the Indians.

The Africans, therefore, remained politically voiceless. Who then looked after their interests? Particularly, what was done about labor conditions? As a result of the 1912–1913 Commission's findings, an ordinance under the heading "Native Registration Ordinance" was promulgated. And what did this mean? Professor George Bennett tells us:

> In the same year (1915) a Native Registration Ordinance was passed, following the recommendation of the Native Labour Commission. Although Ainsworth, the Chief Native Commissioner, said that it was "not a pass-law," it did mean the compulsory registration of all adult native males. Supposed to facilitate the movement of labour, it proved, when amended and enforced after the war, a constant source of complaint among Africans.[3]

Again in 1915, another important ordinance under the heading "Crown Lands Ordinance of 1915" was passed which effectively reversed the ordinance of 1909, which had recognized native land rights.

Now these rights were swept away completely. The Crown Lands Ordinance of 1915 declared all African lands Crown Lands and converted their African owners into "tenants at will" of the Crown, in other words, the

British Government. That infamous seizure of title to every square foot of land remaining in African ownership and occupancy occurred during the first World War (1914–1918), in which at least 23,869 admitted to have given their lives in assisting Great Britain to overcome German resistance to the south in what is now Tanzania. The defenders of the Ordinance hold that it was intended to prevent further encroachment on African lands by the whites. But, as will be shown later, those encroachments continued and the Africans were left without the shadow of a legal remedy in consequence of this abominable legislation.

Section 86 of the 1915 Crown Lands Ordinance read as follows:

(1) The Governor may grant leases on areas of land containing native villages or settlements without specifically excluding such villages or settlements, but land in the actual occupation of natives at the date of the lease shall, so long as it is actually occupied by them, be deemed to be excluded from the lease.

(2) Any land within an area leased which has been in the occupation of the natives shall, on ceasing to be occupied, pass to the lessee.

Although this section bore some resemblance to Section 30 of the 1902 Ordinance, it lacked the same force as the lands had become Crown property. The second part of Section 86 naturally encouraged a settler leasing land partly in native occupancy to use all means within his power to compel the Africans to move elsewhere, and his control of surrounding areas gave him an excellent chance of success. Once the Africans moved they could never return, and it was not they but the settlers who were favored by the Colonial administration in interpreting the Ordinance.

Like Sir Percy Girouard (1909–1912) his successor, Sir Henry Belfield (1912–1917) was also on the settlers' side. After his departure, there was long delay in appointing a new governor and from 1917 to 1919 the Protectorate was ruled by Sir Charles Bowring as Acting Governor. It was at this time that the settlers argued vehemently that the country needed a military governor. This demand persisted throughout 1918 and Colonial Ewart Grogan, who became the settlers' spokesman, was particularly outspoken on the subject.

The Colonial Office yielded and General Sir Edward Northey, who had been in military service in Central Africa, was appointed Governor. The Protectorate was still plagued by the labor shortage, especially so after the war. The other long-standing problem, of course, was better representation in the Legislative Council.

In 1917, Sir Edward Northey decided that "humane and properly regulated pressure" should be brought to compel Africans to work for the white settlers, and in 1919 directed Protectorate officials to exert every effort to that end. This meant that local administrative officers—whose first duty should have been the protection of the Africans from exploitation—were in effect encouraged to supply the whites with forced labor. A further abuse grew from this when African chiefs and leaders were held personally responsible for carrying out the Governor's order.

A case is recorded of one District Commissioner who ordered the supply of 60 Kikuyu girls for work on a white plantation, where some of them were raped by other African employees. It was charged that the District Commissioner subjected headmen to public indignities if they failed to produce women laborers when required; the facts do not appear to have been disputed.

This system was prohibited by the London Colonial Office, but forced labor of a kind persisted in that desertion, perhaps from a cruel or unjust master, was made an offense subject to severe punishment and was provided against by a system of finger printing and identification papers. This system, popularly known as the Kipande system, was introduced in 1921 and is examined in greater detail in Chapter Fifteen.

The missionaries were horrified by Sir Edward's pro-settler attitude and actions. Their protests eventually influenced the Colonial Office, which issued a *Dispatch to the Governor of the East Africa Protectorate relating to Native Labour of 5th September 1921* ordering that Colonial officials should "Take no part in recruiting labour for private employment."

Sir Edward's governorship saw an important change of political status for Kenya. Known for a quarter of a century since the time of Sir Arthur Hardinge (1895–1900) as the British East Africa Protectorate, she was formally annexed by Great Britain on July 23, 1920. This was the culmination of many years of steady encroachment, for Britain had played an increasingly important part in Central East Africa from about 1856 onward.

This meant that the Protectorate was henceforth to be known as Kenya Colony.

5

The African Response

Earlier on, it was mentioned that at least 23,869 Africans of the British East Africa Protectorate were officially admitted to have given their lives in assisting Great Britain to overcome German resistance in Tanganyika (now Tanzania) during the First World War.

Specifically, the historian Anderson writes:

> Africans too made sacrifices in the War. 163,000 were employed as carriers. War casualties, famine and influenza meant the death of 124,000 Kikuyu alone.[1]

The Carrier Corps were responsible for transportation of war supplies, i.e. equipment and foodstuffs. Their usefulness was obvious, particularly in areas where motor transport was impossible through lack of roads.

Notwithstanding these war exigencies, these Africans were willing to pay their contribution to the British Empire.

While serving in the war, Africans widened their horizon and outlook generally. Their thinking was no longer isolated and circumscribed as it had been before the war. Perhaps this is true wherever wars break out; soldiers always learn from outside contacts.

It was natural, therefore, that when the surviving Africans returned to their homes, they had developed a much more sophisticated outlook on the world. The fighting had not made them forget their anger and frustration over the political developments taking place in their homeland. As we have seen, the other developments were not to the Africans' advantage; principally, the *1915 Crown Lands Ordinance* and the *Native Registration Ordinance* of the same year which were noted in the last chapter.

When the war ended in 1918, the Africans returned to their districts to join their brethren, who had also assisted in the war in terms of labor and food production.

Now that it was over, what did the Europeans and Africans gain in the aftermath?

The European gains were evidently enormous and can be tabulated as follows:

(a) They got the military governor they wanted in the person of Sir Edward Northey, whose acts as recorded do not need a Freudian psychologist to predict that their effect, together with the effect of Teleki's activities, would later have a strong influence on Africans.

(b) A new settlement scheme was introduced to encourage ex-soldiers from England, who were offered generous grants of free land and more on lease at low rents if needed.

Free grants started at 160 acres, but later 640 acres (one square mile) for the raising of livestock. The leased land sometimes consisted of blocks of more than 150 square miles (100,000 acres) up to 500 square miles (320,000 acres).

Much of the land disposed of by the Government to European settlers was in actual fact African occupied. A process officially called "alienation" took place. Grants often carried with them entire African villages, and the African owners were frequently evicted from their property. In Kikuyu country—one of the most fertile regions—an appearance of equity was achieved by paying each dispossessed household the sum of four rupees (with a value at that time of about 5x.4d), and permitting the harvest of growing crops. This compensation was supposed to cover the cost of clearing two acres of land elsewhere, preparing the ground for cultivation and erecting new huts, but it was not more than the weekly wage paid by white traders to a single porter. Having found new homes elsewhere, the unfortunate Africans were sometimes evicted again.

In permitting the expulsion of Africans, the British government violated its own Ordinance of 1902 which, to conform to the legal opinion on which the seizure was based, provided that:

> In all dealings with Crown (Government) land regard shall be had to the rights and requirements of the natives, and in particular the Commissioner shall not sell or lease any land in the actual occupation of natives.

The 1915 ordinance described in the last chapter was said to be a safeguard against further white encroachment on African lands, but, as encroachment continued, the main effect was to rob the Africans of all legal remedy.

A case in point was the eviction in 1921 of 1500 of the Nandi tribe to allow the settlement of British war veterans, to whom the land was leased for 999 years—this despite a previous promise that the Nandi would keep their lands forever!

Apart from those seriously interested in settlement, large tracts of land were taken by speculators, in their own names or those of nominees, who made no attempt to cultivate their holdings.

The Agricultural Census for 1938 showed that 5,153,748 acres of land alienated for white settlers were held by only 1,890 persons or corporations, making the average holding 2,670 acres—more than four square miles per unit. Of the 7,900 square miles reported upon, only 10.8 percent was actually under cultivation, while an additional 2.8 percent was pasture improved by sowing and planting forest. The remainder, about 6,890 square miles, remained precisely as it had been before the coming of the whites, the expulsion of its inhabitants excepted.

In addition to getting the kind of governor they demanded and an ex-soldiers' settlement scheme, the Europeans also gained increased representation in the Legislative Council, with power to elect their representatives.

And what did the Africans gain after the First World War?

(a) Kipande system, whereby every African adult male was forced to carry a piece of paper bearing his fingerprints. This differed from that known in the United States of America and the United Kingdom as a social security or identity number, in that in Kenya this piece of paper had economic and political as well as social implications.

(b) Introduction of forced labor.

(c) The making of Kenya into a Crown Colony. The European settlers had hoped that they could gain more politically if the territory was a Crown Colony rather than a Protectorate.

(d) Increase in African taxes, with a corresponding decrease in their wages and salaries. The African laborer had still to plumb the depths of economic misery, for the settlers had decided to reduce wages from an average of ten shillings for thirty days' labor to seven shillings for the same period. This was too much for the Africans.

From 1918 to 1921 various African political associations emerged as a result of the political, social, and economic policies of the new military governor, Sir Edward Northey. Among them were the Young Kavirondo Association (later on Kavirondo Taxpayers' and Welfare Association), and the Kikuyu Association. The Kikuyu Association was dominated by the Kikuyu government chiefs from Kiambu District, who were helped in its formation by the European missionaries who were also unhappy about Sir Edward's policies and his attitudes toward the Africans particularly. These associations were not very forceful in articulating the African concerns, notwithstanding their good intentions. For example, the Kikuyu Association, which was formed in 1919, was led and dominated by the government chiefs; and they were civil servant government employees. Consequently, it was very difficult for them to speak out forcefully against their employer— the Kenyan government.

They, however, continued to operate, giving the impression that they were the official organs of the African people in their respective areas.

In June of 1921, Harry Thuku and his colleagues formed the Young Kikuyu Association as a political vehicle to ventilate the African grievances. Simultaneously, the Young Kavirondo Association in the Nyanza Province was formed by the Rev. Ezekiel Apindi and his colleagues for the same purpose. Both associations were very aggressive in their respective areas. However, the Young Kavirondo Association was neutralized, or rather diluted, in its aggressive tendencies by Archdeacon Owen of the Nyanza Province. The Association was renamed "The Kavirondo Taxpayers' and Welfare Association" in 1923.

In July of 1921, Harry Thuku and his colleagues in Nairobi thought that the title of their movement, the Young Kikuyu Association, implied that it was limited to Kikuyu people only. They wanted to give the movement a name which would cover not only Kenya but Tanganyika and Uganda as well—hence the formation of the East African Association.

Other founding members included Jomo Kenyatta, Jesse Kariuki, Joseph Kang'ethe, George Kirongothi, Mukasa from Uganda, and from Nyasaland (Malawi), J. Sabluoni.

It is interesting to note that the concept of an East African Federation on African lines was actually initiated by Harry Thuku as early as 1919, though many cling to the idea that its inception fell between 1959 and 1960. Credit for this brilliant idea goes to Harry Thuku, although the successful development of his theory was stopped by the Colonial authorities in 1922. It is also interesting to note that the Africans of that generation do not seem to have been troubled with destructive tribalism and were ready to accept Harry Thuku as their acknowledged leader.

Who was this Harry Thuku, political star of the period? He was born in 1894 (and he witnessed the Kenya Independence celebration in 1963). His father was a member of a large Kikuyu clan on the western side of the Kambui Mission Station, about twenty miles northeast of Kiambu

Township, and had many goats, sheep and cattle, as well as a fairly large farm.

According to the Kikuyu tradition of inheritance, all this wealth belonged to young Thuku. The clan could only have taken his wealth if he had died without issue to survive him. This point is vital at this stage of the narrative, because it will have a bearing on what happened to Thuku about ten years later.

Young Thuku obtained his formal primary school education under the guidance of Mr. and Mrs. Knapp of the American Gospel Missionary Society, Kambui, Kiambu, in Kikuyu country. In appearance he was of medium height, handsome and very healthy. He was also daring and brilliant and had a tremendous amount of self-confidence.

On the successful completion of his schooling at Kambui, he joined the Civil Service as a clerk and, in this position, was able to observe African working conditions carefully. He was extremely sensitive to injustice and unfair play and was easily spurred into action. Hence, the young Thuku ignored the traditional code that the civil servant should not take active part in politics, and formed the East African Association. Though he risked dismissal from his job, Thuku felt his people were more important.

As a leader of the Association, Thuku's influence was felt all over the Central Province, and as far as Nyanza Province to the west and Taita-Taveta country to the Coast Province.

Thuku toured the country, making political speeches against forced labor, the color bar, the Kipande system, and reduction in African wages and salaries, as well as land alienation. He could not understand why the Europeans, who were supposed to be Christians and to have read both the Old and New Testaments, did not live and act according to Christian teachings. This can be noticed in his speeches, which had a distinctly biblical flavor.

The government was by now aware of Thuku's chief aim: to unite all the Africans in Kenya and to spread "Thukuism" into Uganda, perhaps even to Tanganyika.

In February 1922, at a general meeting in Fort Hall, the African leaders made it clear that they were not prepared to abandon their campaign against injustice of any kind and specifically demanded that the government should provide that:

(a) Forced labor be stopped immediately

(b) Land alienated for European settlement be returned to Africans

(c) Abolition of the Kipande system

(d) Repayment of African wage and salary deduction

(e) Adjustment of African taxes, which had been increased

The government officials present at the meeting listened attentively, but the talks ended without the officials and the Africans finding common ground for agreement. At the same time, the settlers intensified their campaign against the East African Association, as they were strongly opposed to the African demands, and grave unrest ensued.

As the situation deteriorated, the Kikuyu continued to pray to God that He should guide Harry Thuku in his leadership. Prayers were offered and the most famous of them all was recorded in an official report, *Papers Relating to Native Disturbance in Kenya, Cmd. 1691 (1922)*:

> Christians of all districts of African and Uganda.... We want urgently to remind you to pray for Bwana Harry Thuku, our leader, and the elders, that, with him, they may make us go in the right path at all times and give thanks for us every hour, that there may not be others amongst us who are his enemies; he and his elders, let them come to no harm with any words whatsoever, either now or hereafter, because he and his elders have been set apart by our God to be our guides in our present condition of slavery, which we knew not ... before the Europeans came into our country of East Africa.
>
> Also remember how that our God brought the children of Israel out of the house of bondage of King Pharaoh.
>
> And to Him let us pray again, for He is our God, Also let us have faith, since in the eyes of our God there is no distinction of white or black. All are the sons of Adam and alike before Him, Jehovah, our living God.
>
> Also remember how that Goliath was unable to hurt David when David was a child and not yet full grown. Nor could Saul hurt David, for David was chosen by Jehovah, our God.
>
> Also remember how that the Europeans and ourselves are not ashamed to pray for our King George, and in the same way do not be ashamed to pray for our guide and his supporters.
>
> Thou, Lord Jehovah, our God, it is Thou that hast set apart to be our Master and Guide, Harry Thuku; may he be the Chief of us all.
>
> Guard him from all evil and bad works.
>
> Also guard the elders who are under him, both here and hereafter, in the name of Jesus Christ our Lord, Amen.

After the prayer was published, the Chief Native Commissioner, G. V. Maxwell, considered it highly seditious. He commented:

I consider this publication to be a very dangerous one. When the element of religion is introduced into native activities of this kind, we are liable to get fanaticism, and that may lead to anything very suddenly. The whole tenor of the prayer is to stimulate enmity between black and white, and to get the people to consider that they are in a state of slavery which has been imposed upon them by the Europeans. This I consider highly seditious.[2]

Students of social sciences, and psychology in particular, may interpret the prayer differently. However, to the settlers there was a clear call to "enmity between black and white" in the words "Also let us have faith, since in the eyes of our God there is no distinction of white or black. All are the sons of Adam and alike before Him, Jehovah, our living God."

The situation became ominous in February 1922, after Thuku's bitterest political speech in the Fort Hall District of the Kikuyu. He was now fully committed to an offensive position, and compared himself to Samson in the Old Testament, saying that he had as much strength and that there was no Delilah on earth who could cut his hair!

The government intervened swiftly and, in the night of 15 March 1922, Harry Thuku and other leaders of the East African Association were arrested and taken to a police station in Nairobi.

Poor Harry Thuku! His strength, which he had pictured as equaling Samson's, was now shorn, by a Delilah in the shape of the Governor, Sir Edward Northey. But Thuku took heart, for although he was not properly tried for his supposed crime, he felt that he would one day regain his Samsonian strength, pick up the ass's jaw and challenge these "Philistines" who had encroached on the rights of his people.

On the morning following Thuku's arrest, a large crowd of angry men and women gathered near the police station where he and his colleagues were detained, demanding their immediate release. This demand was flatly rejected and the police officers and guard became impatient with the crowd, who were ordered to leave the station forthwith.

Instead of obeying, the angry Kenyans sang political songs, interspersed with prayers to Ngai who had given them the land they were now struggling to regain. Women shrilled, the police became restless, the crowd more so. What was going to happen?

Kikuyu women, like their sisters the world over, goaded their men folk to action. How? They sang songs and shrilled. They asked the African men who were supposed to have Harry Thuku released to take off their trousers and give them to the women to wear, if women were men. In turn the women would hand their skirts and other clothes to the men to wear. This was a great challenge. It implied that the men were cowards and did not have enough guts to rescue Thuku and his colleagues. "Wake up, you coward men," they shouted.

The men felt humiliated. They had no pangas, arrows, bows, spears or clubs, the police were heavily armed. "What can we do?" asked the men among themselves. The women intensified their challenge: "Thuku must be released; Thuku cannot be banished," they chanted.

The men were exceedingly embarrassed and bitter, urged on by the women, they advanced slowly toward the police buildings. The noise was tremendous and the crowd looked so menacing that the police inspector lost his head and ordered his men to fire.

After the gun smoke had cleared, 200 Africans were said to be lying dead. Officially, it was announced by the government that only 25 Africans had been killed. After crying and lamentation, the crowd dispersed and returned home, beaten by the guns but still nursing their deeply felt anger and resentment.

Some of the leaders who were arrested along with Harry Thuku were imprisoned for a few months, others for several years. Thuku himself was deported to the Northern Frontier District of Kenya for eleven years, having been given no fair trial and no chance to arrange with someone to look after his property should his aging father die in the meantime. Intelligent and forward-looking Thuku was to remain alone in a remote place called Kismayu for the next decade.

After Harry Thuku's arrest and his eventual deportation, there was a jubilant mood of relief among the Europeans as reported in the editorial comment of the *Leader* of March 18, 1922. Under the title, "The Unrest," it said:

> Yes, they have a right to organize but not of the type of East African Association.... Any laxity in permitting mobs of natives to congregate without authority amid a European settlement led by irresponsibles is simply inviting trouble of the gravest character.

Indian leader Mr. M. A. Desai was not well impressed by the Harry Thuku incident. In the *Leader* of March 25,

> I am not in any way that convinced that the recent loss of life was the result of Mr. Thuku's propaganda. I go so far as to emphatically deny that it was.

Mr. Desai's views as a leader of the Indian community at that time demonstrate that the Indians in Kenya, in spite of their few aggressive businessmen, did in fact have the welfare of the Africans at heart.

Did the British Colonial Government in Kenya ban the East African

Association legally or by applying political pressure on its leaders? The East African Association continued its political activities after Harry Thuku's deportation under the leadership of Joseph Kang'ethe as Secretary and Job Muchuchu as Treasurer. The European community continued to be apprehensive about this movement.

In 1923, for the first time, a European missionary, Dr. John W. Arthur, was nominated by the Governor to represent the African interests in the Kenya Legislature. The East African Association, in common with the African population at large, was against this nomination. They felt that naturally the Africans should be represented by their own people. The East African Association protested and sent a telegram to the Colonial Secretary in London.

At that time, the British Colonial Secretary invited European and Indian representatives to a talk in London. The Africans were to be represented by Dr. John W. Arthur, their nominated member in the Kenya Legislative Council. In addition, the East African Association gave a memorandum of complaints to Mr. M. A. Desai, the Indian representative, to take to the Colonial Secretary in London. The Association did not choose to give this memorandum to Dr. Arthur to take to London on their behalf. The outcome of the London talk will be discussed in a later chapter of this book.

In the meantime, the East African Association continued to exert political pressure on the Colonial government. The Kenyan government became increasingly apprehensive about this movement.

In 1925, the Association held a mass political meeting at Fort Hall (now Muranga). Unfortunately for the movement, Joseph Kang'ethe, its General Secretary, was arrested on the pretext that the mass political meeting was held illegally. The East African Association protested against Joseph Kang'ethe's arrest to the British Chief Native Commissioner, Mr. Watkins. Later on, Mr. Watkins pointed out to the members of the East African Association that since the organization aspired to be a multitribal political association, the government was not prepared to have its activities continue. On the other hand, the government was in favor of tribal associations, and not a single political association which could be joined by all tribes of Kenya.

Hearing this from Mr. Watkins, the Africans were depressed and dispirited. In the end, a new political movement, the Kikuyu Central Association, emerged in 1925. Even though the name suggested that it was purely a Kikuyu association, it was hoped that the Kikuyu Central Association would continue to maintain the East African Association's policy, aims and objectives.

6

The Kikuyu
Central Association—
Enter Kenyatta

In 1924, Mr. Amery, who had replaced the Duke of Devonshire as the Secretary of State for the Colonies, was vigorously championing the idea of a closer union of the East African Territories. He was particularly interested in studying about African labor conditions, taxation, and chances of integrating the public services of the area—for example, health facilities, agricultural production facilities, communication, and the African social conditions.

Mr. Amery was also under great pressure from Sir Sydney Henn, a British Member of Parliament who also appeared to have had a conflict of interests because of his business connection with the East African territories. To this end, a Commission composed of three men, all members of Parliament under Mr. Ormsby-Gore, was formed and went to East Africa to conduct its findings.

In Kenya, African associations (the Kikuyu Association, the Kavirondo Taxpayers' and Welfare Association, the East African Association and others) all gave evidence to the Ormsby-Gore Commission unanimously rejecting the idea of closer union in East Africa—especially when they had no direct representation in the Kenya Legislative Council. The Indians of Kenya, Uganda, and Tanganyika all rejected the idea of closer union, because they were afraid that any closer union in East Africa would undoubtedly be controlled by the Kenyan Europeans. In Tanganyika, the idea of closer union was rejected by the Tanganyikan Europeans, the reason being that Lord Delamere, who was the leading European settlers' spokesman in Kenya, wanted to divert trade for Dar-es-Salaam to Mombasa—which meant that Tanganyika would stop building a railroad line from Tabora to Mwanza. In addition, Lord Delamere wanted a part of Northern Tanganyika where Kilimanjaro is situated to be added to Kenya. Consequently, in Tanganyika, a closer union was viewed as both economic retardation and territorial aggrandizement. Hence, rejection of the closer union.

In Uganda the Kabaka (the King of Uganda) and members of his parliament, known as Lukiko, rejected any idea of closer union for fear that it would violate the 1900 Anglo-Uganda Agreement. The Europeans in Uganda also felt that Kenya was not playing equity when taking its share of the revenue which was derived from the Kenya-Uganda Railroad. They also felt that closer union was unacceptable.

In Kenya, Europeans were expected to be enthusiastic about the Ormsby-Gore Commission. However, most of them were cautious about it, lest it bring them under the scrutiny of the Secretary of State for the Colonies.

The main African leaders in Kenya in this period following the arrest if Harry Thuku were Joseph Kang'ethe, Jesse Kariuki, George Kirongothi Ndegwa, Willy Jimmy, Wachiuma Wanjohi, Job Muchuchu, the Reverend Peter Kigondu, Githendu Mukerie, James Beauttah (all from the Central Province and former members of the East African Association); W. K. Mengo of the Taita Hill Central Association, and Ezekiel Apindi of the Kavirondo Tax Payers' and Welfare Association.

Some observers believe that these other organizations were in reality branches of the K.C.A. and that all of them were carrying on the spirit of the former East African Association.

The main preoccupations of the K.C.A. were the return of the African land which had been alienated for European settlement, the release of Harry Thuku, translation of Kenya's laws into the Kikuyu language, the establishment of the Kikuyu chieftancy, and permission for the Africans to be allowed to grow cash crops, such as coffee and tea.

Two of the K.C.A. demands point to the fact that, though the association did try to speak for all Africans in Kenya, it differed from the former East African Association in that it was inclined to be inward looking.

How would the other tribes of Kenya feel, for instance, if the laws of Kenya were to be translated into the Kikuyu language only, which most of them clearly could not understand? Secondly, according to tradition, the

Kikuyu had believed in the Council of Elders, which meant they did not feel that power should be entrusted to one particular person. Nor did the Kikuyu believe in chieftancy. How then could such democratic people circumscribe themselves to the idea of an appointment of a paramount chief?

Although the leaders of the K.C.A. were rich in common sense, they seem to have lacked the dynamism which Harry Thuku had demonstrated. Not until 1928 was this situation remedied with Johnstone Kinyata, who later became Jomo Kenyatta, joining the organization as its General Secretary.

Although Kenyatta helped to form the East African Association with Harry Thuku in 1919, he was still in the full-time employ of the Nairobi Municipality. He only gave this up when he joined the K.C.A. on a full-time basis in 1928. Before this, his participation in politics appears to have been on a part-time basis, and it is interesting to note that the Nairobi Corporation did not seem to mind his extraneous activities.

There were many unnamed loyal men and women who were also mainstays of the K.C.A. They raised money to finance the movement, and later on churches and independent schools.

Who was Kenyatta? He was born in Ichaweri at Gatundu in Kiambu District probably between 1890 and 1896. His father was Muigai and his mother was Wambui. He joined the Church of Scotland Mission at Kikuyu in 1907.

In 1913, he went through the traditional ritual of the Kikuyu circumcision. Hence, he became a member of the age-grade called Mubengi, or Kihiu Mwiri. In 1914, he was baptized by the Church of Scotland Mission at Kikuyu as John Peter Kamau. "Peter" signifying "rock," he changed to "stone," thus giving himself the name of Johnstone Kamau.

In 1919, he was married to Grace Wahu. Out of this union, two children were born: Peter Muigai in 1920 and Margret Wambui in 1928. In October of 1920, he was summoned by the Kirk Session to be tried by the church elders for taking a wife without a Christian ceremony and for drinking locally brewed liquor.

After the Church of Scotland Mission was firmly established in 1898 at Kikuyu Station, a church was built and in 1900, a school was established. In addition, sub-stations were also built in the Kikuyu country. All these were necessary if the process of evangelization was to succeed. A dispensary and a hospital were also established.

Kenyatta, in common with other young men and women in the country, decided to take advantage of the white man's education, so the young Kenyatta had his formal elementary schooling under the guidance of Scottish missionaries.

Like many other young men and women in Kikuyu country, Kenyatta seems to have enjoyed a full normal boyhood before going to mission station to be educated. For example, before he underwent the circumcision ceremony, he danced the Ngucu, then a very popular dance among the uncircumcised boys.

After circumcision, he danced Gichukia, Mugoiyo, Nguru and Kibata. Some of these dances are similar to the ones danced by the native Indians of the Americas, wherein the dancers, especially the males, tie bells (ciigamba) immediately below the right knee. These bells provide a very interesting rhythm and made a good male dancer very popular with the fair sex. This sort of dancing can also still be seen in the summer in England, where it has survived since at least the reign of Elizabeth I and probably dates back to the Middle Ages. The Morris Dancers, as they are known there, wear bells on both legs.

The dances performed by Kenyatta and his friends could be likened to the pop dances and songs of contemporary Britain and the United States, indeed the Western world in general. So Kenyatta had plenty of opportunity to assimilate the Kikuyu social ways and traditions, as well as those of the white man, after joining the missionary station.

Like Harry Thuku, Kenyatta was very keen on matters affecting his people. He witnessed land alienation and, as did Harry Thuku, felt something must be done.

But for Kenyatta the time was not yet ripe. After successfully completing his studies, he joined the Municipality of Nairobi and worked in its plumbing department, where he appears to have been happy. He used to travel on a motorcycle—a luxurious form of transport for an African in those days. He was a hard-working man.

In common with Harry Thuku, he used to feel that as a man he should contribute something to the ideas men discussed round the evening fire, though he seems to have hated idle moments, especially after he became involved in politics.

As soon as he joined the K.C.A., he established an official organ—a political paper known as "Muiguithania," meaning "One who brings unity and makes people compromise." He had by now thrown himself completely into politics.

At that time a controversy was raging between the missionaries and Kikuyu over the circumcision of women. Kenyatta felt deeply that, unlike the missionaries, he understood the full significance of the ceremony.

In order to discourage female circumcision, the missionaries adopted a negative approach to Kikuyu customs generally, condemning them all as "heathen," "pagan," "barbaric," and "primitive." This attack on an entire social structure was naturally resented by the Kikuyu. A strongly political song called "Muthirigu" was composed against the missionaries and sung all over the Kikuyu country and among the squatters working for the European settlers.

The missionaries were, however, as determined as were the Kikuyu. The colonial government sided with the missionaries, so that mass meetings and political songs against them were banned, but the rift between the Kikuyu and the missionaries remained.

In 1929, the K.C.A. sent Jomo Kenyatta to Britain to represent the African people in the political heart of the British Empire—London—but his mission had no concrete result. He did, however, make important contacts and friends and it is certain that his visit to Britain and the impression he made focused British public opinion on Kenya's problems more than ever before.

After his return from Britain, he became acknowledged leader of the Kenyan people. A man of extrovert personality, a vigorous speaker, physically strong, with eyes burning like fire, generous but ruthless when aggravated, independent in his thought, Kenyatta at no time in his political career attempted to represent the interests of the Kikuyu people only, though he was himself a Kikuyu.

In 1931, Kenyatta and another Kikuyu leader from Muranga named Parmenas Githendu Mukerie represented the Africans before the Carter Commission. Both carried out their mission excellently and it was decided that Jomo Kenyatta should remain in Britain to obtain a thorough training. This was not an easy thing for him to do, financially or otherwise.

Fortunately for Kenyatta, he had a good friend in Birmingham, England, Dr. Norman Leys, who had been in Kenya as a medical officer and had practical experience with the Kenyan colonial government and its relationship with the Africans. As a matter of fact, Dr. Leys wrote a book which was like an indictment of the Kenyan colonial authority called *The Colour Bar in British East Africa*. In 1932, as a family friend of Dr. Leys, Kenyatta attended Woodbrooke College, Selly Oak, where Dr. Leys' brother was teaching. For Kenyatta, attending Woodbrooke College meant brushing up on his primary and secondary education in order to prepare himself for higher courses at the London School of Economics and Political Science later on.

Kenyatta got along famously with the students at Woodbrooke College. He was very popular as a mature man among the young students. They referred to him as "Uncle Ken," and he seemed to like his nickname.

To what extent was Kenyatta's representation accepted by non–Kikuyu people of Kenya? The extent to which non–Kikuyu people of Kenya could be said to have accepted Kenyatta's leadership could be demonstrated by the Akamba case in 1938, wherein the British colonial government in Kenya ordered that the Akamba people de-stock their cattle herds, in order, presumably, to lessen the problem of soil erosion. The Akamba leaders contacted Kenyatta in London to represent their case to the colonial office.

In addition to sending their case to Kenyatta in London, the Ukamba Members Association, which had emerged as a political association for the Akamba in the 1930s, organized a big march, in October of 1938, of 3000 Akamba to Nairobi to demonstrate to the governor, particularly that they were bitterly opposed to his policy toward the Akamba. The governor was not receptive, and the Akamba leader Samuel Muindi Mbingu, who had organized the march, was arrested and deported to an island in the Indian Ocean called Lamu.

It has been said repeatedly by British officials in both the colonial office London and in Kenya that Kenyatta in England was representing the Kikuyu people alone, as he was sent to England by the Kikuyu Central Association—implying that the rest of the Kenyan Africans and associations had nothing to do with Kenyatta in England. They were the same officials who encouraged ethnically bound tribal associations after the East African Association was discouraged officially by the Kenyan colonial government in 1925.

In Britain, Kenyatta was representing all Africans of Kenya, irrespective of their tribal background. All Africans suffered from the same fate, economically, politically, socially and culturally. Land alienation was as common in Masai, Ukambani, Nandi, Kisii, Kipsigis and Taita-Taveta as it was in the Kikuyu country. Consequently, the claim that Kenyatta in Britain was merely a Kikuyu representative appears to be unfounded. He was not claiming privilege for the Kikuyu.

Between 1933 and 1936, Kenyatta studied with the London School of Economics and Political Science, from where he obtained a Diploma in Anthropology, under Professor Bronslaw Malinowski. (A University of London Diploma is perhaps equivalent to a general B.A. degree.) Later he traveled widely throughout Europe and attended a few lectures at Moscow University.

In 1938 Kenyatta published his excellent book on the Kikuyu, under the title *Facing Mount Kenya*. In it, Kenyatta advised against value judgments and in favor of functional judgments in respect of western interpretation of a non-literate culture.

In 1940 during the Second World War, Kenyatta had a hard time in England financially. He worked as a laborer in West Sussex. He was amazed to find out that the Britons in Great Britain were as hard working as the

African workers in Kenya. In Kenya, the Europeans relied on the Africans for the hard work.

In 1942, Kenyatta met and married an English girl, Edna Clarke, at the Chancetonbury Registry Office. As a result of this union, the couple had a boy named Magana Muigai Kenyatta. Kenyatta had two other children in Kenya before he left Kenya for England, with Grace Wahu, his first Kikuyu wife. These were Peter Muigai Kenyatta and Margret Wambui Kenyatta. However, the Kenyan Africans did not seem to dwell on Kenyatta's personal lifestyle. They deeply trusted him as their true representative.

Back in Kenya, the K.C.A. was continuing the struggle. Throughout this period, the problem was to educate the children, to build independent schools, and to supply Kenyatta with ammunition to carry on the battle in England to secure the return of the land to its rightful African ownership.

The Africans were happier now, however, because in 1930 their former leader, Harry Thuku, was released from his long detention (1922–1930) and was allowed to re-enter politics on the understanding that he only oppose the government constitutionally.

When Thuku joined the K.C.A., a bitter struggle for leadership developed. He felt he was the acknowledged African leader and could not under any circumstances serve under others. The K.C.A. leaders disagreed for, although Thuku's contribution to Kenyan Africans' political development was great, they had themselves developed further during the eight years of his detention. Indeed, they insisted that Kenyatta, though in England, was their acknowledged leader and that under him there was opportunity for everyone else to play his part. The struggle between Thuku and the other K.C.A. leaders persisted, however, and was embittered by personal differences.

Thuku was accused of being "soft" with the British in their colonial policy and suspected of having been tamed by them—tantamount to being told that he had already been bought by them and was no longer as tough as he had formerly been. Thuku pleaded eight years of detention, arguing that those years had taken their toll and he could not understand why, after such a long ordeal, he could not be more appreciated.

He accused the K.C.A. leaders of not agitating sufficiently for his release and then threatened to resign from the association. The K.C.A. leaders accepted the challenge and Thuku broke away, forming the Kikuyu Provincial Association (K.P.A.) as a rival to the K.C.A.—an unhealthy development for the African leadership. Despite the advantage the K.C.A. enjoyed in its existing membership and years of organization, Thuku's K.P.A. attracted a moderate following. Both organizations functioned side by side, pursuing almost identical proposals to the government, which therefore took little comfort from the split.

There is no evidence, in fact, that his political fire had been dampened by detention, but at this time Thuku was preoccupied with a personal problem. On his return, he found that his father's immense wealth and land had been appropriated by members of his large clan, who had taken advantage of his absence. He was determined to regain that which he felt rightfully belonged to him, since everything had been willed to him by his father. The clan resisted his claim, but Thuku employed an able lawyer and eventually won a complete legal victory.

The case dragged on for a long time and seems to have taken up much time, so that he did not pay nearly enough attention to his K.P.A. But his riches enabled him to settle down on a large piece of fertile land, on which he grew potatoes, maize (corn), beans and later coffee. As well as a beautiful wife, he boasted a splendid house and a nice car.

Was the split-up between the K.C.A. and K.P.A. inevitable? When Harry Thuku rejoined the K.C.A. after his release in 1930, he insisted on a strong discipline among its members. He also insisted that the organization must have an accountant, a treasurer, and that the organization's fund must be audited annually. He further insisted that all members of the organization must have other means of personal income—for example, farming or working—instead of relying on its limited funds for their livelihood. Harry Thuku added that he was strongly in favor of constitutional struggle, and opposed to violence.

In the end, most members of the K.C.A., especially Jesse Kariuki and Joseph Kang'ethe, felt that Harry Thuku's demands were intolerable and dictatorial. Consequently, the split-up occurred in 1935.

To demonstrate that he was a constitutionalist and not a man of violence, Harry Thuku's new organization had a set of rules and regulations which were different than those of the K.C.A. Indeed, Harry Thuku felt that the K.C.A. did not seem to have rules and regulations. One of the rules which he insisted upon very strongly was a stand on constitutionality and loyalty:

> Every member of the organization will be pledged to be loyal to
> His Majesty the King of Great Britain and the established Government and will be bound to do nothing which is not constitutional
> according to the British traditions or do anything which is calculated to disturb the peace, good order, and Government.[1]

To the K.C.A. and its members, this was unacceptable. They accused Harry Thuku of being an apologist for the British authorities.

In 1939, when the Second World War broke out, the Kenya colonial government was sensitive and suspicious of all African political association. Consequently, in 1940, the Kikuyu Central Association and others were proscribed or banned. However, for some reasons unknown to the Africans, Harry Thuku's Kikuyu Provincial Association was not banned. As a matter of fact, Harry Thuku himself went to Kiambu Township to see the District Commissioner about the possibilities of his political association—The Kikuyu Provincial Association—raising money for the purpose of supporting the war efforts. The District Commissioner, Mr. C. H. Williams, expressed his appreciation, after which time a huge sum of money was raised by the Kikuyu Provincial Association and deposited through the National Bank of India in Nairobi.

Harry Thuku himself acknowledges this account in his own autobiography, *Harry Thuku: An Autobiography*, published by the Oxford University Press in Nairobi in 1970, page 64.

7

Closer Union versus African Paramountcy

The grievances which the Africans had been ventilating—especially since Sir Edward Northey became the first military governor in Kenya in 1919, culminating in Harry Thuku's arrest and eventual deportation in 1922—were still outstanding and were, therefore, not rectified. It is also important to remember that since the establishment of the Kenya Legislative Council in 1907 the Africans were indirectly represented by the government officials of the Kenya Legislative Council. The government official members could not effectively represent African interests in the Legislative Council for the simple reason that they were themselves government civil servants. Expressing the difficulties which the official members faced while representing African interests, C. W. Hobley, who was once a District Commissioner, says:

> The present system of safeguarding their interests by an official majority is even in many ways illusory, for it is only to be expected that heads of various technical departments should look more to satisfying the needs of an intensely critical European population than those of the inarticulate black millions. The so-called direct representation of native affairs on the Legislative Council is at present lamentably weak; it consists of the Commissioner of Native Affairs and three provincial commissioners, who appear rather as suppliants for funds before a majority of members who, as a body, are not particularly interested and further, they are not

real representatives for they are by their position subservient to the Governor.[1]

To this end, it would seem as if the nomination of Dr. J. W. Arthur in 1923 to be the first missionary to represent the African interests in the Legislative Council was a direct result of Harry Thuku's incident of 1922, in addition to the missionaries' pressure on the British government. It would seem that the Duke of Devonshire's declaration of 1923, which will be discussed hereunder, was also stimulated by Harry Thuku's unrest.

Dr. Arthur's nomination to the Legislative Council to represent the African interests had mixed reactions from the African people. Some did welcome it as a step forward. Others would have preferred a direct African representation by their own people—while some resented Dr. Arthur who viewed the missionaries as nemesis of the African customs.

It should be emphasized, however, that Dr. Arthur's performance during his tenure as a representative of the African interests in the Kenya Legislative Council was absolutely superlative. His services and his focused devotion to the African people during this period of Kenyan history were beyond any description. He fought very hard, pressing the Kenyan government to demonstrate its fair play. It would appear as if there were no Kenyan African at that time (in the 1920s) who could have represented all Africans of Kenya in the Legislative Council better than Dr. Arthur did.

Maneuvering for position between Whitehall and Kenya's white settlers continued. In 1923, a further attempt was made by the British Government to define their authority and policy at the expense of the settlers. The Devonshire declaration, as it became known, laid down that:

> Primarily, Kenya is an African Territory and His Majesty's Government thinks it necessary definitely to record their considered opinion that the interests of African natives must be paramount, and that, if and when those interests and the interests of the immigrant races should conflict, the former should prevail.... But in the administration of Kenya, His Majesty's Government regard themselves as administering a trust on behalf of the native population and they are unable to share or delegate this trust, the object of which may be defined as the protection and advancement of the native races.

The settlers were greatly disturbed and decided to counter the declaration by advancing the concept of a closer union of all the East African territories. The settlers envisaged a new Dominion like Australia or South Africa in which they would be politically and economically dominant and independent of the Colonial Office. The suggestion was interesting but doubts were raised and so, as Professor Margery Perham writes:

> In July 1924 an all-party Parliamentary Commission, with Ormsby-Gore as Chairman, was sent to East Africa. Its report, published next year, emphasized, almost in Lugard's own words, the concept of the Dual Mandate. It advised against federation, but was in favour of regular governors' conferences. But in a matter almost of months the settlers, led by Lords Delamere and Francis Scott, were trying to get closer union in East Africa accompanied by an unofficial majority in the Kenya Legislative Council.[2]

Earlier, the Africans in Kenya had greeted the British government's proclamation of 1923 with applause. They then, naturally, could not support the idea of closer union of the East African territories, while in their own country they had no representation whatsoever in either central or local governments.

The Kikuyu Central Association, the Kavirondo Taxpayers Association, and the Taita Central Hill Association, in their evidence to the Ormsby-Gore Commission, all strongly opposed closer union which could only be a death-blow to eventual African self-government and independence.

On the land question, on which the Africans had placed special emphasis in their representation, the Ormsby-Gore Commission suggested that a Native Lands Trust Board should be established.

The British Government was still considering the Commission's report when Sir Robert Coryndon died early in 1925. At that time, the Colonial Secretary was Leopold Amery, and he appointed Sir Edward Grigg to succeed as Governor.

This appointment pleased the settlers immeasurably. Why? Professor Margery Perham again explains:

> Their hopes lay in the Conservative Colonial Secretary, Mr. Amery, and their new Governor, Sir Edward Grigg. He drew his inspiration from Rhodes and Smuts. He knew that Amery meant him to bring about closer union and could expect to be himself the first Governor-General....[3]

As a preliminary revitalization of the idea of closer union which the Ormsby-Gore Commission had discouraged, Lord Delamere, now that once again there was a sympathetic Governor, called a settlers' meeting at Tukuyu in Tanganyika. It was attended by Colonel Sanders and C. Burbery Sede from Nyasaland (now Malawi); L. F. Moore, F. G. Clarke, and T. M.

Michlam from Northern Rhodesia (now Zambia); Lord Delamere, Lord Francis Scott and H. F. Ward from Kenya; and J. Stuart Wells, F. Billinge Ullyate and G. H. Hewer from Tanganyika (now Tanzania). No African or Indian representatives were invited.

The settlers' meeting at Tukuyu prepared the way for the East African Governors' Conference, which met in Moshi, Tanganyika, in December, 1925.

Both economic and long term political strategy indicated closer ties between the three East African territories controlled by the British. The essential factors were explained by Sir Edward Grigg as follows:

> The argument for closer union was simple enough. It derived *in primis* from the fact that German East Africa, conquered by a South African General at very considerable sacrifice, would no longer be a barrier to the Rhodes-Milner concept of a British dominion stretching from Rhodesia to Kenya. The mandate system was devised in order to honour the allies' declaration that they had not fought for territorial gains; and Smuts had agreed accordingly that German East Africa should be a Mandated Territory. But he had been careful to have its mandate so framed that Britain retained complete sovereignty and the right to amalgamate the new territory with its neighbours whenever she chose to do so.
>
> For such amalgamation the foreseeable needs of the area gave compelling reason. Being as large as Europe, but sparsely peopled, it could never raise production or revenue or attain a higher standard of living without some considerable development of communications, more particularly of ports and railways....[4]

Despite these persuasive arguments, the East African Governors' Conference as a whole did not favor closer union. Sir Donald Cameron, then Governor of Tanganyika, took the view that the interests of his mandated territory should not be subordinated to those of Kenya and its settlers, and nearly persuaded Mr. Amery, the Secretary of State. Sir Edward Grigg explains that in Sir Donald's conception, German East Africa was held separate from the racial conflicts in other parts of Africa by divine intervention, in order that its indigenous people might be trained to become sovereign over their own territory.[5]

In 1927, Sir Holton Young, then Lord Kennet, headed a special Commission to East Africa with a view to studying possibilities for closer union once again.

The commission included also Sir Reginald Mant, Sir George Schuster, and Dr. J. H. Odham. For the first time, it might be said, a commission on East Africa was composed of people of independent and impartial thinking.

On its return to the United Kingdom in 1928, the Commission reported to the colonial secretary: Despite the economic advantages, they did not favor closer union on political grounds. They stressed again the British declaration on Kenya in 1923, disapproving the settlers' desire for an unofficial majority in the Kenya Legislative Council while the Africans lacked adequate representation.

Mr. Amery, Sir Edward Grigg, and the Kenya settlers were disappointed by the Hilton Young Commission's report. The bitterness of the settlers now extended to a suspicion of the Colonial Office itself.

Mr. Amery, however, did not abandon all hope and, in spite of the forthcoming general election in Britain, he sent his permanent under-secretary, Sir Samuel Wilson, to discuss the matter once again with the East African political leaders.

Sir Samuel's mission was inconclusive and the new Labour government decided to set up a Joint Select Commission of Parliament to investigate closer union yet again.

The committee sat from December, 1930, to July, 1931, and presented its report to the Colonial office in October, 1931, following which a delegation of African, European and Indian representatives was summoned to London. After much argument, agreement on the basic issues proved impossible. Much of the blame for failure falls on the Kenya settlers who by then realized that an East African Federation would weaken, and not consolidate, the increasing control they had been achieving over their own affairs. Professor Margery Perham writes:

> Well, what happened? The Kenya settlers had been pressing on and off for years for a more dominant position in the Kenya constitution and the request had been evaded or refused by the Government. Closer union had certain obvious conveniences and the settlers decided to support the request in the hope that under the general federal control they would be allowed to obtain European self-government in Kenya. But this was refused by the Hilton-Young Commission, by the Imperial Government, and by the report of Sir Samuel Wilson. The settlers then realized that they would get with closer union a federal council with an official majority and with little or no compensating advance for themselves within Kenya. They therefore told the Joint Committee they would give up the idea of closer union.[6]

The Africans should be thankful to Lord Lugard and Dr. J. H. Oldham, for they led the direct opposition to closer union. There should also be added the names of Sir Donald Cameron, the Governor of Tanganyika, and Professor Margery Perham of Oxford University for the part she played in publicizing the issues involved.

Perhaps Lord Lugard did not, after all, forget the importance of the Kikuyu oath which had been administered on both Waiyaki and himself at Dagoretti in 1890. For the fight in which he engaged in his later years on behalf of the Kenyan Africans was in the true spirit of his oath.

8

Intercultural
Relations, Part I

This book cannot deal in detail with the history of the Christian missionaries, but would not be complete without some overview mention of the missionary movements in Africa generally, because these men and the ideas and education they brought with them had an inevitable influence on the political progression of the African people everywhere in the continent.

The history of Africa and Christianity dates back to about the fourth century, with the Ethiopian Orthodox Church. While not attempting to or having any direct effect on the Christian movement in Africa, it inspired the founding of the Independent Churches in Southern Africa. The Independent Churches are a direct result of intercultural relations.

The missionary movements came from Europe with the arrival of Portuguese chaplains at the trading settlements in Africa. These also acted as missionaries to the neighboring African people. In 1500, Benin and Congo were penetrated by them with San Salvador, capital of Congo, becoming the mission. The King of Congo had his son sent to Portugal for training and the son later became Bishop of Congo in 1518. The Jesuits then pushed from the mouth of the Zambesi into Rhodesia in 1561, at which time a priest was martyred. The Jesuits were operating out of San Paulo de Loanda which superseded San Salvador as an ecclesiastical center. The Dominicans finally placed a priesthood in Rhodesia in 1652.

Most of the previously mentioned missions and congregations vanished by the end of the 18th century. The reasons for this decline are:

(a) The Portuguese alliance with slave trade

(b) Difficulty of training African priests with no African seminary

(c) Missionary policy clashed with rights of Portuguese Crown

(d) Effectiveness and number reduced by climate and disease

(e) Problems in Europe: French Revolution, Expulsion of Jesuits from Portugal and Napoleon's actions against the Pope.[1]

There were few traces of the Catholic movement left when the Protestant missionaries began their drive at Sierra Leone. Slave trade had an important part in the establishing of Freetown in Sierra Leone. After the Church of Africa was established at Freetown in 1791, slave ships were captured by the English and men were freed in Freetown. The first group of slaves were already Christian, coming from Nova Scotia, Jamaica, and Britain.

Fifty years after Freetown, Gambia, Gold Coast, Dahomey and Nigeria all had Christian congregations. Missionaries were coming from Europe, America and the West Indies. An example is Thomas Freeman, an American, who preached in Kumasi in 1839, Abeokuta in 1842, and Obombey in 1843.

Liberia also created a home for freed slaves under American initiative, which included Roman Catholics, but Monrovia failed to be another Freetown because of its location. Freetown's harbor formed a natural link with other trading posts and, unlike Monrovia, was easy to frequent.

The movement in itself was very costly. From Sierra Leone to the Gold Coast the C.M.S. suffered heavy losses to climate and fever. The Roman Catholics also suffered the same fate. The Protestants were reduced to a holding operation in the latter part of the 19th century because of this casualty rate.

The holding operation had a positive aspect. It left an opening for African leadership in the Church, but a later setback in this trend reversed this. By 1900, there was greater "missionary" control. The reasons for this were:

(a) A new mood of imperialism

(b) New emphasis on secondary schools and teacher training colleges with the requirements for the staff coming from Europe

(c) New Puritanism from the holiness doctrine of the Keswick Convention.[2]

In Southern Africa there was a new thrust northward by the L.M.S. and the German Monrovians. As a matter of fact, the first L.M.S. missionaries arrived at the Cape in 1798.

Stations in Namaqual, Bechuanaland, and Rhodesia were strung out across Zulu and Xhosa country. They were interrupted by Zulu wars and differences with Boer farmers, but they were not stopped.

Livingstone, Philip, and Moffat are names to remember in the movement because they not only preached the gospel but spoke out for African rights. The rapid growth of the Church in the South-Central region was due to Xhosa and Zulu Christians accompanying the pioneer missionaries as catechists and evangelists.

In East Africa the German missionaries under the C.M.S. reached Zanzibar in 1844, Uganda in 1877, and the first Catholics two years later.

Forty-five men, Protestants and Catholics, were put to death because of their religion within a span of ten years by the Kabaka of Buganda, but so rapid was Christian penetration that they were the driving political force at the start of colonial rule in 1894.

In Central Africa the Baptist Missionary Society entered the Congo in 1870. With others coming in, a foundation of interdenominational societies arose. Why were they able to build under King Leopold, whose methods they condemned? A clause governing the Congo Basin, and accepted by the Berlin Conference of 1884–1885, protected *all* religious institutions. As a matter of fact, the churches in Congo became one of the pillars of Belgian Colonial system.

The Roman Catholics, seeing the success of the Protestants, penetrated the mainland to, and in, the following places and times: 1878, Tanganyika; 1877, Uganda; 1843, Senegal; 1866, Congo; 1851, South Africa; 1884, South West Africa.

There were almost two million Roman Catholics in these countries by 1900 and five million by 1930. Today there are twenty-four million, served by fifteen different orders.

Why did the Catholics succeed where they earlier failed?

(a) They profited from the mistakes of the Protestants and had the ability to overcome opposition.

(b) Control of tropical disease was making headway at the restart time of the Catholic movement.

(c) Catholic orders were limited to Africa, thereby applying greater concentration to particular regions—not so with Protestants.

As mentioned earlier, the Independent Church started to appear in greater numbers. Why?

(a) Revolt against European domination

(b) Revolt against practices of Church against polygamy

(c) Revolt against limitation of spontaneous expression in worship such as drumming, hand clapping, dancing, and any relation of religion to so-called witchcraft

Simon Kimbangu, who actualized the African plight in the lower Congo, was imprisoned for life by the Belgian authorities. He was the black savior for his followers.

In Uganda the missionary movement, as anywhere else, was backed by political motives. Since the English, French, and Arabs were the main parties involved, the morality of Arab slave-trade was used by the English and the French for political intervention. This came in the form of missionaries. Soon after H. M. Stanley came, a marriage between European commercial and social interests occurred. Hence, Christianity was used as a political tool against the Arabs.[3]

The "Stanley Letter" in 1875, opened the door for missionary endeavor, followed closely by charter companies.

The C.M.S. responded to this letter by sending an expedition into Uganda lead by Mackey in 1778, followed shortly by French Catholics. All three groups, Arabs, Catholics, and Protestants, contended for the Kabaka's favor. The missionaries were soon regarded as "chiefs" with no allegiance to the Kabaka. Their individual sources of power came from their congregations.

When the missionaries sought to widen their power, the Kabaka saw the relevance of previous Arab warnings about the greed of Christians. "There was little more cordiality between the Protestants and the Catholics than that between the Anglicans and the Arabs."[4] Because of the deteriorating relationship between Mutesa and the Christians, the French withdrew half of the French Catholics and several Protestants' readers were burned. Between 1885 and 1887, fifteen Protestants and twenty Catholics were martyred.[5]

Because of his actions, Mwanga was constantly under personal attack by the Christians. He decided to rid himself of the ever-increasing power of the missionaries and "all" that was not pagan. The reaction to this was a "united" religious revolution which sent him fleeing from Buganda. His elder brother, Kiewewa, took over only to be displaced for not accepting Islam and circumcision. Kalema, Mwanga's half-brother, was then placed on the throne, which was to be a short-lived victory for the Arabs.[6]

Mwanga wrote a letter to the C.M.S. lead by MacKay, asking for forgiveness and help to return to the throne of Buganda. The Christian forces, reorganized under Protestant General Kagwa, defeated Islam and Kalema in 1890, reversing the bloody expulsion of the Christians previously. "Now all posts of authority are occupied by the Christians. The land falls into their hands and the Kabaka is no longer a king but a puppet."[7]

The Catholics and Protestants were in another bitter conflict because Mwanga, to maintain harmony, was playing one off against the other. He became a Catholic to offset British power. Demands from both secular powers flew fast and furious. The missionaries were no less determined than the C.M.S. to dominate the chastened Mwanga. Captain Lugard from the I.B.E.A.C. had a British-Buganda treaty signed against the Kabaka's will. The French induced Mwanga into signing a Protectorate treaty with the German representative, Dr. Carl Peters. Mwanga was later forced to renounce the German treaty by Lugard. After the I.B.E.A.C. was established as a protectorate, religious conflict continued. Whichever secular power felt it was out of favor with Mwanga made vicious personal attacks on him which brought the whole mess right into his own household.[8]

Due to this secular and political upheaval, Mwanga fled again and was defeated in Buddu in a countermove to regain his throne and oust the British once and for all. This had a tremendous effect on the government of Uganda. Even though the Kabaka at this time had a separation between church and state, the secular factions were still controlling forces in the government. The Catholics and the Protestants are fairly equal with the Muslims—small in number, but holding the balance of power. Uganda is a prime example of nationalism without mass political parties, but also a separatist nation with the need of a common denominator.[9]

The situation in the Congo, as far as religion goes, is similar to that of Uganda. With H. M. Stanley preceding their arrival, the British Protestants and the French Catholics both contended for the royal favor. Before the Berlin Conference in 1885, Leopold was careful not to offend either secular faction. After the Kaiser, Otto Von Bismarck, virtually handed the Congo to Leopold, he no longer had any need for British public opinion or for their missionaries. The political pressure put on Leopold at this time was similar to that put on the Kabaka in Uganda.[10]

Leopold found Belgian missionaries too few in number to replace British Protestants. He also caused an overbalance of state subsidies in favor of the Catholics which generated a tumultuous protest from the Protestants. As in Uganda, the state regime came under verbal attack by the Protestants for alleged atrocities. Because the Catholics did not want to lose their subsidies, they let themselves be used as a counterbalance to the Protestant attack.

The Congo Free State, going inland only as far as Leopoldville in 1885, expanded to what it is today by 1898. It was annexed by Belgium in

1908. The expansion headed by Carl Peters and backed by the military force of Leopold was similar to the force used by Lugard in Uganda.

The Belgian government tried again to replace British Protestants with Belgian Protestants. The numbers were so insignificant that this just tended to swell the ranks of the Protestants.[11]

Feeling they were being discriminated against, the Protestants held a series of conferences from 1902 to 1924 about the subsidy problem and unification. They finally unified under "The Church of Christ in the Congo." Unification of religion happened in Uganda, too. This does not mean Catholics and Protestants, but factions within each religion.

Relations between Catholics and Protestants at this point did not improve. In fact, "A great impetus was given to Catholic missionary expansion by Pope Pius XI, who realized that the Congo represented a unique opportunity for advance, and the Belgian Catholic missionary efforts concentrated on the Congo. Medical missionary work was developed a great deal in this sphere."[12] Unlike in Uganda, Catholics held the position of power at this time.

Peaceful coexistence was just as impossible in the Congo between the two secular factions as it was in Uganda. A bitter fight broke out between them. The Catholics carried on pamphlet warfare accusing the Protestants of being allied with Moscow to overthrow the Belgian Government. The Protestants, in turn, gathered information indicative of mistreatment of their people by Catholic missionaries and allegations against the State.[13]

Unlike Uganda, the Congo Church leaders did not always rate second to the European. After Independence in 1960, African Church leaders were placed in positions of responsibility, and also made up the delegation to the Congo Protestant Council in 1963.[14]

In Kenya, the early missionaries were:

(a) The Portuguese who in the course of their brief stay in the East Coast of Kenya tried to convert the Coast people to Catholicism. After their departure, support for the missions they had established declined rapidly and the impact of Islam filled the vacuum.

(b) The Church Missionary Society of the Church of England sent Dr. J. L. Krapf, a German missionary, to Kenya by way of Ethiopia. In 1844, he reached Mombasa. He worked hard and translated the New Testament into Swahili. In 1846, the Rev. John Rebmann and the Rev. J. J. Erhardt, both members of the C.M.S., joined Dr. Krapf.

(c) In 1862, the United Methodist Mission, again from England, sent Thomas Wakefield to Kenya.

(d) In 1891, the Church of Scotland Mission sent Dr. David Clement Ruffelle Scott, Mr. A. R. Barlow (a scholar of exceptional ability), and Dr. J. W. Arthur.

(e) In 1892, the Holy Ghost Fathers, a Roman Catholic mission, arrived.

(f) In 1895, the Africa Inland Mission came from the United States of America to evangelize the Rift Valley and Central Provinces.

(g) In 1898, another American order, the Gospel Missionary Society led by Krigor and Mr. and Mrs. Knapp, set up its headquarters among the Kikuyu.

(h) In 1902, the American Friends' Africa Mission established its headquarters among the Abaluhya and Nandi.

(i) In 1904, another Catholic order, the Mill Hill Fathers, started work in North Nyanza, South Nyanza, and later in Rift Valley Province.

From the first, perhaps the only thing the different denominations had in common was the evangelization of the Africans. Looking back over the past 120 years, it is easy to criticize the missionaries as they had no special dispensation from ordinary human failings and lack of foresight. They quarreled amongst themselves and at times showed a perhaps understandable inclination to follow government policy at the expense of the people amongst whom they worked. However, in the final analysis, their hard work and moderating influence will stand as a solid and permanent contribution to Kenya's cause.

There is no need to argue a special case to excuse the missionaries. We need try only to understand and to give credit where credit is due. As Spinoza said: "I have made a ceaseless effort not to ridicule, not to bewail, nor to scorn human actions, but to understand them."

There are some Africans today who, because of the anti-colonial struggle, still see everything in terms of Black and White. It is perhaps time for them to give a lead to the South African Government in abandoning such a backward looking attitude which is already, in this fast moving and shrinking world, outdated as much as is the concept of empire. They restrict our vision like blinkers on a carthorse.

All must learn to evaluate what is good and what is evil objectively. Self-criticism and an unprejudiced willingness to consider the ideas and deeds of others is essential if society is not to be fragmented and distorted. The concept of "un–African thought" is as unrealistic as ever was "un–American activity" in the time of the late Senator McCarthy in the United States. The real value lies in truth wherever it is to be found.

Missionary work, as an influence on the development of Kenya, can best be understood in terms of intercultural relations. To suggest that the traditional African society in Kenya was necessarily better in all ways than the society which resulted from the cultural interaction between Africa and Europe, largely due to the missionaries, is to make a shallow and misleading judgment. African ethnic groups should borrow traits from Europeans as well as from each other when necessary.

As indicated elsewhere, Kenyan Africans were thoroughgoing people of the soil before the arrival of Arabs, Asians, and Europeans. The livelihood of some was based on livestock while others were engaged mainly in agriculture. A very few remained as hunters of wild animals. Means of communication were not highly developed, although there was some meeting of neighboring tribes. All lived under a subsistence economy. As they knew no other way of life, they were satisfied as long as they had enough to eat. Each tribe had its own distinctive social, economic and political institutions. There were also different vernacular languages. Some tribes had governments based on chieftainship, while others were highly decentralized, like the Kikuyu, whose government was by decision of a Council of Elders. Within these tribes, loyalty to clans and to other forms of kinship groups was highly important. The coming of the British established all these tribes for the first time under one rule, after which political, economic, educational and social "transculturation" inevitably intensified, although not deliberately encouraged by the colonial regime.

What then, in specific terms, was the missionary contribution? How could the missionaries have aroused desire for Christian and economic education and social improvement without destroying the basis of traditional African society, founded as it was in traditional religious belief?

On their arrival, the missionaries found what anthropologists would call "primitive cultures," in which the local units of cultural level were limited and geographically isolated. Knowledge of the past was limited and what did survive was transmitted orally in tales of a mythological nature. Preoccupation with the future was also limited and interest was largely in present stimulation rather than long term progress. Time was not an important factor in such simply defined economies: no one thought in terms of hours spent.

The missionaries went to work thoroughly. First of all, they learned the local languages and translated the Old and New Testaments. They wrote books on grammar. They built churches, schools, hospitals, and dispensaries right into the interior or "reserves" where communications were extremely difficult.

Strictly speaking, the missionaries were first in doing all these things and were even ahead of the colonial government by which the Kenyan people were to find themselves ruled. All these things made life more enjoyable than ever before for the Africans, who cooperated wholeheartedly, thereby ensuring a spectacular success for the missionaries' work in the earlier stages.

Acceptance of European education and religion, as well as some of the aspects of the European culture, did not mean that the Kenyan people had jettisoned all their heritage. Nor did it mean that the Africans became black Europeans or "detribalized." For it should be known today that what may be called European culture is a mixture contributed by the many different tribes of mankind through the ages. Hence the Kenya people were experiencing "transculturation" or "cultural grafting."

There is no point perhaps in trying to argue whether this process of intercultural relations was bad or good. Cultural diffusion has been taking place all over the world and it is inevitable.

It would also be misleading to suggest, as some have done, that an educated African can very easily revert to ancestral tribal ways of life. By the same token, can an educated Welsh person today easily revert to ancient Druidism? Would educated Italians today easily be able to revert to the ancient rites of the Roman gods? Perhaps only when acting in a play in the theatre by way of entertainment!

While the missionaries were endeavoring to evangelize and help in hospitals and educational institutions, another important factor we can call "urbanization" was taking place. Its effects among the Africans were creeping in gradually but steadily.

As small cities and towns developed, they became melting pots of races, languages, and of multicultural activities. Kinship structures preceding African-European contact broke down rapidly; and, to use sociological terms, "normlessness" and "uprootedness" became apparent. People became of interest to each other as customers and in terms of usefulness.

No one could blame the missionaries for these later changes. Unfortunately, however, despite their devotion, courage, and indefatigable spirit, their approach to the Africans and African custom was often ill-informed and extremely paternalistic.

In some instances it appeared that the European missionaries were sometimes ambivalent, as if they wanted many aspects of the patterns of living in Kenyan African societies to be changed as quickly as possible to make the African societies more similar to European and American societies. Yet, on the other hand, whenever Euro-American missionaries, as standard bearers of culture, came into contact with the Kenyan Africans, only limited aspects of Western culture were presented to the Kenyan Africans.

9

Intercultural
Relations, Part II

In 1939, Lord Halifax proclaimed Britain's duty toward the subject peoples of her Empire as "finely expressed" in Article XXII of the League of Nations Covenant, which defined "the wellbeing and development" of "peoples not yet able to stand by themselves under the strenuous conditions of the modern world" as "a sacred trust of civilization."

If Great Britain's mission in Kenya had been designed to help "peoples not yet able to stand by themselves," there could by that time have been considerable numbers of well-educated Africans in Kenya, and illiteracy would not have been the general rule. What were the facts?

The Report of the Education Department of Kenya "Colony" and Protectorate for 1938 shows the following gross expenditures for education, disregarding general administrative and extraordinary expenses:

For the Education of Non-Africans		Pounds	Percent of Total
Europeans		49,003	27
Indians and Goanese		42,861	24
Arabs		6,711	4
	Total	99,575	55
For the Education of Africans		80,130	45
	GRAND TOTAL	179,705	100

72

No less than 97½ percent of the entire population were Africans, yet more was spent in 1938 on the education of the children of the non–African minority of about 85,000 than on the offspring of nearly 3,300,000 Africans who paid 70 percent of all direct taxation.

The Report of the Education Department of Kenya for 1938 shows the number of African children attending school in that year:

In government schools	5,002
In mission schools receiving government aid	50,232
In unaided mission and independent schools	73,773
TOTAL	129,007

The report indicates that government direct and indirect assistance to the mission schools equaled about 41,000 pounds of a total operating cost of about 98,000 without deducting fees paid by the parents of the pupils. The government contribution was equal, therefore, to the entire cost of educating about 21,000 of the 50,000 children attending those institutions. In other words, of the 600,000 African children in need of education, the Kenyan government was providing for about 26,000 only—about 5,000 in its own schools and 21,000 in the mission schools it aided. The result was that only about 4 percent of the children of school age were being educated at any expense to the government, about 17 percent were being taught by the missions and African contributors, and 79 percent were receiving no education whatever. On the other hand, about 12,000 non–African children were receiving a much more costly education than that of the individual African, although the groups to which they belonged represented less than 3 percent of the total population.

Another evil of African education—or the lack of it—was that government-aided schools were required to collect fees from the parents of all pupils. To most people this was a particularly vicious practice, because the children of the poorest Africans, no matter how bright, were deprived of the most elementary instruction, notwithstanding that their parents paid their share of the taxes collected by the government and the African local councils, the sources of grants made to the schools from which their children were barred.

Historically speaking, African education in Kenya was provided by the Christian missionaries since 1847, when Rebman and Kraft started an African school in Rabai. The Kenyan colonial government assumed its responsibility in providing African education from 1925 onward, but even then the missionaries continued their dominant role. Unfortunately, the missionaries' negative attitudes and attempts to de–Africanize African cultures became a part of their evangelization and education. At the beginning, the Africans did not react directly or indirectly to the constant attacks and demeaning of their cultures. However, their anger was latent. How would the African children be expected to feel when they were taught to hate their culture?

In Kikuyu country, especially, these attacks on traditional customs were highly accelerated—especially on the subject of female circumcision. Many tribes—the Kikuyu, Akamba, Masai, Nandi, and Kipsigis practiced female circumcision. They also used imitative magic, contagious magic, and verbal magic, or what Freud calls the omnipotence of words. It appears as if the missionaries would have been more successful in discouraging these "pagan practices" if they had a finer understanding of sociology, anthropology and psychology, in addition to their knowledge of Christianity. For example, arguments against female circumcision would have been more effective if they had been based on physiological grounds. So far as the Kikuyu were concerned, the Bible recommended circumcision, and they naturally saw no reason to distinguish women from men while it remained the sole authority.

The Old Testament also sanctions polygamy. How can we explain this inconsistency? In order to answer this question, we must define "Christianity," and also try to understand the basis of Western Christianity, i.e., the four apostles, Matthew, Mark, Luke and John, along with the Book of Revelation and the Letters of St. Paul. If, then, these are the bases of Western Christianity, does it mean that the Old Testament is disregarded? If so, why?

Similarly, the strong language used to condemn the African use of magic appears unfair.

It is often difficult, without a true understanding of African society, to demonstrate to some Africans that Christology is any the less primitive or measurably more valid than the verbal magic practiced by tribal societies, such as the Kikuyu, Masai, Nandi, Kipsigis, Wakamba, and the Kisii.

For their part, the Kenyan Africans readily accepted the white man's idea of Christianity, which taught the brotherhood of man, equality, and goodness. At a later stage, the Africans noticed that the commercial, farming, and professional Europeans often failed to practice what their missionary brothers were teaching. This marked inconsistency was puzzling, reflecting as it did on the white man's motives and intentions in dealing with the African people. It was not difficult for some Africans, however wrongly, to see a betrayal in this disparity between theory and practice, for they had believed literally in Christian teaching, and especially in the Ten Commandments.

In other words, the true worth of the missionaries' remarkable achievements became confused and to an extent debased, to the considerable loss of both men and God. For a time—a very important time—there was a tendency among missionaries to remain neutral or, as many Africans would believe, to equate too readily temporal authority with moral right.

In Kikuyu country, after the formation of the Kikuyu Central Association in 1925, the anti-missionary attitudes of some African converted Christians started being expressed bitterly and openly.

In 1929, the split-up between some Kikuyu Christians and the mission churches became inevitable. The defection by the Kikuyu Christians from the missionary churches was not a total defection, however. Some remained loyal to their churches.

The Christian denominations which were particularly affected or involved most were: The Church of Scotland Mission, the Church Missionary Society, the African Inland Mission, and the Gospel Missionary Society—all of them in Kikuyu country.

It should be emphasized that there was a very heavy concentration of missionary stations or centers in Kikuyu country—much more than in other parts of Kenya. This was perhaps due to climate, closeness to towns including Nairobi, the Capital, and the fact that Kikuyu were mainly agricultural people. It should be stated that Kikuyu Christians who defected from the missionary churches were not anti–Christian or anti any religion. They were anti–European Christians who constantly attacked their traditional culture. This book is not meant to excuse all the African cultures, nor glorify them. The Kikuyu who accepted Christianity after the arrival of the European nationalities accepted it literally and seriously. Those Kikuyu who left the European Missionary Churches and Schools established their own Independent Churches and Schools. They were faced with so many problems: finance, lack of sufficient educational facilities, lack of well trained school teachers, and lack of trained clergymen or theologians who could ordain and baptize their followers. Their churches and schools were scattered all over Kikuyu country, although not to the same extent as the European Missionary Churches and Schools.

The problem of having ordained clergymen was very acute and pressing for the Kikuyu Independent Churches and Schools.

In 1932, James Beautah and Permenas Githendu Mukarie, both members of the Kikuyu Central Association, met a South African Archbishop in Mombasa. The Archbishop, the Rev. William Alexander, D.D., was on his way to South Africa from Uganda where he had been for the purpose of ordaining Reuben Spartas, who had defected from the Anglican Church in 1929, establishing his own church under the name of the African

Orthodox Church. James Beautah and Mukerie recommended Archbishop William Alexander to the leaders of the Kikuyu Independent Schools and Churches for the purpose of training and ordaining their church ministers. Legitimization of the clergymen of the Kikuyu Independent Churches, at the time, was absolutely important, and their leaders were desperate about it.

An invitation was sent to Archbishop Alexander who, in his reply, sent his credentials to the leader of the Kikuyu Independent Churches and Schools. He also asked that his ticket from South Africa to Kenya be paid for by the leaders of the Kikuyu Independent Churches. The Archbishop's credentials impressed the leaders of the Kikuyu Independent Churches highly.

On November 8, 1935, the Archbishop arrived in Mombasa. He was met by the leaders of the Kikuyu Independent Churches and Schools. It was planned that he would establish his headquarters at Gituamba in South Fort Hall (now Muranga). He spent a few days in Mombasa and then left for Gituamba through Nairobi.

On November 15, 1935, the Archbishop started teaching five students. He insisted that these students should be married. Another student was added in 1937. In the meantime a disagreement between the Archbishop and the leaders of the Kikuyu Independent Churches and Schools occurred over the duration of training theological students. The Archbishop suggested fourteen years of training. The leaders were unhappy about the length of this time. They suggested two years. The Archbishop agreed and the issue was resolved.

Before the ordination of the six theological students, a split occurred between the Archbishop and the leaders of the Kikuyu Independent Churches and Schools. They felt that it was wrong for the Archbishop to pocket money collected for the purpose of baptisms instead of using these funds for the purposes of the local churches.

In addition, the Archbishop wanted a big church to be built at Gituamba, and be named after him. The leaders of the Kikuyu Independent Churches and Schools disagreed. The Archbishop left Kenya for South Africa on July 6, 1937.

In September of 1937, all leaders of the Kikuyu Independent Churches and Schools met in Nyeri, North Kikuyuland, for important church deliberations. In the course of their deliberations, a split occurred among the leaders. Arthur Gatung'u of Kiambu District and Philip Kianda of Nyeri District both wanted to adopt and follow Archbishop Alexander's methods of conducting the church. Consequently, they preferred to call their churches the African Orthodox Church, like the African Orthodox Church in South Africa. The Fort Hall District (now Muranga) represented by Daud (David) Maina Kiragu and Harrison Gacokia, proposed the name be the African Independent Pentecostal Church. They did not want any link with the Archbishop. There was no compromise. Henceforth, all those churches and schools which accepted Arthur Gatung'u's suggestion came under the auspices of the African Orthodox Church, and all those churches and schools which accepted the Kiragu and Gacokia proposal came under the auspices of the African Independent Pentecostal Church. Consequently, all the schools which were under the control of the African Orthodox Church became known as the Kikuyu Karing'a Schools. The Kikuyu word "karing'a" would imply the word "pure." For example, I am a "pure" Kikuyu ("Nii ndi mugikuyu karing'a"). In this sense, Arthur Gatung'u and his followers wanted to maintain and preserve Kikuyu customs at whatever cost and, perhaps, emphasize a complete break with the European missionary churches. How then would they teach European skills and techniques in their schools? However, it would appear that this was a form of over-reaction, because the word "pure" could also, in this particular case, be limiting and exclusive.

On the other hand, all those Kikuyu Independent Schools and Churches which accepted Kiragu and Gacokia, and consequently were under the auspices of the African Independent Pentecostal Church, avoided anything exclusive which could imply that those schools were meant for the Kikuyu people only. It is also true to say that the Kikuyu Karing'a Independent Churches and Schools were highly influenced by the Kikuyu Central Association, and politically charged.

That African parents had a genuine desire for the education of their children is easily demonstrated:

In the last few years preceding the First World War, two African groups in Kenya endeavored to provide education for their children by building and maintaining schools of their own. These earnest and enterprising people, all Kikuyu, enrolled themselves in the Karing'a Schools Association and the Kikuyu Independent Schools Association.

By 1937, the two organizations had established more than 50 schools, staffed by African teachers and responsible for the education of more than 7,000 children.

Educational standards at the schools varied considerably; one of the finest was Githunguri School, founded some years later as a teachers training college by the first Kikuyu ever to win a Master's degree—for which he inevitably studied in England and America. Others were less satisfactory. The 1937 Report of the Kenya Education Department was able to comment:

> In most of the schools the bulk of the teaching is done by pupil
> teachers who have themselves received education of a standard very
> little in advance of those whom they are trying to teach.

But, however slowly and imperfectly, a genuine movement toward mass
education of the African people was under way, and would have progressed
much more dramatically if the Independent Schools had not been opposed
at all times by the Kenyan government. Once again there was a misunderstanding, tragic in retrospect: African political advancement was not acceptable, mass education would lead to political demands, the African insistence
on education was in itself a political demand and those concerned with it
only one remove from political agitators.

The government was not reassured by the fierce pride of the Africans
in their schools and their resentment of governmental attempts to control
them. Suspicion was in fact inevitable: It was not until 1932 that the government officially recognized the independent schools and only then so it
could directly supervise school activities through an official appointed for
the purpose.

It is true that many of the schools were bad and should have been
closed if the government had been willing to provide something better, in
fact, any alternative. But there was no alternative, the schools were closed
anyway, the opening of new schools was refused, and eventually the government itself created what it had most feared. The Independent Schools
movement took on political significance.

In 1938, the Report on African Affairs disclosed that the schools of
the Karing'a Association had been taken over by the Kikuyu Central Association, an organization for the improvement of the status of Africans in
Kenya and a political body. Two years later the government took the disastrous, but by then inevitable, step of passing through the Legislative Council an ordinance making it a criminal offense for any person to take part
in the management, control or conduct of a private school ordered to be
closed by the Director of Education, or opened without the Director's
consent.

The new crimes were punishable by a fine not exceeding fifty pounds
or three months' imprisonment. No African could pay the fine, so prison
was inevitable. All the independent schools were of course closed, the
K.C.A. and two similar organizations were suppressed by the governor as
"dangerous to good government" and, as Mr. Creech Jones reported to the
House of Commons in March 1942, "All (African) political institutions (in
Kenya) have been placed in concentration camps."

More even than most government actions, the closing of the independent schools struck at the weakening faith of the ordinary African people in the goodwill of the colonial administration, and was a key factor in determining the political development of Kenya from then on. The British government, being certain of the rectitude of its policy and out of touch with the people, had little idea of the significance of its action. The Second World War was an interlude, but as such served to consolidate the loss of faith. After the war, and after numerous appeals by the Kikuyu, the schools were allowed to reopen and the number increased from 50 to 180, but the damage was done and other events soon overtook this particular issue. In October of 1952, the "Mau Mau" emergency was declared and the schools were closed again as being "dangerous to good government of the Colony"—a phrase reminiscent of 1940, and indeed one that might have been used again sooner but for the war.

It is easier to study history than to create it. Some of the finest intelligences have been led astray by the confusion of contemporary events and perhaps the ultimate test of a man is his willingness in retrospect to admit his error, especially in public. The British government has stood this test; however, the fact remains that the bitterness engendered by the attitude of the colonial government to mass African education could well have been avoided by a simple adjustment of mind at an early stage to those principles which the League of Nations attempted to establish and to which, even today, not all those who are members of the United Nations fully subscribe.

It is worth adding, as a postscript to the last chapter, that the missionaries also made serious mistakes, though theirs was the most sincere good will of all. They preached that Mau Mau was specifically an anti–Christian revolt and therefore those Kikuyu who resisted were Christian martyrs. Mau Mau, as the culmination of a national movement, was nothing of the kind. It was simply national and political and even Christianity allows force against an oppressive government, though it does not condone all methods.

As a matter of principles, education is the means by which people are prepared to do a job, and by which culture and tradition are handed down; it is also the process by which people develop their own attitudes toward life and their opinions about art, philosophy and the rest. Unfortunately, however, in colonial Kenya education was not meant for every African in the multi–African societies. Racial, economic, political, and social considerations were used as criteria to determine which race would get a "big piece of the cake," so to speak. In other words, educational facilities were stratified according to the colonial racial make-up or structure. Specifically, the European community had the first priority when it came to the distribution or allocation of the educational funds and facilities, the

Asian community was second, the Arab community was third, and the African Community was fourth.

The main argument in favor of this colonial system was that the European community was the main backbone of Kenya's economy and development, and that the European technical skills and capital endeared Europeans for the first priority. However, this argument did not take into consideration the traditional use of African cheap labor in the idea of economic backbone or economic development. Could the "White Highlands" function as a successful basis for the Kenyan economic backbone without exploitation or the use of the squatter system? The cheap squatter labor force was always and readily available in the "White Highlands." Generally speaking, cheap African labor was used in all walks of life, let alone the Kenya colonial civil service.

The argument of the settlers and the European community generally that they were the backbone of Kenya's revenue was tested in 1932 by the Lord Moyne Report. The Report concluded that:

> Considering the services provided in return it is evident that the natives have long paid ample contribution towards the general revenues of the country and the indivisible services on which some of the native taxes were spent were of little present value to the natives.[1]

Unfortunately, the cause of Christianity suffered in Kenya because of the confessed identification of some of its ministers with the ruling power. Today, the churches are regaining their strength as they have remembered their true doctrine of justice for all; in political terms, social and economic equality.

To conclude, as a warning to all those who deal with Africa, whatever their religious or political beliefs, one authority has observed:

> The Church, to her glory, provided plenty of martyrs during the Mau Mau insurrection. And it was a significant moment when one Christian leader, now a bishop, declared that he was only prepared to be described as one of the "loyal Kikuyu" provided that it was understood that he was loyal to Jesus Christ but not to the British Government, because he was just as anxious to see Kenya independent as any of the Mau Mau.

This is true Christianity—and this is Africa.

10

The North Nyanza Gold Fields

The Luo, Kisii, and Abaluhya country is on the eastern shore of Lake Victoria, Nyanza, and extends somewhat to the north of that great body of water. Like the Kikuyu, the Luo, Kisii, and Abaluhya, formerly known as "Kavirondo," are agriculturalists, fishermen, and some own considerable numbers of livestock.

Under the British rule, their country was divided into three "reserves": South Kavirondo, Central Kavirondo, and North Kavirondo. The original western terminus of the Kenya-Uganda Railway, Kisumu, is in Central Nyanza on the lake shore, where the climate is tropical. In this book, peoples who have been inhabiting what became the Nyanza Province will be classified as the Kisii in the South, the Luo in the central area and the Abaluhya, or Luhya, living in the north.

The Luo escaped the major evils of settlers' domination—not because they were overlooked, but because their "reserve" was too low for inclusion in the highlands and its climate rather unhealthy for white men in the rainy season. However, the impact of forced labor legislations which will be described later on in the book, did seriously affect the Luo people.

The Kisii "reserve" in the south is one of the best tea growing areas in Kenya and for this reason it was of great importance to the European settlers. On European expansion into the Kisii country, one authority says:

> [I]n the middle of 1905, expeditions against the people of Sotik and against the Kisii led to the first opening up of that south-western

81

area of the Protectorate, though a much larger expedition had to be undertaken, in 1908, before the Kisii were finally pacified.[1]

In common with the other Kenyan Africans, the Luo, Kisii, and Abaluhya were compelled to pay taxes for the support of a government which appears to have done little to aid them, and when a tribesman, perhaps old and infirm, was unable to pay his share of the tribute, he was evicted from his hut—which was sometimes burned if the default continued.

In 1930, the Kenya Legislative Council, under strong pressure from Lord Passfield, Secretary of State for the Colonies, passed a Native Lands Trust Ordinance, which promised Luo, Kisii, and Abaluhya "the use and benefit" of their reserve "for ever," and supplied the local "native" councils with maps defining the territory which was to be theirs until the end of time.

But the Abaluhya had scarcely familiarized themselves with their maps when disaster descended upon many of them in the most unexpected and curious way. Gold was discovered in the Kakamega area of the North Nyanza Province. Logically, the landowners should have been in the fortunate position of the Oklahoma Indians, who have reaped immense wealth from oil found on lands reserved to them by the United States Government.

However, the British Government decreed that minerals should be excepted from the grant of land to the Abaluhya and they could not therefore take any share of the new wealth. Further, as possession of the land was necessary for exploitation of the gold, the government evicted the African landowners. The process by which eviction was to be achieved was still to be devised—at the time of the gold strike, the recent Native Lands Trust Ordinance at least provided that, if it became necessary to move tribesmen, they should be given new land in compensation.

The Ordinance of 1930 had been law for less than eighteen months when the gold prospectors began to invade the North Nyanza Province. The prospectors, who roamed among and disturbed their crops, alarmed the Africans, and *The Times* of July 26, 1932, reported from Nairobi:

> In view of the big influx of miners into the Kakamega native reserves following the gold discoveries there, many natives are apprehensive they will lose their land. In order to dissipate their fears, Sir Joseph Byrne, the Governor, addressed a meeting of thousands of natives near the gold diggings and assured them the Government had no intention they should be deprived of their land.

The governor was Brigadier-General Sir Joseph Aloysius Byrne. His promise to the Abaluhya may have been made in good faith, but it had to be honored by the Secretary for the Colonies, who was no longer the considerate Lord Passfield. Meanwhile, Ramsay MacDonald had quarreled with the British Labour Party and, as a result of the 1931 general election, now headed a "national government." The majority of his supporters in the House of Commons were Conservatives who were represented in the Cabinet by Stanley Baldwin and others, Lord Passfield being ousted in the process.

Measures to deprive the Abaluhya of their gold-bearing land without providing them with land elsewhere were rushed forward in an atmosphere of haste and secrecy. On December 7, 1932, Cunliffe-Lister, Lord Passfield's successor, made a statement in the House of Commons on the Government's gold mining policy in Kenya, namely, "I am not yet in a position to make a statement." Yet, less than two weeks later, on the 18th of December, 1932, Sir Robert Hamilton and other members of the House were cabled from Kenya that the Legislative Council was about to amend the Native Lands Trust Ordinance of 1930 to provide that no land would be given to evicted Africans in the mining region and that any compensation would be in the form of cash only. An official admission of this was made in the House of Commons on the 20th of December, and eleven days later the Kenya Legislative Council amended the Ordinance of 1930.

> Land may be excluded temporarily from a native reserve under this section for the purpose of granting a lease for the development of the mineral resources of the Colony, and in such cases it shall not be obligatory on the Governor during the period of the currency of such lease or any renewal thereof to add to such reserve any land as provided under sub-section (2) of this section.

The Abaluhya are not lacking in physical courage, and it may well be asked why they did not violently resist this legislation and their eventual expulsion from their homes. The answer is simple: Section 97 of the Mining Ordinance (No. 1 of 1931) decreed that any person "who interferes with any mining or prospecting operations authorized by or under this Ordinance shall be liable to a fine of 300 Pounds or to imprisonment for three years, or both." Three hundred pounds represented the gross cash reward of fifty years of hard work at the average rate of wages then paid to Africans in Kenya. Resistance would have inevitably meant a long jail sentence.

It might be thought that the violation of the British pledge to substitute other land for that expropriated was largely offset by the promise of cash compensation, but if a farmer loses his land, his whole livelihood goes with it. The dispossessed could not claim other land in the area as of right, for the Abaluhya have their own system of land ownership. Furthermore, there was a ban on Africans buying land outside their own tribal reserves. The extent of this injustice was admitted by the Chief Native Commissioner on December 20, 1932, in the course of a Kenya Legislative Council debate, although he clearly thought it unnecessary to oppose or offer any honorable alternative despite the nature of his office:

> I am afraid we have got to hurt their feelings, we have got to wound their susceptibilities, and in some cases I am afraid we may even have to violate some of their most cherished and sacred traditions if we have to move natives from land on which, according to their own inalienable law, they have the right to live, and settle them on land from which the owner has the indisputable right to eject them.

It might have been expected that at the least the Abaluhya would have had the chance to prospect their own lands, but the Legislative Council had decided that only Europeans were to benefit. In addition to a substantial fee for a prospector's license, the Mining Ordinance of 1933 provided that a right to prospect should not be granted:

(b) to any person who is unable to read or to any person not capable of understanding this Ordinance in such a way as to form a reasonable guide to and restriction on his actions.

We have already seen the strong desire by the Africans for education and the determined efforts of the settlers to deny this, whether sponsored by the government or by the Africans themselves. We can now see why.

The matter was pursued by Lord Lugard and Archdeacon Owen of Nyanza Province in letters to *The Times* and *Manchester Guardian*, and was debated on a question by Lord Lugard in the House of Lords on February 8, 1933. Lord Passfield, who, as Secretary for the Colonies, had been primarily responsible for the inviolability of the Africans' "reserves" contained in the Kenya 1930 Native Lands Trust Ordinance, took part in the debate and his speech was summarized by *The Times*:

> The inviolability of the native reserves was accepted from the first and was given sanctity by the declaration of the Government to all parties. That being so, he felt that the action of the Colonial office and the Kenya Government amounted to a definite breach of faith with the natives.

The severest criticism of the government came from Sir Robert Hamilton and Sir Herbert Samuel, then leader of the Liberal Party. Sir Robert

Hamilton's opposition was especially significant, for he had spent many years in Africa and was a former Chief Justice of the British East Africa Protectorate before its annexation as Kenya "Colony."

Cunliffe-Lister's replies showed quite clearly that he thoroughly approved the action of the Kenya Legislative Council. He expressed himself just as anxious as his opponents to provide land for the evicted Abaluhya. Stressing the fact that up to then no African in the gold-bearing region had actually been dispossessed, he expressed the novel thought that:

> It would be criminal, unless it was absolutely unavoidable, to take such a man (an evicted native) away from where he is living today and put him 20, 30 or 40 miles away as the Labour Party suggest. Therefore the man is going to be left either in the part of the holding where he and his people are now, or if it is not practicable, settled among his neighbours.

In other words, the solution to one injustice was to perpetrate another; the neighbors of the evicted Africans were expected to surrender to them such land as might be necessary to their maintenance in a reserve already intensively cultivated in one of the most densely populated areas of Kenya.

Cunliffe-Lister made much of the fact that practically all the mining operations then in progress were alluvial and, for that reason, confined to the banks and beds of streams and rivers where there was little cultivation. He then proceeded to baffle his critics by indicating that the objectionable amendment passed by the Kenya Legislative Council might, after all, be only temporary because he had referred the entire matter to the Kenya Land Commission then in session. Meanwhile:

> The Governor has estimated it is an outside estimate the area for which the surface is likely to be acquired in this interim period as being 1,000 acres, which is one and half square miles out of a total reserve area of over 7,000 square miles. That gives one some idea of the magnitude of the matter.... At the outside it is probably a question of moving, or partly moving, 300 natives including their families.

To say the least, this statement was totally misleading. It had never been suggested that the mining operations affected the whole of the 7,000 square miles of the three Nyanza Province reserves. The operations were concentrated in a much smaller area in the North Nyanza Province only, described by Sir Albert Kitson, a geologist employed by the Kenya

Government, as follows: "The field comprises a strip of country extending roughly, west to east, some thirty miles, and north to south some fourteen miles."

Further evidence of the value of Cunliffe-Lister's statement on the surface area involved is found in the Annual Report of the Mining and Geological Department of Kenya "Colony" for 1933: "The total area covered by Lode and alluvial claims in the Kakamega goldfield at the end of the year was approximately 65,000 acres."

Sixty-five thousand acres is more than a hundred square miles and, while no statistics are available on how much of this was lode and how much alluvial, it represented about one-quarter of the entire gold-bearing area of which the beds and banks of streams and rivers form no very considerable proportion.

The reports of the Mining and Geological Department of Kenya show the value of gold mined in 1933 as 67,665 pounds. By 1940, the value had risen to 643,783 pounds, in spite of the fact that alluvial mining had declined considerably in the interval.

In the House of Commons debate of February 8, 1933, Sir Herbert Samuel laid much emphasis on the fact that the breach of faith with the Abaluhya was condemned by such men as Lord Lugard, Sir Robert Hamilton and Archdeacon Owen, men who knew far more about the Africans of Kenya than those who sought the approval of the House.

He pointed out also that Sir Edward Grigg, Governor of Kenya, who had opposed the addition of land to the reserves in substitution for land taken away, agreed that the pledge contained in the 1930 "Native Lands Trust Ordinance" had been violated by the passage of the 1932 amendment.

As a result of the agitation fostered by Lord Lugard, Archdeacon Owen and Sir Robert Hamilton—all men who had known the Africans of Kenya when they were relatively free and independent—the Kenya Legislative Council passed a remedial ordinance (No. 36 of 1934). However, although their policy was modified slightly, the settlers gave up not one iota of their profit. While the evicted Abaluhya were given land at a distance from their old homes, away from relatives and friends, to replace that of which they were forcibly deprived, they received no share whatever of the gold found in the territory which they and their fathers had occupied from time immemorial ("kuuma tene na tene").

11

The Kenya Land Commission, Part I

The Kenya Land Commission was appointed in April of 1932. Its purpose was to report to the British Government on the land needs of the African population, "present and prospective," and the desirability "of setting aside further areas for their present and future occupancy." There were no Africans on the commission, which consisted of three members only: Sir Morris Carter, Chairman, a former judge of the adjoining mandated and later trust territory of Tanganyika; R. W. Hemsted, a settler who had spent most of his life in the service of the East Africa Protectorate and Kenya; and Captain F. O'B. Wilson, a settler and prominent character in settler politics.

Although perhaps well-intentioned in its inception and painstaking in its collection of information, the commission was to prove a failure in the recommendations it made, particularly when these were interpreted by the Kenya Legislature.

Throughout their report the commissioners stressed that European land rights should be inviolate, but took a different view of African rights.

The Commission noted importantly the constricted nature of the official Native Reserves:

> The native reserves are 48,149 square miles, or approximately 22 percent of the whole area of the Colony. Of this area, the three Kikuyu and the three Kavirondo districts comprise between them 8,556 square miles. *The population is 1,518,578, or approximately* (1)

The areas of Crown Land described in Government Notice No. 394, published in the Official Gazette of the Colony dated the thirteenth day of October, 1926, are hereby declared to be native Reserves and are reserved and set aside for the use and benefit of the native tribes of the Colony forever, and a copy of this Ordinance duly authenticated together with maps showing the boundaries of the Native Reserves concerned shall be delivered to each Native Council throughout the Colony.

The Africans who had suffered most from encroachments of the settlers were those whose ancestral lands adjoined the main line of the Kenya-Uganda Railway, as good lines of communication and transport were essential to the settlers. At the time of the commission's inquiry, the principal tribes involved and their numbers were:

Akamba	391,669
Masai	48,381
Kikuyu	599,853
Nandi	50,844

The Akamba

The Akamba, a partly agricultural and partly pastoral people, originally occupied a considerable part of the territory east of Nairobi and nearly all north of the Kenya and Uganda Railway. The whites were allowed to encroach on the western limits of this land, where it bordered on the highlands, and the Akamba were confined in two reserves—Machakos and Kitui. The Machakos Reserve, at the date of the appointment of the commission, comprised 2,166 square miles with a population of 238,910, and the Kitui Reserve 5,911 square miles, with a population of 152,759. In the Kitui Reserve, "large areas are not inhabited during the dry season owing to lack of water."

The establishment of these two reserves, of course, limited the Akamba and severely restricted their chances of expanding their territory to meet the demands of increasing population. However, at least the reserves belonged to them.

The commission confirmed that the Machakos Reserve was badly overstocked for the amount of pasturage available, but if anything, that the people had rather fewer animals than were necessary for their support.

This semi-pastoral people possess no more livestock than they require (although many of those which they have are of a useless type), but, notwithstanding this, they own several times more than their country in its present condition can well support.

The commission therefore recommended that a tract of 512 square miles be given to the Akamba in exchange for an area of 389 square miles south of the railway from which 3,194 Akamba would have to be removed, and commented that:

> We do not consider that there is any obligation on Government to compensate individuals for disturbance caused by the move. Should the Kamba feel that any of the 3,194 natives concerned suffer undue hardship, the Local Native Council, in consideration of the substantial addition to the tribal land, should make provision for the necessary compensation.

The eviction of the 3,200 Akamba is an interesting object lesson in itself, because the land from which they were to be driven was unsuitable for white settlement. One reason given by the Commission for their removal was that there was a shortage of water in the Kyulu subdivision of the Akamba country in which they lived, whereas the land to which they were to be transferred was free from that defect and alleged to be more desirable in other respects, but there was also another:

> A second argument is that the proposal would have the effect of concentrating all the Kamba North of the railway line, thus consolidating the Machakos Reserve and facilitating the administration of the tribe and the provision of road and social service centres.

In fact, the Akamba of Kyulu had solved the water shortage by securing what water they needed from a pipe line along the tracks of the railway in which, as taxpayers, they had an interest. The commission described this "unofficial arrangement with the Railway Administration" as "irregular" but it must have served its purpose, for otherwise a large part of the African population would have had to move elsewhere without any legal incentive to do so. The Commission conceded the Africans themselves wished to remain in Kyulu despite the supposed advantages of the new location. While the Commissioners estimated that at least 70 percent (approximately 2,200) of the 3,194 Akamba involved were living on former tribal lands which had not been included in the Kyulu subdivision of the reserve, it was obvious that about 1,000 of them were settled on land set aside for their use "forever" by the "Native Lands Trust Ordinance of 1930," and that this group had an unquestionable right to decide for themselves whether they wanted to move to the new location recommended by the Commission.

Now they were to be thrust out of their homes, not as a matter of necessity but as one of administrative convenience. No arrangement was made for new huts or other amenities on the new land and, it will be recalled, no compensation had been recommended.

There was a considerable delay between the submission of the recommendations of the Kenya Land Commission to the two Houses of Parliament in 1934, and the actual eviction of the 3,200 Akamba did not begin until 1939, after which any African who refused to leave Kyulu became subject to "a fine not exceeding fifty pounds or to imprisonment not exceeding six months, or to both such fine and imprisonment."

The only other recommendation made by the commission to ease the strain on the Akamba pastures was the addition to the Machakos Reserve of 300 square miles adjoining it on the Yatta Plateau. Thus, the area available was increased only from 2,166 to 2,589 square miles. Clearly the problem had not been solved. The Commission had found that they could not question the number of livestock but, as they would not recommend a larger increase in pasturage, they could only find an "administrative" answer in a reduction of the livestock. Accordingly, Chapter 10 of the report dealt entirely with the advisability of compulsory "de-stocking"— the seizure and slaughter of animals without the consent of their African owners.

The Commission's main argument for the reduction of African herds was:

> We have therefore at the present moment a preposterous state
> of affairs in the Colony which can be summarized as follows:
> A human population of under 3,000,000 (natives) owns about
> 6,000,000 cattle and probably more sheep and goats....

However, they forgot to add that a white population of about 17,000 at the date of its report also owned a considerable number of cattle. The Agricultural Census of Kenya for 1938 showed that a white population of about 21,000 owned more than 300,000 cattle and about the same number of sheep. Why was it "preposterous" for the Africans of Kenya to average two head of cattle per person while the white population averaged fifteen? The quality of the Africans' stock may not have been of the highest, but it was their wealth and livelihood, and de-stocking was an irrelevant answer to the question which had been posed.

The commission continued:

> It is, in our opinion, a mistaken kindness to await the time when
> the almost inevitable recurrence of drought and pestilence will take
> its toll on hundreds of thousands of animals and so bring a tempo-

rary respite to the over-grazed pastures, only to be followed by dreary cycles of overstocking and epidemics of disease.

We therefore recommend, with all the emphasis at our command, that action be taken with the least possible delay to inaugurate the culling of surplus stock and to pursue unremittingly a policy of controlling the cattle population within the limits that the grazing facilities from time to time dictate.

This was as welcome to the Kenyan government as water is to a duck, and the slaughter of the "surplus" Akamba cattle began in 1938. A delegation of Akamba attempted to protest to the Governor in Nairobi and this event was chronicled in the Annual Report on "Native Affairs" for 1938:

At the end of July a party of some 1,500 Kamba—men, women and children—proceeded to Nairobi with the avowed object of requesting His Excellency to accord them an interview and, as this request was not acceded to—remained in Nairobi for six weeks. They were well organized and behaved in an orderly manner and no disturbance resulted.

Thus these poor and oppressed Africans who came to present their grievances to the head of the Kenyan government in a perfectly orderly and legal manner were denied a hearing.

The Report on "native affairs" relates that the Akamba delegation was organized by Samuel Muindi—"A semi-educated ex-policeman." Soon after Samuel returned from Nairobi, the government was baffled by a sudden halt in the slaughter of cattle in his reserve. The authorities were almost entirely dependent upon a group of Akamba "yes-men" for the execution of its cattle reduction program, and it was to these people that Samuel turned his attention when the governor refused to listen. To have had these slaughtermen speared would have been simple, but that would have meant collective punishment of the whole people, and Samuel, perhaps because he was a former policeman, disapproved of violence. Instead, he persuaded the tribe's medicine men to put their most malignant curse on the offenders. The curse was uttered with appropriate ceremony, and the magic was so awesome that the rest of the tribe completely shunned the "yes-men" and their families. Facing misery and damnation here and hereafter, their participation in cattle spotting and slaughtering abruptly ended, and there were no volunteers for the jobs they had been forced to abandon.

The Kenyan government soon discovered that Samuel Muindi had been the medicine-men's inspiration, and the 1938 Report on "Native Affairs" records that he was arrested on September 13, 1938, and deported to Lamu, a small coast town hundreds of miles from his family and friends, without benefit of a proper trial. The Report remarks that this event "had a steadying influence on the tribe." It also seems to have had some effect on the Kenyan government, for in December 1938, "de-stocking by compulsory culling was postponed."

While clamoring for a reduction of the number of cattle in the Africans' reserves, the Kenyan government had done its best to prevent the owners from finding a market for their surplus stock by establishing a system of quarantine areas, ostensibly to prevent the spread of disease. On March 3, 1939, the *Kenya Weekly News* published an article on "Native Policy" by the Honorable S. V. Cooke, an elected member of the Kenya Legislative Council who represented an area far removed from the highlands. He wrote that while the British government had for years encouraged de-stocking and encouraged the natives to sell their stock, they had at the same time "bolted and barred the door of egress from the Reserves." He continued:

> Two years ago the then Acting Director of Veterinary Services ... confessed with refreshing and commendable candour that the only reason why the cattle could not leave the Reserves was that the market would be flooded and the European farmers would in consequence suffer.

Mr. Cooke had spent over twenty-five years in Kenya. At various times in the course of his career he collided with the white settlers and reached the peak of his unpopularity by releasing from illegal detention an African boy against whom no charges had been preferred. The youth had been guilty of displeasing his employer and had committed no offense involving legal punishment. The employer, a prominent politician, then alleged that Mr. Cooke had been transferred from another district as a result of secret pressure for his removal by the local white settlers. Mr. Cooke demanded an inquiry, and the Commission appointed for that purpose reported that the movement of officers "because of grievances alleged by planters, without full investigation, could only lead to a most unwholesome condition."

12

The Kenya Land Commission, Part II

The Masai

The position of the Masai reserve was such that all the Kenya Land Commission was able to do, apart from a few unimportant adjustments, was to take advantage of an opportunity to increase the number of its inhabitants.

In 1860, a powerful Masai clan, the Uasin Gishu, was almost wiped out by a hostile section of its own people. The survivors fled south to escape utter extinction. Some of the vanquished settled in what was later known as the Ravine District in the Northern Mau area, where they were living when an early government station (Eldama Ravine) was established in their neighborhood. The Commission reported they had "rendered considerable assistance to Government in the early days of administration."

The white settlers drove the Uasin Gishu Masai away from the land on which they had grazed their stock for more than forty years, but just as it seemed they would lose everything a friendly District Commissioner obtained 9,000 acres for their use. Later, when their numbers were increased by other members of their clan who had found refuge with the Nandi people, 41,400 additional acres were added, making a total of about eighty square miles.

This area was not proclaimed an African reserve in 1926 because the governor of Kenya did not recommend it, his reasons being that the land was "of low cattle-carrying capacity and subject to droughts," that it was insufficient to sustain livestock in good condition "so that trespass upon neighboring European farms had for long been a matter of increasingly frequent occurrence," and that the several areas of land the Masai had been given were inconveniently situated with respect to each other.

The Governor's conclusion was that the Uasin Gishu Masai would be far better off in the Masai Reserve, if they could be persuaded to go there voluntarily. A number of the unwanted Africans adopted the governor's suggestion and moved into the reserve, but others clung to the Ravine District where fate, in the guise of the Kenya Land Commission, overtook them once more a few years later.

Without the slightest hesitation the commission recommended their expulsion. To the commissioners the removal of these people from their homes was a matter of only trifling importance because:

> The total population involved is only some 1,431 natives owning approximately 6,300 head of cattle and 5,200 sheep and goats. Rather less than half are anxious to move, while rather more than half are anxious to remain where they are.

The commission's method of stating the number of Africans who were "anxious to move" as opposed to those who were "anxious to remain" casts suspicion on the thoroughness of their investigation. All the Masai involved had a long-standing invitation to move into the reserve and, had any of them been really "anxious" to move, they would not have been still in the Ravine District waiting for the commission to recommend their expulsion under penalty of fine and imprisonment.

Whatever may have been the truth, the fact remains that many of the Uasin Gishu Masai were driven out of an area in which they were acknowledged to have settled sixty years previously and about thirty years before Great Britain made any claim to sovereign rights in their territory. It was further acknowledged that they had helped, so far as they were able, in establishing British rule. The treatment they received threw doubt on Great Britain's sincerity in subscribing to Article XXII of the League of Nations Covenant which proclaimed that "the well-being and development" of "peoples not yet able to stand by themselves under the strenuous conditions of the modern world" was "a sacred trust of civilization."

The Kikuyu

The Kikuyu, a prolific and agricultural people, occupied a narrow strip of hilly country of which the southern boundary was northwest of Nairobi, and extended in a northeasterly direction to the southern slopes of Mount Kenya, about a hundred miles distant. The entire area had originally been covered with dense forest which the Kikuyu cleared and burned away to make room for their plantations.

By 1902, Kikuyu cultivation had practically reached the open plains to the east, but to the north and west was the great Aberdare Forest, into which the population increased. They were careful not to hew themselves out into open country and were thus protected from their enemies by a forest barrier. Prudently, they would sometimes build their villages in patches of forest left standing among their plantations. The winding pathways, approachable only through thick undergrowth, made surprise attack extremely difficult. Inside the forest belt Kikuyu plantations stretched as far as the eye could see, and the density of the population was surprising.

In the later years of their encroachment on the forest to the south and west, the Kikuyu had not advanced unchallenged. The ground they cleared had earlier inhabitants who claimed title—the Dorobo, a group of skilled hunters who thought little of creeping up to a herd of elephants feeding in the bamboo forest and hamstringing one of the huge creatures before it became aware of their approach. The Dorobo, it was alleged, did not permit the Kikuyu to take their forest from them at will, and the Kenya Land Commission was obliged to admit that various payments of sheep and goats had been made to them for specific pieces of land from which the Kikuyu were subsequently evicted to make room for the white settlers.

It has been shown earlier that the justification for the seizure of native land for white settlement was a legal opinion of 1899, that the declaration of a Protectorate enabled the British government to claim sovereign rights over land, subject to recognition of any private rights then existing; the Crown Lands Ordinance of 1902, the local law under which the earlier seizures were effected, provided that the commissioner (the direct representative of the British government) should not sell or lease any land in the actual occupation of natives.

The "actual occupation" of land used intermittently for grazing purposes by nomadic or semi-nomadic people might be questioned, but in the case of the Kikuyu farmers the seizure of land for white settlement was in violation of all existing law—a violation the more contemptible because it was committed by the government itself, the enacting authority, for much of the land taken from the Kikuyu was actually under cultivation, and the remainder was used largely for the supply of firewood and the grazing of livestock.

The Kenya Land Commission conceded that at least 4,810 Kikuyu were evicted from the Kiambu District of Kikuyu alone for the benefit of the settlers, and that they were paid the magnificent compensation of 3,872 rupees (about 259 pounds), computed by the commission at two rupees (about 1s, 4d.) for each acre of cleared and cultivated land, including the living accommodations of its owners. The official record of payments terminated in 1908 and the commission noted that "it is certain that between that date and the present time many families drifted away, most of them uncompensated."

In a later portion of its report the commission estimated the number of families which received no compensation as between three and four hundred—from 1,500 to 2,000 persons under the commission's system of estimating. The total number of Kikuyu driven out of this part of Kikuyuland alone was thus from 6,300 to 7,300, although the Kikuyu claimed this number to have been many times greater. Large numbers of the tribe were also dispossessed in areas to the east and, in a lesser degree, to the north, but the commission did not attempt to estimate the number.

The Kikuyu attitude toward these inequities was set forth in a petition presented to a Parliamentary Commission by the Kikuyu Association and quoted by the late W. McGregor Ross:

> When the Whiteman first came we did not understand that we were to be deprived of any of our land, nor that they had really come to stay. A small piece of land here and there was sold to a few of the first pioneers and to one or two missions voluntarily by its owners in the time of the Imperial British East Africa Company. When the British Government took over the administration of the country we were still unaware that our possession of land would be questioned or challenged.
>
> Then from about the year 1902, increasing numbers of Whitemen arrived and portions of our land began to be given out to them for farms, until large areas in Kyambu, Limoru, station Kikuyu, Mbagathi, about Nairobi and at Ruiru and lands were not bought from their Kikuyu owners and any compensation they received (for land under cultivation only, and at an extremely small rate per acre) was quite inadequate. The natives on them had either to become squatters (on what had been their own lands) or else move off. Many of them today are squatters on up-country European estates and many have become wanderers moving from one estate to another.

This assessment was supported by the Kenya Land Commission, who estimated that the population per square mile in the Kikuyu Reserve in 1931 was almost the same as it had been in 1902. The commission noted that 110,697 Kikuyu were estimated to be living outside the reserve, and:

The conclusion suggested is that in 1902 Kikuyuland was inhabited in very much the same density as it is now and that, although the population has increased greatly, the method of dispensing with the surplus has been by a resort to squatting on alienated lands.

The portion of the petition dealing with the compensation paid for eviction was also confirmed by the commission:

Each householder who left received Rupees 4 and he was also allowed to reap his crop. The assumption made by Government was that other land was available to which he could go and that the Rupees 4 would be enough to reimburse him for the actual expense of moving—that is to say the moving of his goods, the building of new huts, and the clearing of the land for the new garden.

Four rupees represented about 5s.4d. at the then rate of exchange.

What happened to some of the evicted Kikuyu who found "available" land elsewhere may be learned from other portions of the Commission's report. These people, number unknown, had spread themselves over about 31,000 acres of land, of which it was estimated they had made whole or partial use of about 14,000 acres:

Between 1902 and 1907 some Kikuyu who had been dispossessed from lands alienated to Europeans and particularly the Limoru farms began to colonize the Escarpment Forest and the lands east of Limoru in considerable numbers.... The whole of these clearings, except the very few existing before 1902, had been made in contravention of the Forest Rules of 1902 which were applied to this area and prohibited the cutting, damaging or removing of any tree, timber or grass and the pasturage of any stock.

The existence of the Forest Rules of 1902 was not called to the attention of the Kikuyu offenders while they were reestablishing themselves in a location which seemed likely to afford them a living. After they had completed their labors, however, the government became aware of their existence and herded them into an area of 8,750 acres.

All of this, of course, appears to be ancient history, but the comparatively modern view of the Kenya Land Commission of the treatment accorded the twice-evicted Kikuyu is exceptionally interesting:

This was not ungenerous treatment. In spite of the fact that their clearings were illegitimate, the natives were given a fair equivalent for all that they had effectively occupied. No doubt this was because it was felt these natives, having lost their lands on the Limoru farms should be allowed something in compensation.

The commission laid the foundation for further evictions when it concluded that many Kikuyu were living on land outside their reserve, and that others were still residing on their own original holdings which the government had sold or leased to the whites in violation of the law. The commission's comment on the illegal sales is either strangely naive or irresponsibly lenient to the government:

> There are cases of natives who were in occupation of certain lands which have since been alienated as freehold and are still resident upon them. These cases must be held to have occurred by accident, since it is provided under Section 30 of the Crown Lands Ordinance, 1902, that no land which is subject to native rights may be alienated as freehold. In so far as such cases exist and so far as the natives are still in occupation, we consider their rights no less entitled in equity to be regarded than the rights of natives on leasehold land which are protected under the clauses cited.

Notwithstanding their equitable rights, Kikuyu living lawfully on leased land were a source of annoyance to the white lessees, on which point the commission reported:

> The lessee can feel no confidence as to what land is his and what is to be deemed excluded from the lease as the property of some Kikuyu right-holder, who in his turn would not be safe against a counterclaim by the Dorobo on the ground of pre-existing rights and that again might be contested on the ground that the Dorobo were vassals of the Masai.

Having drawn this exaggerated picture of the uncertainties by which white leaseholders of alienated African property were alleged to be confronted, the commission, with unconscious irony, made much of the security of land tenure:

> As a Land Commission we are bound to have great respect for the principle of security, without which no agrarian legislation can possibly prosper, and we deem it extremely detrimental to security and to progress that a state of things should exist in which leaseholders have developed their rights in reliance on a document of lease they hold from Government, only to find it contains a clause of such doubtful significance that their position is jeopardized.

This reasoning is clearly absurd and, as English judges have held for centuries, "ignorance of the law excuses no one." Anyone of intelligence reads a lease before signing, and the settlers knew perfectly well that their leases were subject to the Crown Lands Ordinances of 1902 and 1915, which were quite clear as to African rights, and that they would be responsible for any breach of their covenants.

The remedy proposed by the commission, so phrased as to appear for the benefit of the Africans, was:

> We consider it essential to the peace and well-being of the tribe that the areas over which its land-rights or the rights of its members extend should be consolidated and that the addition to the Reserve of the grant of land which we shall recommend shall be accompanied by the extinction of all private rights outside the Reserve....

The recommendation was accompanied by what the commission evidently considered almost reckless generosity:

> Generous compensation for disturbance must accompany this extinction of rights. We consider it should take the form of a payment in cash and we believe 2,000 pounds to be a fair assessment of the total sum that should be paid.

The commission furnished no exact statistics of the number of Kikuyu among whom this immense sum was to be divided, although in a later section of its report it was estimated that those affected were "not more than two to three hundred." This estimate was in itself an admission that there had been no proper investigation of the exact number of Kikuyu to be evicted and, consequently, of the equivalent amount of land that should have been made available for their use elsewhere. It is evident that in the absence of such an investigation, the commission's recommendation on land area was virtually a blind guess and, as we shall see, greatly inadequate. In fact, the commission's assessment was hopelessly wrong.

The annual report of the Commissioner of Lands and Settlements for 1938 noted that:

> The Land Commission has established the fact that many natives living on European-owned farms, chiefly in the Kiambu and Limuru areas, had been in occupation of this land before the farms were allotted for European settlement. The number of natives concerned has proved on investigation to be about ten times the number mentioned by the Commission.

So the Kikuyu evicted from their homes without just cause numbered from 3,000 to 4,000 instead of from 300 to 400 as estimated by the commission. The 2,000 pounds awarded them as compensation for compulsory removal thus averaged perhaps ten shillings a head—not greatly different from the 5/4d per head paid years before by the government and disapproved by the commission.

Contrary to the claims of the Kikuyu, the commission calculated that only about 109 square miles of land had been taken from them for white settlement and that they had been given, or were about to be given, a total of about 265 miles which was not, however, of equal quality to that of which they had been deprived. The net result of the commission's recommendations was two additions to the reserve—about thirty square miles—in settlement of all private claims (which the commission had underestimated by nine-tenths) and an area of 383 square miles in the Yatta District, considered once to be chiefly suitable for grazing purposes rather than for the intensive cultivation characteristic of the Kikuyu.

The total size of the Kikuyu reserve after these additions was about 2,350 square miles for a community numbering 600,000. The population of the reserve before the additions was such that the density was 253 persons per square mile.

The additions made to the Kikuyu reserve by the Kenya Land Commission were grossly inadequate for another reason. The report noted that: "We have to face the fact that unless remedial measures are taken, a state of general congestion is threatened within thirty years."

While giving 600,000 Kikuyu 2,350 square miles of land for their immediate necessities, the commission recommended that no less than 16,700 square miles be set aside for the exclusive use of a white population which numbered little more than 20,000 at the date of the report.

Legal measures were also taken by the Kenyan government to dispossess a majority of the 100,697 Kikuyu estimated to be living outside the reserve as squatters. A Resident Native Labourers Ordinance passed by the Legislative Council in 1937, and amended by ordinance number 38 of 1941, legalized their wholesale eviction. Many of those evicted were driven away without any provision for their personal needs or those of their livestock, until the situation became so bad that the Secretary of the Colonies in London ordered evictions to be suspended until suitable land could be made available to the Kikuyu.

The Nandi

The last people we have to consider are the Nandi, who dwell to the north of the Kenya and Uganda Railway. Their territory begins on the western edge of the Mau Escarpment, about fifty miles east of Lake Victoria, Nyanza, and extends to the north. Although small in numbers, the Nandi are sturdy in heart and have the distinction of being the first people in the East Africa Protectorate to revolt against the British government and fight for their freedom and independence.

The Nandi are a partly pastoral and partly agricultural people, and their plantations crowned the hills to the north of the valley, where they were plainly visible to travelers on the caravan road below, whom they attacked occasionally when the prospects seemed favorable.

On the last fifty miles of the western end of the old main line of the Kenya and Uganda Railway, the altitude decreases rapidly from about 5,500 feet to less than 4,000 feet at the Lake shore and this, combined with a distance of more than 500 miles from the coast, made the Nandi country unattractive to the earlier white settlers. But the Nandi knew what was going on to the east and asked for assurances that their land would not be taken away from them. The outcome of this request is recorded in the Report of the Kenya Land Commission:

> In the Nandi Political Record Book, the following entry appears under the date of November, 1907: "Deputation of Nandi elders informed that the land is theirs forever." There is reason to suppose that this assurance was given them when the Right Honourable W. S. Winston Churchill [sic] visited the tribe as Under-Secretary of State for the Colonies.

A further and similar assurance was given the Nandi three years later, and the Kenya Land Commission remarked that "these agreements with the Nandi were of a particularly formal character and were in the nature of a pledge given the tribe." But the pledge of the British government, although twice given in this instance, had no lasting value, and the commission's report continued:

> For some reason which is not fully explained the existence of the agreement appears to have been overlooked. In July, 1912, Government approved of the alienation of 17½ square miles in the Kaimosi area, which was included in the Nandi Native Reserve both by the agreement of 1907 and the agreement of 1910. The extent of this land, which is now alienated as farms, is approximately 16½ square miles, and the remainder has reverted to native occupation.
>
> In 1919, the existence of the agreement still being overlooked, the Chief Native Commissioner informed the Governor that a hundred square miles of Nandi Native Reserve could be alienated for Soldier Settlement farms, there being ample room in the remaining part of the Reserve to accommodate the whole of the Nandi tribe. As a result of this recommendation 129½ square miles of land in the Kipkarren area was surveyed into farms; allotment proceeded under the Soldier Settlement scheme, and a number of farms were alienated on 999 year leases. Compensation at the rate of Rupees 50 a hut was paid to all natives disturbed.

The commission estimated that approximately 497 huts and 1,500 Africans were involved in this last repudiation of two solemn promises. The amount of compensation paid per hut was approximately six pounds.

The Report continues:

> Shortly after alienation had begun it was realized that such action was not in accordance with the undertaking of 1910, and also that so large an area could not be taken out of the reserve without hardship to the Nandi.

The result was that the British government decided to violate its pledge only to the extent of taking about forty-three square miles of land from the Nandi, and directed that the rents paid must be expended for their benefit. However, although the government was at last fully mindful of its obligations, two more farms of 713 acres were alienated in 1924, and in 1925 a further 653 acres were taken over in one district, also a farm elsewhere, acreage unstated. The proceeds of the last transactions, amounting to approximately 2,800 pounds, were turned over to the Nandi Native Council.

The commission admitted the gross amount due to the Nandi for illegal seizure of their lands might be calculated as 35,527 pounds, but recommended settlement at a much lower figure:

> We do not think the true loss to the Nandi was anything like as great as would appear. Taking into consideration that they have been compensated to the extent of 2,485 pounds for disturbance and are receiving stand premia in the total amount of 2,807 pounds, and rents amounting annually to 310 pounds, we consider the Nandi would be amply compensated by a payment of 5,000 pounds as a comprehensive compensation for the loss suffered by them through the transactions we have described.

No additions to the Nandi Reserve were recommended by the commission, which made the astounding suggestion that the British government was justified in breaking its pledges to the Nandi because "there was no consideration on the other side," once again a total misunderstanding of the principles of English and international law.

The recommendations of the Kenya Land Commission regarding the African reserves were accepted in their entirety by the Secretary for the Colonies, Sir Philip Cunliffe-Lister, and it remained for Neville Chamberlain and his Cabinet of February, 1939, to provide the legal machinery by which they were made effective. Altogether, 1939 was a poor year for Chamberlain's reputation.

13

"Star Chamber" Legislation

The Report of the Kenya Land Commission was completed in September 1933, and presented to both Houses of Parliament in London in May of 1934 as a Command Paper. Simultaneously another Command Paper, No. 4580, entitled "Kenya Land Commission Report, Summary of Conclusions reached by His Majesty's Government," was also presented to Parliament and included the following:

> (10) The Commission recommends that the boundaries of the Reserves and of the Class C lands (native leasehold areas) and of the Highlands should be declared by Order in Council. This will give added security in that these boundaries could not thereafter be altered by local ordinance. His Majesty's Government approved of this recommendation and propose that in due course these boundaries should be declared by Order in Council.

Orders in Council have the force of law when approved by the reigning sovereign of Great Britain with the advice of selected members of the Privy Council (an appointed body), without any preliminary examination or debate by the two Houses of Parliament such as would be accorded domestic legislation affecting the lives and welfare of the small proportion of British subjects (less than 10 percent) who are actually residents of the United Kingdom. Reports of meetings of the Privy Council at which Orders in Council are made effective receive little current publicity, and it is evident that legislation enacted in this manner does not represent a democratic process.

Orders in Council had been frequently used to empower colonial democratic process. The process is one that lends itself to flagrant abuse. Orders in Council had been frequently used to empower colonial legislative councils to enact laws—possibly affecting the lives of millions of subject peoples—which would otherwise be beyond the scope of their limited constitutional authority. The Kenya Orders in Council fell within this category.

The two Orders in Council which resulted from the recommendations of the Kenya Land Commission were so long delayed that it is not unreasonable to suppose their promulgation may have been regarded as sources of possible future embarrassment to Ramsay MacDonald's Cabinet and to those headed successfully by Baldwin and Chamberlain. We have seen that, so far as the Kenyan Africans were concerned, the proposed Orders were to legalize the eviction of thousands of people from the districts in which they were living, and that among them were many whose right to live on the land they occupied was indisputable, even by the Kenya Land Commission itself.

The area of the so-called "White Highlands"—reserved for European settlement exclusively—was to be increased from about 10,000 square miles to about 17,000 square miles, although the total white population was then only about 20,000, of whom less than 2,000 persons and corporations were actually owners or lessees of the land which had been appropriated for them. For the benefit of this minority about 3,300,000 Africans and other non-white minorities were to be barred from the ownership or use of land in the White Highlands area. Land thus set aside averaged nearly one square mile for every white man, woman and child then living in Kenya. In the Kikuyu country less than two and a half acres for each African man, woman and child was considered ample for people who lived solely by their skill in agriculture.

The years 1934 and 1935 passed without the production of the Kenya Orders in Council. The following year, a discussion regarding them arose in the House of Commons during a debate on the supply of funds for the Colonial Office. It was customary on such occasions for a member of the House who was dissatisfied with some phase of colonial administration to introduce a motion for a reduction of the amount of the proposed appropriation, and the Secretary for the Colonies then became a target for every member of the House who wished to criticize his methods.

In anticipation of the debate on the Colonial Office estimates, which was bound to occur early in July 1936, a number of letters appeared in The

Times from the few tireless defenders of the Africans of Kenya. One of the most important, from Lord Lugard, was printed on May 27, 1936, and read in part as follows:

> The Morris Carter Commission (the Kenya Land Commission) recorded the opinion that certain of the lands now in European occupation belonged to the natives "unequivocally and of right." It is now proposed to "expunge" these rights with compensation in land or money.

Lord Lugard's letter provoked a reply from the leader of the Kenya settlers, Lord Francis Scott, who happened to be in London on an extremely interesting mission, described by *The Times* of May 31, 1936, as designed to raise a government guaranteed loan of between 200,000 pounds and 500,000 pounds for the benefit of those white settlers in Kenya who needed money to develop or retain their holdings. *The Times* reported the government as being critical of this scheme "because the guarantee involves a risk to be borne by the taxpayers of all races." The Africans of Kenya, it seemed, were about to be committed to another burden.

Scott's reply to Lord Lugard's letter was printed by *The Times* on May 29, 1936. No moral or legal argument was advanced to justify the eviction of the Kikuyu, whose right to the land they occupied was absolutely unquestioned, and to whom Scott assumed (most conveniently) Lord Lugard had referred. As already noted, the Kenya Land Commission didn't report the exact number of Kikuyu in this group of proposed evictees, but estimated that "not more than two or three hundred" were involved. We have seen that this was to be proved in 1938 to be no more than one tenth of the true figure. However, Scott's letter to *The Times* made much of the Land Commission's erroneous estimate to show that the act of gross injustice which was to be inflicted by their expulsion was of minor importance only, and quoted Section 1857 of the Commission's report to demonstrate, if such demonstration were possible, that the morals of the Kikuyu were of so low an order as to warrant a complete disregard of the most elementary principles of justice in the consideration of their acknowledged rights. The quotation reads:

> Our investigations have satisfied us that as a tribe they have certain legitimate grievances which we have been at pains to rectify, but their claims and pretensions were exaggerated out of all proportion to the truth.

Scott failed to inform the readers that the Kikuyu people were one of the two principal reservoirs from which he and his fellow settlers drew the sweated labor that enabled them to exploit the human and material resources of Kenya so profitably, and without which they would be almost as helpless as a cloud of locusts that had landed on a barren desert.

Scott failed to call attention to the numerous other evictions involved in the proposed Orders in Council, which included the 3,200 Akamba who were to be moved north of the Kenya and Uganda Railway, the 1,400 Uasin Gishu Masai who were to be relegated to the Masai Preserve, and certain members of the Dorobo people of whom the Land Commission reported "many of them have good claims of right to the areas where they now reside."

Scott soon came under the fire of Sir Robert Hamilton, former Chief Justice of the East Africa Protectorate. In a letter to *The Times* on June 3, 1936, which described Scott's arguments as tending to obscure the real issues, Sir Robert wrote:

> If Mussolini were to reserve a large area of land in Ethiopia for Italians and other Europeans to the exclusion of Abyssinians, and forbid their bringing claims in respect to land to Court, we would hold up our hands in horror and exclaim, "Such a thing would be impossible in a British Colony!"

Even the British Anti-Slavery and Aborigines Protection Society, hitherto rather mute on the wrongs of the Africans of Kenya, was stirred into action, and *The Times* of May 30, 1936, recorded its protest against the proposal to "incorporate in the Order in Council a prohibition against sale or lease to any person of colour."

The Orders were debated in the House of Commons on July 9, 1936, on the usual motion to reduce the Colonial Office estimates. By this time Cunliffe-Lister had become Air Minister and W. G. A. Ormsby-Gore, later Lord Harlech, was Secretary for the Colonies. The quality of the defense of the Kenya Land Commission's recommendations is best indicated by a quotation from the remarks of Earl Winterton, a Conservative of high standing in his party. On the charge that the Africans in Kenya were being subjected to a form of most unjust discrimination, he said:

> I would point out that it is discrimination against British settlers, in the sense that they are not allowed to take up some of the most valuable land in Africa in the native reserves.

The settlers were represented in the debate by Captain F. E. Guest (Conservative), who, although not himself a settler, had spent much time in Kenya. He said, in part:

There are not happier 3,000,000 natives in the world than the
3 million natives of Kenya Colony and that is because we have
accepted the word "trusteeship" in its proper sense.

Guest described the Kenya settlers as in a state of high emotional
excitement about their future, and informed the House that they had organized a "Vigilance Committee." Dreadful things might be about to happen
because they had so many grievances, one of which was that "the burden
of taxation was far too high."

> Many of them were intimate friends of mine at school and in the
> Army and I am entitled to say that when they get to breaking point
> they cannot be coaxed anymore.... It may be a tinder pile which
> only needs a match to set it alight.

Sir Archibald Sinclair, Leader of the Liberal Party in the House of
Commons, subsequently referred to this portion of a Guest speech as "a
note of warning that amounted to a threat." Actually it was only a varia-
tion of the old game of bluff and bluster by which the settlers had always
achieved their ends, excepting that threatening the House of Commons
directly was a new and interesting development. Heretofore it had only
been tried successfully on Governors and Colonial Secretaries.

Sir Edward Grigg, who as Governor of Kenya had always nobly supported the white settlers, made "a special plea on their behalf."

As Secretary for the Colonies, Ormsby-Gore assured the House that:
"The whole spirit and tradition of British Colonial administration in the
Colonies is to consult local opinion in the Colonies."

He meant, of course, that it was "the whole spirit and tradition" to
consult the settlers—in this instance about one half of one percent of the
total population.

The Labour members were not disturbed by the prospect of a white
revolt in Kenya, feeling, no doubt, that it would not present a serious military problem to the King's African Rifles—the local African troops who
later fought so gallantly against the Italian forces in Ethiopia. Major Milnes
said:

> I have some figures here which I have taken from the Annual
> Agricultural Census and the Annual Report of the Department
> of Agriculture for Kenya and they show that the land alienated to
> 2,102 Europeans is over 10,000 square miles and that the only culti-
> vated portion thereof amounts to 869 square miles; something like
> 3,600 square miles alleged to be used for the grazing of livestock
> and 2,200 miles alienated but lying unoccupied in 1934; and a

further 3,600 miles alienated but not used for cultivation, grazing or fallow. So that in 1934, there were no less than 5,815 miles of the European Highlands lying unused and yet the Government propose, if they bring in the Order in Council, to add a further 6,455 miles, making a total of 16,700 square miles in all. That proposal is outrageous, and particularly so when one sees the area cultivated year by year in Kenya declining progressively.

And D. Grenfell: "The small majority of white settlers have an area equal to that of all the cultivable land of the native population." The motion to reduce the Colonial Office estimates was defeated by 171 to 86.

About eighteen months were still to pass before the Kenya Orders in Council became law. An indication of the emotions of the settlers in face of this further delay may have been revealed on July 21, 1937, when the Colonial Secretary was asked in the House of Commons whether "a settler owning a farm at Karamba-ini in the Limuru District near Tigoni burnt three huts and one grain store with all their contents, including 1,250 shillings in cash, the property of a Kikuyu named Karanja wa Wainaina." The answer does not seem to have been recorded.

On June 14, 1938, a Labour member, Mr. Creech Jones, addressed a new Colonial Secretary, Malcolm MacDonald, who had been appointed a month earlier, in these moving words:

> I should like the Minister to reconsider the position in Kenya Colony. He will shortly be called upon to issue an Order in Council in respect to the Highlands. I believe that discrimination will occur at the expense of the non–European people. I hope such discrimination will be avoided, but I would ask him most seriously to consider this policy of tearing away from their ancestral lands certain native people who have for generations lived in these Highlands. It seems to be a cruel and wicked policy to transfer these people from their old territories to land unsuited to them and to which they do not wish to go.

This appeal was useless, for MacDonald acted as did his immediate predecessor, W. G. A. Ormsby-Gore, who failed to disapprove the labor law of 1938. Yet even Ormsby-Gore had avoided the Kenya Orders in Council. MacDonald was in no hurry, however, and eight days later was talking to the Duchess of Gloucester and others about "our" duty to see that a "new happiness" came to the Africans of Kenya.

The Munich conference met in the latter part of September 1938, and resulted in agreement that Chamberlain did not regard as "a defeat either for democracy or the cause of law and order." The world outlook in the months that followed was of unprecedented gravity. The Kenya Orders in Council, so long delayed, might well have been put aside indefinitely during those anxious days, yet in this period of acute international crisis, Chamberlain and his Cabinet found time to convert into law those further measures for the increased injustice to more than 3,000,000 Africans of Kenya. To make the Orders effective, a meeting of the Privy Council was held on February 2, 1939.

To save further controversy, the Highlands Order, a short, three-page document, was drafted in a manner that concealed its true purpose, for nowhere does it say explicitly that land in the Highlands may not be sold or leased to non–Europeans. Instead, this intention was achieved indirectly. The Orders merely define the boundaries of the Highlands by reference to another document and established a "Highlands Board" with absolute control of all land within the specified area. The Board consisted of seven members to be selected in accordance with section 4(w) of the Order, which directed they should be the Chief Secretary of the Colony, the Commissioner for Lands and Settlements, a person nominated by the Governor, and

> (c) four persons not holding office in the public service of the Colony, appointed from time to time by a majority of the European elected members of the Legislative Council of the Colony present and voting at a meeting of the European Elected Members convened for that purpose.

In simpler language, the control of the Board, and the Highlands themselves, was vested in a minority of settlers. Four members of the Board were sufficient for a quorum. The Board's functions were defined as follows:

> (a) To protect the interests of the inhabitants of the Highlands in the land situate in the Highlands and in particular to make representations to the Governor when in the opinion of the Board anything in relation to the administration, management, development or control of the land in the Highlands is not in the best interests of the inhabitants of the Highlands;
>
> (b) to give or withhold its consent in all matters in which its consent is required by any Ordinance for the time being in force in the Colony;
>
> (c) to advise the Governor in all matters relating to the disposition of land in the Highlands; and the Governor shall consult the Board in all such matters as are referred to in paragraph (c).

On February 28, 1939, *The Times* commented on the peculiar ambiguity of the Highlands order:

> The order relating to the Highlands does not include any reference to the reservation of the land for Europeans, but the Imperial Government have already agreed that the existing practice of excluding non–Europeans from the ownership of agricultural land must be continued "as a matter of administrative convenience."

The Order in Council dealing with African lands provided for the creation of a "Native Lands Trust Board" to consist entirely of the Europeans specified below, absolutely no provision whatever being made for any representation of the African population over whose land the Board had control:

(a) The Chief Native Commissioner of the Colony.

(b) The two white members of the Legislative Council nominated by the Governor to represent the natives.

(c) An elected white settler member of the Legislative Council selected by a majority of the European elected members.

(d) A person nominated by the Governor.

The administrative provisions of the African Lands Order in Council were made effective by Kenya Ordinance No. 28 of 1938, which had been passed in advance by the Kenya Legislative Council to become effective after the Order in Council became law.

Section 70 of the 1938 ordinance extinguished the legitimate rights of Africans living outside the "Reserve":

> (1) With effect from the commencement of this Ordinance all native rights existing at the commencement of this Ordinance in any land in the Colony situate outside the boundaries of the native reserves and the native leasehold area, irrespective of whether such rights relate to tribal group, family or individual holdings, are hereby declared to be of the Crown Lands Ordinance, 1902, and of Section 86 of the Crown Lands Ordinance, 1915, shall no longer have any effect in respect to land alienated under such Ordinances respectively.

Sections 49 and 60 of the 1938 Ordinance showed how the evictions were to be carried out and the penalties to be imposed on any Africans who resisted, who were liable upon conviction to a fine not exceeding fifty pounds or to imprisonment not exceeding six months or to both such fine and imprisonment.

The 1938 Kenya Ordinance also provided in Section 65 for "compulsorily reducing the numbers of stock, flocks or herds in any native land unit."

The granting of licenses to non–Africans and others to enter the African Reserves was permitted by Section 38 for the following purposes:

(1) The grazing of livestock

(2) The removal of timber and other forest products

(3) The removal of sand, stone...

(4) Rights of way

Under Section 32, African lands may be leased for 33-year periods or, with the consent of the Secretary for the Colonies, for 99 years.

With loopholes of this description, it was obvious that the Africans of Kenya had little more security within the boundaries of their reserves than before the Kenya Land Commission commenced its labors.

The Africans had no machinery for presenting their objections to the Kenya Legislative Council except through the Europeans appointed by the Governor to "represent" them in that unique organization. Those two representatives seem to have preserved a discreet silence, but at a meeting of the Council held on April 21, 1939, Mr. Isher Dass—an elected Indian member—announced he proposed to read a petition into the official report of the proceedings. The following are extracts:

> It must be stated that in view of the incidents of the past, not much trust can be placed upon the solemn promises and solemn undertakings of the British Government. The principle of the declared trusteeship of the natives is a mockery.... The Africans can never agree to be contented with what is allotted to them under the Ordinance while the best Land in Kenya is given to the white settlers. They can never agree to the reservation of the so-called "Highlands" for Europeans while they are themselves relegated to the poorer land in the country.... The reservation of the Highlands provides yet another example of the doubtful value of British pledges as they are not worth the paper they are written on so far as their execution is concerned.... The Africans strongly object to the statement that only part of the land in Kenya belongs to them by historic right. This is brazen fraud. All land was the property of the Africans and if any part of it has been lost it is because the same has been taken away without the consent of its owners. Land is regarded like a mother and the Africans have never considered themselves free to abandon it.

Their spokesman, unfortunately, was beating the wind, doughty opponent though he was of "Star Chamber" legislation.

14

Tyranny over the
African Labor Force

In Chapter 12, we noted that the basic weakness (and injustice) of every colonial system is a deterioration sooner or later to the permanent relationship of master and servant—the servants being of course the indigenous people. Free land and low taxes are helpful, but the keystone of colonial development has always been a controlled supply of cheap native labor. In this respect, as in many others, British rule in Kenya was a classic example.

From the earliest days, labor was more or less available as the Europeans brought with them many things which attracted the Africans and which could only be bought for cash, which in turn meant working for the settlers. The problem for the settlers was to insure a stable work force, conceding in return the lowest possible wages and the absolute minimum of rights. The answer was quite simple; the introduction of criminal sanctions into the civil contract of employment—something long since discarded by the law of civilized England.

Early on, Kenya became for the Africans a police state. It would be inappropriate to examine the development of legislation in this book but we can look at the consolidation of labor law affected by Ordinance No. 2 of 1938, an ordinance to provide for the control of the employment of servants.

First of all, the *Annual Report on Native Affairs of Kenya "Colony" and Protectorate* for 1938, gives the following information on wages paid to Africans for a "thirty-day ticket."

112

Casual Labour: Tea, Sugar and Sisal Plantations	9/– to 10/– shillings*
Casual Labour: Other	10/– shillings
Indentured Labour	11/– shillings
Resident	8/– shillings
Mining: Alluvial and Surface	9/– shillings
Mining: Underground	11/– shillings

A thirty-day ticket represents thirty days' straight labor without any allowance for Sundays, holidays or other rest periods. The number of hours to be worked daily was not fixed by law and was thus within the discretion of the employer. A nine-hour day appears to have been normal, which made a thirty-day ticket good for approximately 270 hours of actual work for an average payment of ten shillings. In addition, a laborer received free board which the 1938 Report estimated to be worth a further six shillings a month, making the total of cash and food equivalent to sixteen shillings a month.

This unbelievably low scale of wages prevailed for many years in spite of periodical labor shortages which, in white-labor countries, would have brought about an automatic increase in pay. African wages remained stable in Kenya for so long because the settlers were strongly organized and the Africans were forbidden any kind of labor organization. Since low wages meant that the Africans could not afford to educate their children, a high level of illiteracy ensured cheap labor in the next generation, and so on. Suffice it to say that, despite an enormous increase in the cost of living throughout the world, immediately after World War II the scale of wages paid to African labor in steady employment was far lower than it had been forty years before.

Trade unions were illegal and therefore organized strikes were impossible. The 1938 Ordinance guarded the white settlers from any pressure of this kind by defining new crimes punishable by a fine of 150 pounds (twenty-five years' pay for the average African) or imprisonment for not more than six months. These penalties might be inflicted upon any person:

(a) inducing or attempting to induce any servant to leave the service of his employer under circumstances that amount to a breach of the contract under which the servant is employed or any of the provisions of this ordinance; or

(b) who, without permission of the employer, enters upon the premises of such with intent to induce or attempt to induce the servant to leave the service of such employer whether before

Twenty shillings = One English pound.

or after the completion of such servant's contract with such employer.

The second provision was particularly abominable. Why should it be considered a crime to advise an employee not to renew a contract after its expiration, which, in point of law, automatically frees both parties from further obligation?

It may surprise anyone without first-hand knowledge of a colony to learn that the provisions of the 1938 Ordinance applied to children, namely servants, laborers and herdsmen of twelve years of age or more (originally ten years of age but altered as a result of outside pressure) who were under a contract of service "whether in writing or oral, whether express or implied"—the broadest possible definition in favor of the employer.

An employer's contract with an adult was limited to one year with certain minor exceptions, but a child of from twelve to sixteen years of age might, with the consent of his parent or guardian, enter into a contract of employment for any period up to five years. A child might thus be placed at the mercy of a single and unchangeable employer during the period that a white boy of similar age would be receiving the most significant part of his education. Yet the employer was under no obligation whatever to ensure that the African boy received any form of schooling during the contract period. Further, a parent might be prosecuted under the provisions mentioned above if he visited his son in circumstances which the employer considered might lead to a boy's desertion. In other words, the child's parents had the simple choice, whether or not to sell him for the required period. Poverty makes such decisions for us.

If an African under contract left his work without the permission of his employer, he could be arrested forthwith without the slightest investigation to determine whether his absence was justified. If found guilty of desertion, he could be fined a sum not exceeding five pounds (ten months' pay) or be sentenced to a prison term not exceeding six months in default of payment. Africans who could readily produce the equivalent of nearly one year's pay were even rarer than white men enjoying that financial capacity.

As the law was originally devised, the penalty for desertion was relatively mild compared to the punishment of "any person knowingly engaging, employing or harbouring any servant who had unlawfully left the service of his employer." Those guilty of "harbouring" a deserter were most likely to be his best friends or his nearest relatives—his wife, father, mother, brothers, sisters, etc. For thus responding to the ordinary instincts of humanity, these unfortunates were liable to a fine of 150 pounds or six months' imprisonment.

A fine of this magnitude would have taken the average African at least twenty-five years to accumulate, if he saved every penny he could possibly earn. Obviously, it was not intended to be within the capacity of the victims to pay; its purpose was to make imprisonment inevitable. After these penalties had been in force for eight months, the fine was reduced to ten pounds and the alternative period of imprisonment to one month. As a result, friends and relatives who were imprudent enough to help deserters were able to escape a month's confinement by paying a sum they might possibly earn in as short a period as twenty months, if still physically fit! It must not be assumed the reduction in fine and sentence was due to any spontaneous working of the dull consciences of the Governor or the Kenya Legislative Council. It was brought about by outside agitation by the late W. McGregor Ross, Archdeacon W. E. Owen of Nyanza Province and others.

Among the trivial offenses for which an African could be fined half a month's pay or jailed for a period not exceeding one month were:

> If, during working hours, he unfits himself for the proper performance of his work by becoming intoxicated.
>
> If he neglects to perform any work which it was his duty to have performed or he carelessly or improperly performs any work which from its nature was his duty under his contract to have performed carefully and properly.
>
> If he uses any abusive or insulting language or is guilty of insulting behaviour to his employer or to any person placed by his employer in authority over him, calculated to provoke a breach of the peace.
>
> If he refuses to obey any command of his employer or of any person lawfully placed by his employer over him, which command it was his duty to obey.

All these misdeeds are of a character which, in England, would indeed justify summary dismissal, but the introduction of criminal sanctions assured the servant's total submission to his employer—a form of disguised slavery. Who but the employer can decide whether work has been performed carefully, carelessly, or left undone, and whether it was really the duty of the accused to have done the work he is alleged to have neglected? Those are matters of judgment and opinion over which there might easily be genuine misunderstandings; the person "placed by his employer in authority over him" might well be another African, who, like many of his white brethren, might be unfit to exercise such authority. Any responsible magistrate would be most reluctant to judge such cases if justice, not discipline, was expected of him.

Other offenses which subjected the African to a fine not exceeding five pounds (ten months' pay) or prison for not more than six months were:

> If he willfully or by willful breach of duty or through drunkenness does any act tending to the immediate loss, damage or serious risk of any property placed by his employer in his charge or placed by any other person in his charge for delivery to his employer.
>
> If he, by willful breach of duty or by neglect of duty or through drunkenness, refuses or omits to do any lawful act proper and requisite to be done by him for preserving in safety any property placed by his employer in his charge, or placed by any other person in his charge for delivery to or on account of his employer.

Both these hypothetical offenses, unless caused by intoxication, again involved questions of judgment and opinion. Any employer suffering a loss which he thought might have been avoided was tempted to characterize it as a "willful breach of duty" by the African, and of course, the employer would again be the main witness.

If the African happened to be a herdsman in charge of grazing animals, the perils of the labor law were multiplied for his special benefit and his chances of keeping out of jail correspondingly reduced. For he was subjected to the usual five pounds fine or six months' imprisonment:

> If he fails to report to his employer the death or loss of any animal placed in his charge at the earliest opportunity after he has discovered, or at the earliest opportunity after he should in the ordinary course of duty have discovered, such death or loss.
>
> If he fails, after having received an order from his employer to preserve for the use and inspection of his employer any part or parts of an animal which he alleges to have died, to preserve such part or parts and is unable to prove to the satisfaction of the court the death of the animal which he alleges to have died.
>
> If he loses any animal placed in his charge and it is proved by his employer to the satisfaction of the court that such animal could not, in the circumstances of the case, have become irretrievably lost without the act or default of the servant.

It should be noted that only in the last of these offenses was the onus of proof placed specifically on the employer. Further, although the underlying intention of the last two offenses was to prevent dishonest misappropriation by the herdsman, it was not necessary for the prosecutor to prove dishonesty, merely to cast doubt on the herdsman's explanation—a complete reversal of the practice in English criminal courts. The first offense on the list is of course indefensible as it made absent-mindedness as much a crime as deliberate theft.

The subsidiary provisions of the 1938 Ordinance were pernicious. A magistrate was empowered to turn over to an employer all or part of a fine collected from an African if he decided that the employer had suffered damage. Or he could authorize the employer to deduct the amount of his alleged loss from the employee's salary in installments not exceeding half the amount earned. The magistrate could also add to the African's contract with the employer the term of imprisonment inflicted for any violations of the law. This last provision was tantamount to slavery, because the African had no voice whatever in the additional term he was compelled to serve, and the fact that he would be paid adds nothing to the argument: payment might be no more than five shillings a month anyway if the magistrate had authorized deduction of damages.

Apart from the 1938 Ordinance, there was another long-standing law which, for all practical purposes, should be considered part of the labor law. This instrument, Native Registration Ordinance No. 56 of 1921, was so successful in fulfilling its purpose that over the years only minor amendments proved necessary. It provided that every male African "apparently above the age of sixteen years" should register at a designated government office, and, after being fingerprinted, should receive a registration certificate which he was bound to carry at all times.

Having secured his registration certificate, the African youth at once qualified for "a fine not exceeding fifteen pounds (two and a half years' pay) or three months' imprisonment, or both fine and imprisonment," if he:

(1) Shall be in unlawful possession of or shall make use of any certificate belonging to another native; or

(2) Falsely states that he has not previously been registered or shall make any other false statement or commit any act or omission with the object of deceiving a registration officer; or

(3) Hand over his own certificate to any other native to be used by such other native; or

(4) Shall be found in any district without a certificate issued in pursuance to the provisions of this Ordinance; or

(5) Shall refuse or neglect to produce his certificate when required to do so by any police officer or other person lawfully entitled to demand the production of such certificate; or

(6) Shall mutilate any certificate issued to him or shall add thereto or erase therefrom any material particularly; or shall knowingly be in possession of a certificate containing false entries or from

which dishonest erasures or excisions have been made; or

(7) Shall obtain or attempt to obtain a new certificate from a registration officer without first reporting to such registration officer the loss, mutilation or destruction of any such certificate which may previously have been issued to him or the fact that he has been previously registered; or

(8) Shall become registered more than once and omit to give up to the registration officer any certificate issued to him on previous registration which remains in his possession.

Much could be written about the abuses made of this "Kipande" law but it is at least worthwhile to consider a letter to *The Times* on June 10, 1938, from Archdeacon W. E. Owen of Nyanza Province, who pointed out that no fewer than 50,000 Africans in Kenya had been jailed since 1920 for lack of registration certificates—an average of about 3,000 a year. The Archdeacon characterized the penalties imposed by the 1938 Ordinance as "really rather a disgrace to our Empire."

The British government reserved the right to veto any ordinance approved by the Kenya Legislative Council through the Secretary for the Colonies. The man who failed to veto the 1938 Ordinance was W. G. A. Ormsby-Gore, later Lord Harlech.

On June 22, 1938, less than two months after the infamous labor ordinance became effective, *The Times* carried an item captioned "Native Progress in Kenya," describing the opening by the Duchess of Gloucester of an "Exhibition of Photographs illustrating African Progress and Activity." Malcom MacDonald, who had succeeded Ormsby-Gore as Secretary for the Colonies on May 16, 1938, presided and part of his speech reported by *The Times* as follows:

> The recent history of that country (Kenya), where a new colony is being created and a new civilization established, was one of the romances of Empire.... It was our duty to see that not only a new development of life, but a new happiness came to the Africans.

MacDonald's own achievements in bringing "a new happiness to the Africans" are recorded in Chapter XIII, namely the implementation by Order in Council of the recommendations of the Kenya Land Commission, which took away all rights, legitimate or otherwise, which the Africans had in "white" areas.

The laws of Kenya were based on the assumption that a large proportion of the African population was so inherently dishonest that severe punishment, or the threat of it, was necessary for the protection of the European.

The War brought about a further deterioration in the status of African labor in Kenya, for between twelve and fifteen thousand Africans were forced to work for settlers engaged in raising crops essential to the war effort. In time of war or national emergency, the use of compulsory labor for essential public works or services can be justified—assuming it is sanctioned by the elected representatives of the persons affected and invested with proper safeguards. But the use of forced labor for private profit is repugnant to all free men, especially when the appropriate legislation is enacted by unrepresentative government in which the prospective conscripts have no voice.

Following Italy's entrance into the War, the closing of the Mediterranean route to the Middle East threw a heavy burden on British shipping, which was obliged to transport supplies for Egypt and other fighting areas by way of the Cape of Good Hope. It was obvious that increased crop production in Kenya would lead to a corresponding savings in tonnage. Thus in 1943, the Kenya Legislative Council passed Ordinance No. 7 which provided free grants of from fifteen to fifty shillings per acre for plowing virgin land or land not in cultivation since March 1, 1938. After the land so plowed was planted, the settlers were guaranteed a minimum profit per acre as follows:

Wheat	40 shillings
Corn	35 shillings
Rye	37½ shillings
Flax	50 shillings

Although the settlers depended on the Africans to raise the war crops so urgently needed, and although they were on the threshold of a wartime boom, they did not want the Africans to share their profit. The basic plan was that the settlers should cultivate increased acreages, with yields at guaranteed prices, but that their workmen should be paid the same old ten shillings for thirty days' labor, plus sixty pounds of corn to keep them in tip top condition for the national emergency. About 47,000 Kenyan Africans were by this time serving in the British Forces (in Ethiopia, Ceylon and Burma) at rates of pay which ranged from one pound to thirty shillings per month.

The absence of the African volunteers had whittled down the Kenya labor supply, and a committee was appointed to consider methods of overcoming the manpower shortage. On March 26, 1942, the following comment on the committee's report was made by Mr. Creech Jones in the House of Commons:

The Committee admitted with, as it seems, a guilty conscience that the farm work for which the African was asked to give his labour was unattractive because of the pay and conditions operating on the farms.... There is the further admission that there would be no difficulty in securing Africans if pay and conditions were right.... But at the present time wages are 3½ pence for a solid day's work as indicated in the report. If you allow for food, accommodation and other essentials, wages are not more than 7 pence a day.

The white farmers have guaranteed prices and markets and now they have to have cheap subsidized labour, subsidized by the native reserves.

No doubt I shall be told that we have labour conscription in England, and if in Britain, why not in Kenya? We have responsible government, and the right of free criticism, and there is a check on the Government's activities. In the case of Kenya, the African people are governed by an alien race. The black people have no voice whatever in government; there is segregation of land and many of us feel that our native policy in that country has been reprehensible. The racial and economic structure of the two countries is vastly different. There is no analogy between England and Kenya.

The Churchill government was defended by Harold Macmillan, Under-Secretary for the Colonies, who assured the House every possible effort would be made to increase rations and improve wages. He added: "There will be a Central Wage Board; in effect it will fix the wages not of course only for compulsory, but for voluntary labour."

It is sad to reflect that it took the emergency of a World War and an attack in the Commons to rouse the colonial power to attempt an alleviation of the wage freeze the Africans in Kenya had suffered for 30 years or more. It would be naive to suppose that successive colonial secretaries were unaware of this embarrassing problem but of course the settlers' lobby was always well organized and, on ten shillings per month, it was difficult for Africans to post a letter, let alone finance the needed delegation.

15

The Crisis

When the Second World War broke out on September 3, 1939, members of all races in Kenya united in the face of their common enemy, Nazi Germany. Political grievances were temporarily set aside.

The Kenyan Africans enlisted in large numbers in the armed forces, both young and middle-aged. Those who did not join up helped to contribute toward the war effort by growing food stuffs in their fields ("digging for victory").

The Kenyan Africans were willing to help in the fight against Fascism and Nazism until there was victory, proposing to challenge Britain afterward to treat them with fairness.

The month of May 1940 found the fortunes of the British Empire rapidly approaching their lowest ebb. By May 13, the Germans had invaded Holland and Belgium, compelling the British Expeditionary Forces to begin their historic retreat to Dunkirk. Italy was powerful in East Africa and Kenya was menaced from the north and east. Yet, on May 13, *The Times* reported that only 40 percent of the male white population aged eighteen to forty had enlisted in the local Defense Force and that more volunteers were urgently needed.

Two months later the Italian forces captured Fort Moyale on the Kenya-Ethiopia border and it was not until November 1941, that Gondar, the last Italian stronghold in Ethiopia, surrendered to the British.

Who accounted for the severest part of the fighting which led to that surrender? A communiqué issued by the British East African Military and Air Headquarters at Nairobi, capital of Kenya, contained the following, dated November 28, 1941:

Principal credit for the final battle must, however, be given to East African and patriot troops. The assault on this final position was carried almost exclusively by East Africans. More East African soldiers took part in this battle than in any one battle in the campaign.

It is fitting that the African soldiers who played a part in the whole campaign should have the honour of finally overthrowing Mussolini's East African Empire.

Nor did the services rendered by East African troops end with the conquest of Ethiopia. In May 1942, Associated Press reported they were being used to meet the Japanese threat to India and Ceylon, which had a population of about 357 million, more than 70 percent of the population of the British Empire.

Titled "British send Africans to protect India," the news item read:

London, May 8. Britain has reinforced Ceylon with African troops and is now ready to protect India, it was announced today "Troops include Africans from Kenya, Northern Rhodesia, Uganda and Nyasaland," the official statement said.

The story of the assistance given by East African soldiers to the British Empire was continued on September 20, 1943, when the New York Times printed a cable from Colombo, Ceylon, headed: "Askaris training to fight Japanese: Native troops from East Africa are hardened in Ceylon for thrust in Far East: Adapted to jungle warfare, Negro soldiers little affected by malaria; Have beaten Italians in Ethiopia." The troops were described as "recruited from the tribes of Tanganyika, Uganda and Kenya." Subsequently, they fought in Burma with their accustomed bravery.

The contribution of the Africans of Kenya to the British war effort was twenty times as great in numbers of men as that of the settlers, even though some of the whites were drafted while the Africans were volunteers. In a House of Commons debate on March 26, 1942, Harold Macmillan, then Under-Secretary for the Colonies, stated that at the end of 1940 there were 2,332 Europeans (volunteers and draftees) in military service in Kenya, and 47,000 African volunteers. He added that after the 47,000 Africans had volunteered, the Governor prohibited further recruiting because the white settlers complained that a labor shortage was created!

Since the Africans had been fighting for the cause of freedom and democracy, they began to wonder whether freedom and the democratic way of life would fall to them after the war. The first answer they received was tantamount to a slap in the face: the Kikuyu Central Association was banned in 1940 as "subversive." They were made subject to a law which decreed that no three Africans could get together for a meeting without permission from the District Commissioner. There were no uprisings during this intensely provocative period.

While the war was slowly coming to an end in 1944, the Kenyan government made an announcement that as a result of brilliant military contribution by the Kenyan Africans in East Africa and South East Asia, the Africans of Kenya would now be represented by one of their own in the Kenya Legislative Council. However, that *one* African would still be nominated by the Governor. No election for the Africans. That African, Mr. E. W. Mathu, would then join the European missionary who was previously nominated by the Governor to represent the African interests in the Legislative Council, the Rev. L. J. Beecher.

The Rev. Beecher, who was nominated by the Governor in 1943 to represent African interests in the Kenya Legislative Council, amply and emphatically demonstrated his interest in African affairs. Even after E. W. Mathu joined the Rev. Beecher in the Kenya Legislative Council, Mr. Beecher continuously argued that African representation by the two members was still inadequate and should also be a direct representation, meaning that the African people should elect their own members to the Legislative Council. The Rev. Beecher, in common with Mr. Mathu, continued to represent the African interests until 1947. He resigned his position that year, after which three more Africans were nominated by the Governor to the Legislative Council. Now, there were four Africans to this important and country-wide law making council.

Who Was Eliud Wambu Mathu?

Mathu was born about 1910 at Kikuyu in Kiambu District. He obtained his elementary and primary education at the Church of Scotland Mission at Kikuyu. In 1926, he attended the famous African high school in Kenya, the Alliance High School. He was a brilliant student. After completing Form 4 at the Alliance High School, Mathu became a teacher in the same school from 1929 to 1930.

In 1932, Mathu left the Alliance High School for South Africa. In South Africa, he enrolled at Fort Hare College from where he obtained the Matriculation Certificate of the University of South Africa in 1934, after which time he rejoined the Alliance High School.

In 1938, Mathu left Kenya for England to take up courses at Exeter University College and at Oxford University, from where he obtained a B.A. degree. He rejoined the Alliance High School once again. In 1942, he left

Eliud Wambu Mathu, the first African member of the Kenya Legislative Council, from 1944 to 1960.

Alliance High School to become headmaster of Waithaka Independent School. He had a beautiful home by African standards of the time, and a beautiful wife.

In 1944, he was nominated as the first African to represent the African interests in the Kenya Legislative Council. Mathu was a fiery speaker, like the American Adlai Stevenson or the British Aheyrin Bevan.

In 1944, after the nomination of Mathu to the Kenya Legislative Council, a country-wide political body for Africans was allowed, hence the Kenya African Study Union, which was a trans-tribal organization. The first founders were: Francis J. Khamisi, Albert Awino, James S. Gichuru, F. M. Ng'ang'a, Jimmy Jeremiah, Sincion Mulandi, Harry Nangurai, Harry Thuku, S. B. Jackayo, John Kebaso, J. D. Otiende and W. W. Awori. Mathu, the first African member of the Kenya Legislative Council, in common with other African leaders like Harry Thuku, was instrumental in the formation of the Kenya African Study

Union which was renamed soon afterward the Kenya African Union, and whose president was James Samuel Gichuru, formerly a school teacher and a graduate of Makerere College in Uganda. After the formation of the Kenya African Union, other previous political parties which had been banned since 1940 did not resurface. However, in 1945, many members of the Kikuyu Central Association, which also had been proscribed since 1940, were ambivalent as to whether to fully support the Kenya African Union or maintain their underground movement. In the end, most members of the K.C.A. decided to have dual membership, and became dual supporters.

In 1945, the K.C.A., still underground, went on giving or administering what may be described as the "light oathing" practice to its members and its new recruits. Why was this nec-

James Samuel Gichuru, president of the Kenya African Union until 1947.

essary when there was already a country-wide political organization and an African member in the Kenya Legislative Council?

Most members of the Kikuyu Central Association had become dispirited and discouraged about the importance of clinging to constitutional struggle only. They argued that in the case of Kenya, where European settlers had exclusive use of the best land in the country and introduced a policy of racial discrimination, constitutional means would have to be supported by something else as an extra force.

Mathu did his best as the nominated member of the Kenya Legislative Council. J. S. Gichuru did his best as the president of the Kenya African Union, given the political environment of Kenya at that time.

There were many restrictions imposed by the Kenyan colonial government on the Kenya African Union. For example, freedom of speech and the freedom of the assembly were very severely and deliberately curtailed. The Kenya African Union could not hold a meeting anywhere in Kenya without police permission or permit. In some instances the police commissioner would even ask the Kenya African Union to provide a list of topics which would be covered at the meeting, as well as the names of those who would speak on these topics.

Even Mr. Mathu, the Honorable Member of the Kenya Legislative Council, was not immune from the police restrictions. He could not hold or address a public meeting in his constituencies without police or the district commissioner's permission. It was very frustrating. To this end, Mathu gave a passionate speech in the Kenya Legislative Council that said, in part:

> Those who still cherish their former freedom and common rights bitterly resent having to apply for permission to meet together for any purpose whatever. Naturally the law is evaded and they meet at night behind locked doors with a sentry outside; they meet in caves, in the depths of banana groves or in swampy alleys away from the habitations of their fellow men to avoid detection. Yes, they meet together, these "free, happy Africans" of His Majesty's Colony of Kenya, like felons, with all the humiliating circumstances and methods they are forced to adopt, whispering and cursing the Europeans and their own headmen, who administer an oppressive and unjustified law. One day their repressions are bound to burst out with the usual unhappy consequences for all.[1]

Since the Waiyaki-Lugard oath of 1890, one of the Africans' main complaints had been the lack of freedom of speech, assembly, and association, hence when the Kenya African Study Union (later Kenya African Union) was formed in 1944, one of its first demands was that these rights should be accorded to the Africans. For no African in Kenya could hold a public meeting without informing the Government beforehand as to the nature of the meeting, its agenda, who was speaking, where it would be held, and how long it was likely to last. It was only when government officials (mainly the police) were satisfied on these points that a permit for the meeting was issued.

In 1947, one year before Mathu made the speech quoted above, he asked permission to speak in one of the constituencies in the Northern Kikuyu area. He got permission, but on arrival was told by the district commissioner that the meeting could not be held immediately and that, in any case, not many were likely to attend.

"I am absolutely sure that many people will attend," said Mathu.

"How sure are you?" asked the D. C.

"Doubly sure," Mathu replied.

"Are you also sure that the meeting will be orderly?" the D. C. asked.

"I give my personal guarantee."

"But there are not enough policemen at such short notice to supervise the meeting in case—just in case of disorder."

"May I ask you, sir, to preside at the meeting so you can yourself see that it is well conducted?" Mathu asked the D. C. humbly, and the D. C. agreed.

As they approached the market place where the meeting was to be held, they saw a large crowd waiting for them.

"I am surprised," the D. C. said, turning to Mathu as they walked.

"Why surprised?"

"I do not know how all this could have been arranged," said the D. C., looking a little bit embarrassed and annoyed.

"Well, sir, we asked your permission fourteen days ago, didn't we?"

"Yes," replied the D. C. "But do you mean to tell me that all these people could have been informed of the meeting in such a short time?"

"Certainly!"

"All right," the D. C. concluded in a somewhat irritable tone.

When they arrived, they both sat by the table. Mathu took out his papers, and then the chairman of the Kenya African Union in the district introduced both Mathu and the D. C. People stood up and applauded the two men heartily. Everybody sat down.

Now, it was for Mathu to speak to the gathering. As always, there was dead silence when he rose to speak. He began in his usual fiery manner, speaking at length and touching on all the issues which he wanted to drive home to his audience. He stressed and explained the implications of Colonial Paper No. 191 and the difference between it and the other one, Paper No. 210, which was substituted after a heated protest from the settlers.

As the meeting progressed, people applauded Mathu more and more. The D. C. joined the audience in their applause; there was no disorder of any kind, and everyone left peacefully.

When Mathu returned to Nairobi, he and the organizing members of the Kenya African Union in the district where the meeting had been held were charged with having held an unlawful meeting, not authorized by the D. C. or the police commissioner in charge. Mathu was absolutely furious. He went to the highest authorities and the charges were dropped. This incident left a serious scar on many people. Why would the D. C. who had agreed to preside over the meeting then turn against Mathu and other members of the meeting, accusing them of holding it unlawfully?

16

Kenyatta
Returns to Kenya

In England, Jomo Kenyatta, Kwame Nkrumah, T. Ras Makonnen, and Peter Abrahams, along with George Padmore, organized the fifth Pan-African Conference in 1945, at which all the leaders pledged themselves to return home and fight for independence. Each was to wait until the strategic moment. Jomo Kenyatta and Makonnen were commissioned to maintain a branch of the Pan-African Conference in Manchester and to publish a magazine called *Pan African*. At the same time Kwame Nkrumah, Kojo Bosio, and Bankole Awannor Renner established an organization in London called the West African National Secretariat and began to issue their own magazine.

The first of the Pan-African group to go home was Jomo Kenyatta, who returned to Kenya from Europe to assume the leadership of the recently formed Kenya African Union. His arrival concentrated efforts on the national purpose of the Union.

When Kenyatta arrived at the port of Mombasa in September 1946, the people greeted him with great joy. Some had traveled all the way from up-country to meet him; they were too impatient to wait for him in Nairobi.

As his ship dropped anchor, Kenyatta appeared on deck and started waving to the big crowd waiting by the pier. The crowd waved back enthusiastically and women shrilled endlessly as though a Kikuyu baby boy had just been born.

The crowd got even more excited when Kenyatta disembarked and began moving toward the customs and passports offices, and the police had a difficult time trying to prevent people from trampling each other into the ground. On this momentous occasion one could see the pride and happiness in the numerous African faces that their greatest hero had come home.

Eventually Kenyatta went to a hotel, where the Africans had arranged for him to rest for a few days before taking the train to Nairobi, where an even larger crowd was awaiting him. As he entered the train to the capital, news traveled ahead that he was on his way. There was tremendous excitement in Nairobi. The train left Mombasa in the afternoon and was due at Nairobi the following morning at nine o'clock. That morning, people working in the offices were especially anxious, and there were numerous telephone calls between people asking whether he had arrived.

At Nairobi Station, the platform was packed with people from all walks of life. Women started shrilling while the train was still seven miles away and kept going long after it arrived!

It had rained that morning and the platform was a sea of mud. Some of the bystanders climbed on top of the roof, hoping at least to catch a glimpse of the old man. The Commission Officer, his deputy, and numerous policemen were at the station.

When the train arrived, the police went straight to Kenyatta's coach and removed him swiftly. The station entrance was narrow and, though the police had managed to reach Kenyatta before the crowd got near, they still had to pass through it to get him away from the station. The crowd surged forward to see him and people were trampled and crushed. Women shrilled repeatedly and the many columns of people on the station platform looked as though they were performing a Japanese snake dance.

As Kenyatta was being shepherded by the police through the crowd, he waved happily at everyone, and now and then he recognized his old friends. He was heard shouting to one man: "Hey, you, 'Njuki ng'eni,'" meaning "Hey, you, strange bee." This man to whom Kenyatta was calling was an old friend with whom he had traveled on the same boat in the early thirties when they had both left Kenya for Britain. They used to call each other "strange bee" because they were the only two Africans on a boat full of Europeans.

Kenyatta did not want to stay in Nairobi long and most Africans did not want him to either. He moved to Githunguri, about 28 miles north of Nairobi by car.

The problem with Nairobi at that time was that there was no proper hotel in which he could stay or at least any place where he could rest and be able to meet his fellow men casually and talk to them. Racial discrimination was rampant and this meant that the Africans could not hold a

Jomo Kenyatta, the first African prime minister of Kenya in 1963, then president of Kenya from 1964 to 1978.

reception for the old man in any of the Nairobi hotels. Nevertheless, people were very happy indeed to see him and one could hear those working in the offices breathing hard and sighing happily—as Stephen Foster's young man would sigh for his "Jeannie with the light brown hair!"

Members of other races in Kenya, however, were cool about Kenyatta's arrival. The Governor, Sir Philip Mitchell, asked Kenyatta to stay out of politics for at least a year, until he had become familiar with changes that had taken place during his absence. While Kenyatta would give no such pledge, he did refrain from active politics until June 1947, the date of the next meeting of the Kenya African Union, at which he was unanimously elected president and where he made a fiery speech.

"Abrogate Highlands reservation, abolish pass laws in Kenya!" he demanded in an impassioned appeal.

Earlier on it was decided that Peter Mbiyu Koinange should represent the Kenya African Union in London, Kenyatta taking over from him as principal of the Kenya Teachers' College while he was away. One of the tasks assigned to Koinange was to persuade Creech Jones, Labour Colonial Secretary, to change the then system of representation in Kenya; elections in which Europeans voted for Europeans, Asians for Asians, and Africans were not allowed to vote at all. Koinange was also supposed to take a break and take some economics courses at the London School of Economics and Political Science.

Koinange's mission was not successful but he did succeed in rallying a number of prominent British Members of Parliament to the African side. It was he who sent a bitter message of complaint to the United Nations Trustee Council, then meeting in Paris in September 1948, an action which shocked the Kenyan settlers and the Kenyan government officials. Two days later, the office of the Kenya African Union in Nairobi was thoroughly searched by two detectives from the C.I.D. (equivalent to the F.B.I. in the United States). They were particularly interested in a copy of Koinange's memorandum to the U.N. and were curious as to whether he had been actually instructed to write this by the Union's headquarters.

At this time, an almost endemic political issue had been going on. Earlier in 1945 the Colonial Office had, too, an interest in a federal union of Kenya, Uganda, and Tanganyika had grown more clamant than ever. To this end, the Secretary of State for the Colonies issued a white paper, Colonial Paper No. 191, in which proposals were set out in detail for an East African Central Legislative and Executive Commission. These proposals were sent to East Africa for discussion.

The Kenyan governor, Sir Philip Mitchell, had been impressed by the cooperation demonstrated by the three East African territories during the second World War. Sir Philip Mitchell, however, was not in favor of the East African political fusion, but was in favor of economic cooperation. To this end, he put forth proposals toward the formation of an East African High Commission, with a Central Legislative Assembly whose membership composition would have equal representation of all races from each territory. This was particularly surprising, because Sir Philip Mitchell did not have a reputation of being in favor of equality between Europeans and non–Europeans. The European settlers did not appreciate Sir Philip Mitchell's proposals, especially when they "implied" equality of all races.

When the proposals were sent to East Africa for discussion in the Legislative Councils of the three territories, the Kenyan settlers bitterly opposed them. They held numerous political meetings throughout Kenya; they carried on their fight against the Colonial Paper so vehemently that the Colonial Secretary felt compelled to make concessions to them. The Africans and the Asians in Kenya accepted and supported the proposals contained in Colonial Paper 191.

What was so objectionable in the Colonial Paper? The proposals were that the European, Asian and African races should each have equal representation in a new East African Central Assembly. The Kenyan settlers did not approve of racial equality and the Africans and the Asians on their part joined forces to oppose the settlers. In a quandary, the Colonial Secretary decided to appease the settlers by withdrawing Colonial Paper No. 191 and replaced it by another (No. 210) which accepted the principle of majority representation for the white settlers.

When the final vote was taken in the Kenya Legislative Council, the Afro-Asian representatives were of course outnumbered and Colonial Paper 210 was approved by the Council in 1947.

At the final voting, Mr. E. W. Mathu, the only African member in the Kenya Legislative Council, decided to support Colonial Paper 210. This was particularly discouraging to some Africans and Indians because earlier on Mr. Mathu had supported the proposals of Colonial Paper No. 191. The Kenya African Union had supported these proposals wholeheartedly.

Why did Mr. Mathu change his mind on this very vital issue? Mr. Mathu argued that under the principles of Colonial Paper No. 210, African representation would increase to four African members. In addition, the European settlers under the terms of Colonial Paper 210 did not get their "Rhodesia," or otherwise a Kenya Constitution based on the Rhodesian Constitutional model. Consequently, to Mr. Mathu, Colonial Paper No. 210 was like a synthesis—that is to say that the Colonial Office Paper No. 191 was a thesis and the settlers' demand of a self-government controlled by them or a Kenya Constitution based on the Rhodesian Constitution as model was anti-thesis, and therefore Colonial Paper No. 210 was a synthesis of the two choices.

It is true, however, that some members of the Kenya African Union did not agree with Mr. Mathu's final decision in this case. A near split-up was avoided, only because of Jomo Kenyatta's efforts. Kenyatta argued vigorously that Mr. Mathu was the only African member of the Kenya Legislative Council, and it would be a mistake to sacrifice him, notwithstanding his change of mind.

In spite of Kenyatta's efforts to plead for Mr. Mathu, Mr. W. W. Awori, the Treasurer of the Kenya African Union and the chief editor of *The African Voice* (*Sauti ya Mwafrika*), the official newspaper of the organization, resigned as a protest. Mr. Awori, after resigning both positions from the Kenya African Union, started his own newspaper called the *Radio Posta*. He did not discontinue his membership in the Kenya African Union, but his dislike of Mr. Mathu's action was very deep. Mathu valued the increased African membership in the Kenya Legislative Council much more than the equal African representation in the East African Central Legislative Assembly. A certain R. Mugo Gatheru was assigned as the assistant editor of *The African Voice* after Mr. Awori's resignation.

It is true to say that the Africans of Uganda and Tanganyika were not particularly enthusiastic about Colonial Papers 191 and 210. They were afraid of the Kenya settlers' dominating political and economic power. Tanganyika was under the auspices of the United Nations Trusteeship and did not want the Kenyan European settlers' influence and domination. Uganda was particularly sensitive about Kabaka's position in an anticipated East African Federation.

Incensed that the Labour Party had countenanced so unfair a piece of legislation, Africans realized that they would have to depend upon their own strength if they hoped to secure their rights. The Kenyan Africans had put their faith in the British Labour Party, seeing in it their last hope. It was not that they were interested in European party politics, but that the Labour Party had been regarded by the Kenya people as being more sympathetic toward the African cause. They had hoped that when it came to power, most of the African problems in Kenya would at least be alleviated.

It was natural, therefore, that there should be great expectations of Creech Jones, the Colonial Secretary, and when he failed the Africans in 1947, all the repressed bitterness, anger and suffering were intensified. The Labour Party had been their last hope, but unhappily it was the Labour Party which conceded the principle of a white majority in the legislature.

Everywhere in Kenya one could hear Africans murmuring: "I see we are now being governed by '210.' The settlers have won again." The Africans were furious and frustrated, and it was the implementation of this decision which made inevitable the violent period of the Africans' struggle: the Mau Mau period, from 1952 to 1956.

Kenyatta's responsibility in 1947 was very heavy. His task was to lead the Kenya African Union and also to help raise money for the Kenya

Teachers' College. In addition he was charged with the responsibility of attempting to coordinate the activities of the Kikuyu Independent Schools.

People of all age-grades in the Kikuyu country united to support the Kenya Teachers' College; there were also enthusiasts from Nyanza Province and the Ukamba country who rallied to its support. At that period, the Kikuyu in both Nyeri and Fort Hall Districts were experiencing difficulties arising from the digging of terraces for soil conservation. The government, through the chiefs, headmen, and the agricultural instructors, wanted to impose a compulsory system of digging terraces throughout the entire Kikuyu country. The Kikuyu did not welcome compulsion. The most enthusiastic opponents were the young men—particularly those who were circumcised in 1940 and consequently were known as the "Forty Boys."

Undoubtedly there was a complete misunderstanding of the Kikuyu motives in refusing to cooperate in this particular scheme. The Kenya settlers and their supporters had often declared that even if the Africans were allowed to farm in the Kenya Highlands, they would ruin the land because of their primitive methods of farming. This unfortunate chorus was repeatedly echoed even by the former Governor of Kenya, Sir Philip Mitchell, who himself resided in the Kenya Highlands after his retirement. Now, Kikuyu refusal to dig the terraces was cited as proof.

Why then were the Kikuyu hostile to the scheme, however beneficial for them it might have been? Their argument was that the land in the reserves was too overcrowded and that the digging of the terraces was not an adequate remedy. A better plan would have been to relieve the obvious congestion by using the empty Kenya Highlands. After all, they argued, why should the Kenya Highlands lie fallow when people were in dire need of land? Small strips of land in the reserves could achieve nothing significant even with the terracing system. The Kikuyu saw in the imposition of the system another device of the government to ignore the issue of opening up the Kenya Highlands for the Africans.

African anger was intensified when government agricultural instructors resorted to total compulsion, threatening "If you do not do this and that, I shall deal with you accordingly, or report you to the District Commissioner." This threat was also resorted to by the chiefs.

Instead of compulsory digging of the terraces, the Kikuyu wanted the African District Councils to vote money from the public funds, the grant to be used for digging the terraces, as with money for road construction, hospitals and other social welfare organizations. This suggestion was not taken up by the Kenya government.

There were also certain Africans who opposed the Kenya African Union, notably the chiefs and some of the more devout members of the

Christian mission churches. The "Forty Boys" were bitterly opposed to this kind of individual; their anger against these dissident chiefs and others who were "sitting on the fence" was sometimes expressed by using clubs against the "unpatriotic ones."

The youngsters, particularly the "Forty Group," had something in common with the Maquis in France under Hitler. They considered Kenya an occupied country, and themselves as a resistance movement. It must be remembered that some of these young men had fought in the Allied armies overseas and had picked up political ideas during the war, as well as military skill, while others were still attending schools in Kenya.

As early as 1947–1948, the European politicians helped also to intensify the crisis by making offensive political speeches and writing articles in the Kenya press assuring the public that "they were in the Kenya Highlands to stay," and that asking them to share the Kenya Highlands with the other races was a waste of time. The governor, too, was responsible for this embitterment. He continued to address meetings in the Kikuyu country, advising the Africans not to listen to "those foolish young men who talk and write hot-headed nonsense." The governor and the European community were misled. They seem to have underrated the slow-bucking intensity of African resentment to alienation of their land, however many years before. It was not the problem of these young men alone.

During this phase there were many unemployed in Kenya, especially in the big cities. When the people found they did not have enough space for reasonable farming in the rural areas, many moved into the towns in search of employment, another means of relieving population pressure and economic distress in the reserves in which the Africans were living at a bare subsistence level.

Unfortunately, there was not sufficient industry in the cities to absorb the large numbers of unemployed. It was only too natural, therefore, that some of them should develop into petty criminals. They could perhaps have obtained jobs as laborers on the European farms in the Kenya Highlands, but it is almost unnecessary to point out that this would have meant humiliating capitulation of principle, as land ownership in the Highlands was reserved for European settlers alone.

To the Kenya Africans in general, land was accepted as a gift from God. For an outsider to have appropriated this gift, one directly offered to the Africans by Ngai, created serious problems—psychological, political, social and economic. In particular, it was impossible for the Kikuyu to adjust their minds to the idea that the Highlands would never be theirs again and that instead they should be forced to dig the terraces by way (as government officials described it) of soil conservation.

The Kenyan Africans tried hard for over thirty years to alert Britain to the need for drastic changes in Kenya. They had many allies there, men of the caliber of Lord Lugard, W. McGregor Ross, Dr. J. H. Oldham, Norman Leys and numerous supporters in Church circles. The changes were not made in time. So the story of Ireland, Palestine, Cyprus, Algeria, and the American Revolution was repeated in Kenya. As in so many like instances, moderate leaders were swept aside and the crisis was inevitable.

Following Parliamentary Paper No. 210, which was approved against the Africans' wishes, the settlers published what they called "The Kenya Plan" in 1949, through the auspices of their political organization, known as the Electors' Union. This union, incidentally, was merely the old settlers' body, the Colonists' Association, under a new name. Only one European, S. R. Cook, refused to support this "Kenya Plan."

The Kenya Plan clearly stated that the settlers would not accept African representation in the Executive Council and were opposed to increasing the number of Africans in the Legislative Council. In essence, the Kenya Plan revived the same old scheme for which the settlers had been clamoring since Delamere entered Kenya—self-government for the European settlers, followed by the creation of a white dominion in East Africa, which would then join hands with the Union of South Africa.

The maintenance of the European leadership was so stressed in the Kenya Plan that one would be tempted to think perhaps there was biological justification for European claims to lead other races. As it happened, the slogan "European leadership" was repeated so frequently that the whole concept became hateful to the Africans.

From this time on, the African political temper rose very high. The situation was particularly dangerous when one considers that most Kikuyu had already by this time taken the first K.C.A. oath "muma wa tiri"—"the oath of the soil"—to fight for, unite, and defend the African lands. Yet the settlers' bellicosity regarding European supremacy persisted, and the determination of the Africans to succeed at last hardened.

By 1952, almost everything that could be said had been said. Neither side would yield and sporadic assassination of colonial government headmen began. The Africans saw these men of their own kind as appointed to oppress them, and there was little sympathy at their deaths.

Amidst all this political tug-of-war, James Griffiths, Secretary of State for the Colonies, visited Kenya. His visit, however, was not fruitful and did not improve the situation. For their part, the Africans felt that they had already seen too many Colonial Secretaries and that, as neither the Kenyan colonial government nor the British government seemed willing to take decisive action, they would have to fall back on their own resources.

In June of the same year, Sir Philip Mitchell resigned his governorship, and there was a delay of more than two months before Sir Evelyn Baring was appointed to replace him.

When the new governor arrived in September 1952, the Mau Mau war had just begun and over fifty "unpatriotic" Africans had already been killed. The colonial government moved swiftly. On October 21, 1952, a State of Emergency was declared in Kenya, followed by the immediate arrest of Jomo Kenyatta and over 80 African leaders.

The Mau Mau war had begun.

The Kenya African Union was banned. At his trial, Kenyatta denied being a member of the Mau Mau or managing the Mau Mau. The British judge did not believe him.

After the outbreak of the Mau Mau rebellion, Harry Thuku collaborated with the British colonial authorities. He was well guarded. He denounced the Mau Mau rebellion. However, it would appear as if there was a prior declaration by the leaders of the movement that Harry Thuku should not be harmed, in spite of his public denunciation of the Mau Mau rebellion. They argued that in spite of his anti Mau Mau utterance, he had saved Kenya from becoming Southern Rhodesia or South Africa. What does Harry Thuku say about all this?

> [B]ut the most interesting thing about my own safety I heard after the Emergency from George Ndegwa. He had just been released, so I offered him a lift to Nairobi, and we had a discussion in a milk-bar there. He told me that Kenyatta had issued an order from detention that I was not to be killed by the Mau Mau; this letter was even taken to the forest fighters. He said I was to be left safe, for I had been the bridge they had crossed to get to where they were today.[1]

What Harry Thuku said in his autobiography is very interesting because at his trial at Kapenguria in 1952, Kenyatta flatly denied being a leader of or managing any secret society whatsoever.

If this was so, how then and on what authority would he be able to send an order or a letter to the freedom fighters in the forest and order or tell them not to kill Harry Thuku? Did they listen to him? When Kenyatta became Prime Minister in 1963 and then President of Kenya in 1964, he never denied Harry Thuku's above quoted statement. Harry Thuku died in 1970. Kenyatta died in 1978. The statement was made by Harry Thuku in 1958.

17

What Was Mau Mau?

Some historians, social scientists and government officials have tried to explain Mau Mau as a movement and its methods of administering the oath—the techniques, the objects, and the invocation of the words used. However, some of these authorities have failed to discuss the root causes of the Mau Mau movement or what caused such intelligent and hard-working people, the Kikuyu, to use such techniques or methods in their organization—some of which might not have fit in their own traditional culture or society.

One such example would be C. T. Stoneham, who seems to postulate that the Mau Mau had some peculiar meaning connected with the early religion and Kikuyu tradition, even before the arrival of the white man in Kikuyu country.[1]

Others, like the government official experts, would explain that the Mau Mau was the violent manifestation of a limited nationalistic revolutionary movement confined almost entirely in the Kikuyu, and that it was the evolutionary child of the first subversive Kikuyu political organization—the Kikuyu Central Association, formed in 1925.[2]

Two authorities, and two conflicting views. Still less satisfactory is the opinion of Dr. L. S. B. Leakey in *Mau Mau and the Kikuyu* that Mau Mau was simply the Kikuyu Central Association under a different name and using different methods. As mentioned in the Introduction to this book, it will be clear by now that it is the colonial history of Kenya that explains Mau Mau and that it cannot be considered in any other context. It was not the Kikuyu alone who had cause for complaint.

It should be reemphasized at the outset that the early missionaries, like the CMS, CSM, AIM, and the Catholic Fathers, as well as ethnographers like Major Richard Crawshay in 1902, and anthropologists like W. Scoresby Routledge and Katherine Routledge in that same year, all came to the general consensus that the Kikuyu people were highly intelligent people of considerable drive and initiative. Indeed, the Church of Scotland Mission noted that:

> As with all Bantu peoples, the Kikuyu have a conception of one High God behind all created things, but they believe that He is altogether too great and too remote to trouble Himself about ordinary individuals. Yet He holds the destinies of men and the forces of nature in His hands; so in any national extremity such as war, drought, or epidemic, He may be approached by selected elders who have made the appropriate sacrifices.[3]

All these very early people and the church organizations did not seem to report any sign or an appearance of something like or closer to the Mau Mau movement in the Kikuyu institutions.

The truth is that the Mau Mau rebellion was the revolutionary expression of a national feeling, becoming a national movement, led by members of the largest tribe and influenced in its organization by the ways of that tribe. It is the emphasis on tribalism that misled the government to underestimate the movement at the time and, against the proven facts, still misleads some of the theorists.

Historically, the roots of Mau Mau can be traced to the oath taken by Lord Lugard with Waiyaki at Dagoretti in 1890. We have traced the resentment following the repudiation of that oath by the British (despite Lugard's protests) to the arrest of Harry Thuku in 1922, and the formation of the K.C.A. At the same time, we have touched on some of the parallel incidents affecting other tribes who had equal cause for complaint but who, being smaller in numbers and in some cases less sophisticated in organization, did not at first direct their complaints in orthodox political ways.

We have seen the delegations to London led by Kenyatta and others on behalf of all the Africans and the increasing interest of the Indians in their political future. We have seen the banning of the K.C.A. in 1940, and how the political movement then went underground until the formation of the Kenya African Study Union (later the Kenya African Union) in 1944. Finally, we have seen in the Kenya Plan and its explicit policy of permanent European domination the final blow to African aspirations to political and economic equality in their own country.

However, by 1950, Africans, the Kikuyu in particular, had learned some hard lessons. Other tribes could certainly cite many instances of trickery and injustice. However, because of their large numbers and the attraction of their rich lands, the Kikuyu can be said to have suffered most as a group, and most consistently. Again because of their numbers, the Kikuyu had greater powers of protest (and eventually of violent opposition) and their tribal structure gave them a cohesion in action. They had their system of oaths which, from being a useful practice for the moderation of tribal society, was easily adapted to produce the organized discipline of guerrilla warfare—and many had fought in the World War which had recently ended.

When public assembly became difficult and the K.C.A. was banned in 1940, recruitment became difficult. The underground movement devised the first of the K.C.A. oaths, to protect the land.

The first plan to be seriously attempted was the subversion of African officials working for the government and the "elimination" of those who proved intractable, and this continued roughly to be the emphasis throughout the whole of the rebellion, as is borne out by the casualty figures.

It will be seen therefore that in the decade after 1940 the banned Kikuyu Central Association gradually built up a quasi-military structure which received an impetus from the soldiers returning after the war to find that once again they had fought for democracy, the fruits of which were still denied to them. That the political theory was elementary is clear, and besides the "professional" African politicians like James Gichuru were otherwise concerned with the new Kenya African Union. What, if any, was the connection between the two? The K.C.A. planned violence and was essentially Embu, Meru and Kikuyu; the K.A.U. still sought resolution of the problems by peaceful political means and on a national scale.

From 1949 onward more and more K.A.U. men took the Mau Mau oath, although the party did not officially recognize the practice. Thus, some members of K.A.U. at last began to consider violence as a last resort, or at least the threat of it as a political weapon backed up by the incipient Mau Mau movement. At the same time, Mau Mau began to receive more effective political direction and wider horizons.

Where did Kenyatta stand in all this? He was, of course, arrested in 1952, and put on trial at Kapenguria with Fred Kubai, Bildad Kaggia, Achieng Oneko, Kung'u Karumba and Paul Ngei. The trial dragged on for five months, and eventually they were all convicted of managing Mau Mau and sentenced to seven years hard labor with unlimited preventative detention to follow. It is not only Kenyans who say that the conduct of the trial was a sad travesty of British justice. One of the main witnesses for the prosecution later confessed his perjury, and therefore we learn little from the trial verdict. The truth lies elsewhere.

Kenyatta consistently refused to condemn Mau Mau publicly. He would hardly have been likely to do so as a consistent supporter of the K.C.A. before 1940 and a father figure of the movement, as indeed he was for the whole of black Kenya. Further, although after the war his heart was in the organization of K.A.U., he was too much of a realist to think that his condemnation of a potentially violent movement which shared at least his long-term political aspirations would be countenanced by the authors of the Kenya Plan with African majority rule.

He knew in fact that a background of unrest, rather than the violence itself, was more likely to strengthen his own peaceful program than the total confusion which would have resulted from a condemnation of his own people. In any case, would the K.C.A. leaders have obeyed him in 1952? Again realism dictates that, at least after 1949, the movement to violence had taken on so much momentum that for Kenyatta to have condemned it without qualification would certainly have been regarded by the people as an appalling betrayal which would in itself have precipitated the violence it would have been meant to avoid.

Therefore, Kenyatta stood aloof. He neither condemned nor, unlike some of his colleagues in K.A.U., did he actively participate. This in effect meant that he condoned the movement, and nothing he has said since disputes this, but for what it is worth today, he was innocent of the charges of which he was convicted at Kapenguria.

Despite this, was there anything Kenyatta could have done to avert the Mau Mau rebellion? The answer is certainly, yes, if the colonial government had only had the sense to treat with him realistically. One of the greatest mistakes made by Governor Mitchell in his term of office was to underestimate not only the feeling of the African people, but also Kenyatta's prestige and political sense.

Mitchell regarded Kenyatta first and foremost as a political agitator, a threat to the existing colonial system, a man with whom he could not treat on reasonable terms and whose only use might be to throw the Africans into confusion if he could be bribed to do so. His attitude was extraordinarily naive, and still more astounding is that he had the backing of the colonial office in London.

If for once he had been prepared to contemplate a change in the system, and discuss with Kenyatta what concessions might be made and on what timetable, the whole senseless war might have been avoided. But colonial powers traditionally dislike negotiating until the other "side" has surrendered unconditionally—a theory which bears its own fatal flaw to this day—and Sir Evelyn Baring who replaced Mitchell instead arrested the one man to whom the Africans would have listened had he been able to tell them of an honorable compromise.

The arrest and trial of Kenyatta and his companions seriously weakened the Kenya African Union as an organization. Of the other leaders, F. W. Odede was also arrested and put in detention. Joseph Murumbi was on a tour of India, Egypt and Britain, with the intention of going on to the United States as a guest of the American Friends Service Committee of Philadelphia, although the U.S. State Department in fact refused him a visa.

In Egypt, the British Embassy protested that the Egyptian government should not allow Murumbi to speak on behalf of an organization proscribed by the British government (the K.A.U. having been banned in June 1953). The Egyptian government refused to "suffocate" democracy, and eventually Murumbi joined Mbiyu Koinange in London where he had been since before the declaration of emergency. In a desperate, final effort to achieve advancement by peaceful means, Koinange had come to London with Achieng Oneke to ask for a constitutional conference, denied in the circumstances. As we have seen, Oneke in fact returned to Kenya just as the emergency was declared and was tried and imprisoned. Koinange and Murumbi remained in exile in London for the next eight years, until 1960.

The banning of K.A.U. and the arrest or neutralization of its more effective leaders for a time robbed the Africans of organized political leadership, and this situation seemed likely to continue—one colonial official declared that the national organization would never be allowed again in Kenya. Yet, the rebellion continued and clearly had effective leadership. If Kenyatta was not the director of the movement, who was? What was the Mau Mau hierarchy?

In his book, *Gangs and Counter-Gangs*, Frank Kitson says:

> The supreme Mau Mau body was the Central Committee; at least one man from each of the main districts of the Kikuyu Reserve was a member of it. Attached to the Central Committee was a body known as the War Office and Headquarters of the Land Freedom Army. In theory this had authority over all the terrorists in the Colony and its chairman was officially known as the Commander in Chief, Kenya. In practice its functions were concerned with the mechanics of collecting together recruits and supplies and passing them over to the parties from the Aberdares or Mount Kenya. Under the Central Committee there were in Nairobi itself other Committees representing every district in the native reserves. Under these district committees were committees representing

every division in the district, and under them again committees
representing locations in the divisions. In each case the chairman
of the lower committees formed the next committee up. Thus
the Fort Hall District Committee in Nairobi would have consisted
of the Chairman of the four Fort Hall Divisional Committees in
Nairobi, plus perhaps a few extra such as Vice-Chairman, Treasurer
and so on....[4]

To the above could be added that the supreme Mau Mau body was
centered in Nairobi City. Members of the headquarters staff came from the
Kikuyu-Embu-Meru, and included also a few Wakamba, Luo and Abaluhya,
the last two being particularly vital at one stage when it seemed the Kikuyu-
Embu-Meru would be removed from Nairobi entirely.

The Secretary-General of the Supreme Mau Mau Council was a very
bright, educated young Kikuyu from Muranga, Isaac Gathanju. The
Supreme Council in Nairobi was the real center of authority, even of the
fighting forces in the forests.

Many people wrongly believe that the authority in the forests was in
the hands of Mau Mau generals, such as China, Kimathi, Kahiu Itina, or
Mathenge. This was not the case. They were controlled from Nairobi, and
this involved a lot of intelligence work, since the Mau Mau leaders did not
have telephone, cable or wireless systems. This explains why people
entrusted to transmit intelligence messages underwent a very severe type
of oath unpracticed in the old Kikuyu society.

To overcome the intricate system of intelligence work, and arms and
money transmissions from Nairobi into the forests, the British government
also deployed its intelligence systems and in 1954 the Kenya Colonial Government Intelligence Services discovered the working of the Mau Mau
Supreme Council in Nairobi.

The British intelligence men recognized one of the members of this
all-powerful Supreme Council. He was a Kikuyu named during the 1954
Operation Anvil. He tipped the British off, and agreed to lead them to the
headquarters of the Mau Mau Supreme Council.

The whole thing was so arranged that the supreme Mau Mau body
was caught red-handed while in session. All the members were arrested
except one, who was absent at the time on a mission. This incident was
very important because at one blow it diluted civilian influence over the
fighting forces in the forests, even though the Supreme Council in Nairobi
was quickly reorganized.

The generals in the forests and elsewhere in the country decided that
some powers and decisions should be in their hands. The vital power of
concerted military action began to fragment, as there was no effective

central coordinating body. Even variations of the Mau Mau oath became commonplace.

As to the actual fighting, following the arrest of Kenyatta and the declaration of Emergency at the end of 1952, the British government brought in more troops (among others the Lancashire Fusiliers) and the settlers were mobilized. It was now open war, which affected the ordinary non-combatant Kikuyu very seriously. As fighting progressed, a concept of collective punishment was introduced whereby if an individual who was supposed to be pro-government happened to be killed in a village, the village was invaded by the security forces, as they were known. The villagers would then be punished collectively, whether they knew the wrongdoers or not.

Collective punishment could take many forms. In the European settled areas, it could mean wholesale removal of all African squatters from, for example, a town or village in the Rift Valley Province to the Kikuyu Country. This was usually done in such an unceremonious manner that people had to leave their belongings behind and had no idea what would happen to them afterward. In other cases, the collective punishment was the total burning of a village as a deterrent to neighboring villages. Nothing caused so much bitterness as these collective punishments.

At the height of the fighting, two new groups of people emerged, calling themselves the "Kikuyu Loyalists" and the "Kikuyu Christians." These two groups combined to form the "Home Guard," siding with the colonial government to oppose Mau Mau. The so-called staunch Christians became the spearheads of the new group. It is reported that the inspiration for the formation of these two groups was revulsion against what happened at Lari—afterwards known as the "Lari Massacre." This was the massacre by Mau Mau forces of an entire village, suspected of aiding the government. There is a question here whether only the Mau Mau forces committed the massacre at Lari or whether the opportunist "Home Guards" also contributed to the massacre.

While Mau Mau leaders were accused of perverting the principles of the traditional Kikuyu oath, members of the Home Guard also violated Kikuyu tradition by raping women in the villages and towns. Indeed, one of the staunchest Christian leaders in Muranga (Fort Hall), whose father was a respectable church minister, was said to be notorious for leading the way in raping other people's wives in the villages. It was also reported from reliable sources that, in certain cases, after raping had taken place, the rapists would then insert an empty Coca Cola or mineral water bottle into a woman's private parts, as further punishment to her husband.

Brutality was shown on both sides. Mau Mau generals became recognized for their organizing ability and their intelligence services, and their fighting initiative grew in strength. The settlers pressed the government for permission to carry firearms. The government agreed, and "shooting to kill" became commonplace in Kenya. All the paraphernalia of war appeared, including detention camps, which were established in various parts of the country to imprison both men and women.

The strategy of both sides need not be deeply explored. There were some staged battles, but largely the Mau Mau relied on guerrilla tactics, particularly after the capture of the central committee. Government troops relied on patrol, arrest, screening of suspects and the occasional "break" when a suspect under "questioning" would betray a forest camp or line of intelligence. Discipline and morale were high among most people, men and women, forest fighters and villagers; the young fought, and the very young and the old supported them as best they could.

All along it looked as if the Mau Mau could not win a war against modern British arms, but they did not need to. The longer the struggle, the more the people of Kenya, not just the Kikuyu, realized that in all ways but military strength the settlers were vulnerable. Confidence and self-respect came creeping back. The government would win a war, but time was running fast on the side of the Africans.

Sometime in August of 1953, General Dedan Kimathi, one of the "Chiefs of the African Fighting Forces," sat down in his forest hideout and wrote a letter which was published by the *East African Standard*. In his own way he pointed out that only a political solution could solve the Kenyan problem. He said:

> I am explaining clearly that there is no Mau Mau, but the poor man is the Mau Mau and if so, it is only Mau Mau which can finish Mau Mau, and not bombs and other weapons....
>
> Now, it is the responsibility of the government (Colonial) to see whether these things are true or not. The foundation of lawful cooperation is also the foundation of peace, wealth and progress.

Kimathi expressed the prayer of all the people and indeed he restated the British General Erskine's belief that the problem would never be solved by military means alone. But the government decided that militarily there should be no quarter, the Mau Mau must be wiped out. They did not entirely succeed in this for the Mau Mau leaders would not surrender and were hunted one by one. Eventually, the fighting died down as the Colonial Office in London at last began to impose political changes on the settlers. But some stayed in the forests, ready to fight again if need be, until the very day of Kenya's Independence, December 12, 1963; more than ten long years.

After that day, Kenyatta went himself to the forests to tell these men that their vigil was over, the day had come. They came back with him. But Kimathi did not return, nor did he see Kenya independent. He was taken by police to Nairobi in 1957 and hanged as a common criminal, castigated as the most "savage and bestial" of all the Mau Mau leaders.

In his book, *Mau Mau Detainee*, Josiah Kariuki quotes the Song of Kimathi—

> If you drink from the cup of courage
> The cup I have drunk from myself
> It is a cup of pain and of sorrow
> A cup of tears and death.

At the beginning of this chapter, we asked the question, what was Mau Mau? Two of many sources and authorities were cited.

It should be stressed in a deeper sense that the movement which became popularly known as the Mau Mau began with African frustration over the land issue. But the question remains to be answered, how did the name "Mau Mau" happen to be used as applicable to the movement nationally and internationally?

In October 1967, a Kenyan student named Johnstone Muthiora was attending George Washington University in Washington, D.C., with a view to obtaining the Ph.D. degree. While in Washington, he wrote a long letter to the editor of *Africa Report* in which he describes, among other things, the cross questioning of a Kikuyu named Kodogoya, who resolutely insisted that because of a secret commitment, he would never tell what those things were. When asked by the magistrate what he meant by "those things," he answered, "Just those things ... those things I was told never to tell." Translated into Kikuyu, the statement came out "*Maundo maumau nderiruo ndikoige.*" Newspapermen then seized on the term. He continues:

> Mau Mau is an expression which Kikuyu use very commonly to refer to objects or ideas whose names are unknown or forgotten, or which are difficult to classify or to name specifically.[5]

Due to an obvious linguistic misunderstanding, the movement became widely known as the Mau Mau, taken out of the phrase "Maundu mau mau nderiruo ndikoige" ("those things which I was told not to reveal").

What was the real name of the movement before the Naivasha incident in May of 1950? As has been mentioned earlier on, the Kikuyu Central Association, in common with other African associations in Kenya, was banned by the Kenyan colonial government in 1940.

The K.C.A. became an underground movement thenceforth, recruiting its new members by administering the oath "Muuma wa tiri"—the oath of the soil. At that time the association was operating under the name "Kiama Kia Ndemwa Ithatu": "The Association or Council of Three Letters," which was basically the K.C.A. This name was applicable in all the Kikuyu-Embu-Meru reserves and in the Rift Valley Province from 1945 to May 12, 1950.

It was at the trial of Kodogoya and his colleagues at Naivasha on the above date that the words "Mau Mau" were coined—through, as we have said, linguistic misunderstanding.

How can we alter substantially the conventional interpretation of the Mau Mau crisis in Kenya? It's worth noting that after May 12, 1950, even the leaders of the "Kiama Kia Ndemwa Ithatu" including the generals and the fighting forces in the forests used the new misleading name, the mau mau, instead of sticking to the original name. Even D. L. Barnnet and K. Njama, who wrote a book, *Mau Mau from Within* (MacGibbon and Kee, London, 1966), and who seem to interpret the Mau Mau rebellion as a peasant revolt—almost equating the Mau Mau with the Chinese Peasant Rebellion of 1949—use the name Mau Mau.

Historians and other scholars who wrote about the movement continued to refer to it as the Mau Mau. Perhaps this is not surprising because even the famous Christopher Columbus, upon reaching San Salvador on October 12, 1492, called the native inhabitants of the island "Indians" because he felt, quite mistakenly, that he had arrived in the Indies.

18

The Psychology
of the Oath

There has been a great deal written about the Mau Mau oath, in which it is described as "horrible, filthy, and degrading." In fact, the nature of the oaths, as practiced in the Kikuyu society before the coming of the Europeans, after their arrival, and as later modified by the Mau Mau leaders, has been somewhat misunderstood, especially by those outside the events which transpired.

In the old days there were what may be described as minor and major oaths. A minor oath was one which the Council of Elders administered in minor disputes, as for example where a young man was accused of making a girl pregnant but denied responsibility. This oath involved only the young man concerned; it was not administered to the pregnant girl. The effect of the minor oath was supposed to have effect on the accused party in about seven days to seven months.

The major oath involved land disputes, larceny, or criminal acts like poisoning. For example, if two parties were in dispute about a piece of land, they brought their case to the Council of Elders, who acted as judges and juries. If the Council of Elders failed to settle the claim then the last resort was the oath, which would be binding on the two disputants. Before a man took a major oath of this nature, he had to talk it over with his family and clan, since they would also be implicated by the oath even though not parties to the dispute.

The psychological effect of an oath on Kikuyu society was considerable. For instance, taking a major oath meant that the man's life as well as the lives of his family and clan were in danger. The oath was so regarded that if one were not telling the truth, one was also lying to Ngai, the Creator, and consequently the ancestors' spirits ("ngoma") would cause the death of the individual concerned, his family and kinsmen.

If taken untruthfully, a major oath was to take effect after three and a half years ("imera Mogwanja"), after which time a person who took it might die. Should he not die then, his eldest son might die first, followed by his wife, the rest of his children (if any), his sheep, goats and cows.

After one had taken an oath, it was impossible to be de-oathed; there was no concept of de-oathing in the traditional Kikuyu system. Otherwise, people might have continued taking oaths under false pretenses, knowing that they could be de-oathed eventually in order to prevent death. This is a highly important point.

It is also significant to note that women were entirely excluded from taking either a minor or a major oath, although there was a peculiar type of oath exclusively limited to women, one which was rarely used and only then in extreme cases. In this special type of oath a woman would take hold of a big empty cask or clay pot and break it into pieces, cursing a wrongdoer or wrongdoers, saying that their life or lives should be shattered in like manner.

Circumstances under which a woman might resort to this type of oath were, for example, if she were barren or had been raped, as a result of which her husband had neglected her, or she had been unreasonably "picked on" by her husband, and could not put up with this any longer. Where a woman had made this type of oath, she was convinced that she could not live with her husband again.

If a woman with children was raped and broke the cask or pot (Kuuraga Nyungu) against the man who had defiled her, she was purified by a medicine man (Mugo) before any further contact with her husband or her children. If she were not thus purified, she would not be permitted to cook food for her family. Also, she could have no sexual relations with her husband until she had been purified, otherwise a bad "mugiro" would fall on her and her entire family.

Why then did the Mau Mau introduce the oath in the rebellion against the British administration? The answer lies in the causes which led to this rebellion. It is significant that the type of oath administered in the course of the revolt, though basically a Kikuyu oath, was different from the accepted custom in Kikuyu society. For example, it was administered indiscriminately to both men and women, which suggests that it was more of a military nature—an emergency measure—than the usual oaths administered in civil and criminal cases.

After the Kikuyu and other Kenyan Africans generally had appealed to the Kenyan government for social, economic, political, educational and agrarian reforms (appeals which had repeatedly fallen on deaf ears, chiefly because of the settlers' pressure on the Kenyan colonial government) they felt that the situation had become desperately intolerable. They were convinced that no political speeches or political organizations could unite people so effectively as the custom of oath-taking, respected by the Kikuyu people from time immemorial. They felt also that for military and security reasons, women should also take the oath, otherwise their plans might be divulged to the colonial government.

Before we consider the oaths themselves in detail, it is worth remembering that each society has its own special taboos and customs. It is unthinkable for a Hindu to slaughter a cow for food, as reverence for this animal is an integral part of the Hindu religion. Other peoples do not have this reservation.

It should also be remembered that the sacrifice of animals in religious or quasi-religious ceremonies is neither new nor out-of-date in the world, nor something considered by most peoples in any way wrong or irreverent. The same thoughts apply to the consumption of sacrificial animals by participants in a ceremony and the use of one particular part of an animal rather than another. Consequently, the reader is asked to consider the oaths in anthropological and sociological (rather than sentimental or dietary) terms if he or she is to understand something of their true nature and purpose.

The first oath was introduced on a small scale in the period between 1940 and 1949, by the Kikuyu Central Association. It involved the public in general. It was called "Muuma wa Tiiri" ("the oath of the soil"), to signify that the public had solemnly affirmed that they would fight and defend the land that was theirs. In its initial stage it was actually meant to arouse people's conscience and create a spirit of nationalism. Its paraphernalia included the blood of a he-goat mixed with soil, and waste matter from the large and small intestines. This mixture was put in a calabash and circled seven times around the head and legs of each candidate. It was simple, not so complicated as the later, more serious, oaths.

The second oath was called the "Mbatuni" oath, and was used from 1949 to 1952. It was intended for the fighting forces in the forests. It was taken in that part of a house where the kitchen was situated, and where an altar was temporarily set up. The altar was made from banana trees and sugar canes, and decorated with sweet creepers. This was the time when the three tattoos were introduced, all candidates being thus marked on their arms. A piece of meat was then smeared with blood from each candidate, subsequently to be eaten bit by bit by each person, thus implying that all candidates have now shared each other's blood, strengthening the unanimity, brotherhood, and determination to achieve their objective.

During the oath's administration the specialists sat in a circle with the altar in the center. The candidates entered singly, and when one had taken the oath he or she was led to another house to avoid contact with candidates who were still awaiting their turn.

Considering the vast geographical locations or areas in which the Mau Mau fighting forces were located, there were variations in methods used in administering the second Mau Mau oath. To this end, Josiah Mwangi Kariuki, in his book *Mau Mau Detainee*, writes:

> Naturally, as there was no central control of the organization,
> there were minor variations in the different districts and oath
> administrators did not everywhere use exactly the same technique.[1]

Generally, a candidate was given a slice of meat whose length would equal the distance from this mouth to his penis, with a hole on the end where the penis was located. A candidate would be naked, in order to emphasize the fact that he was now returning to his mother's womb to be reborn.

The candidate would then be asked to put his penis inside the hole of the lower part of the slice of meat given. He would then hold the other part with his left hand, as if the piece of meat was like an umbilical cord from the lower part of the stomach to his mouth.

The oath administrator would then recite a verse and the candidate repeated the same verbatim, as follows:

> I (name of candidate) solemnly swear that should I ever be asked
> to go get somebody's head, be it even that of my father, or of my
> mother, or of my brother or of my sister, I will arise and do as com-
> manded without question, and should I go against such an order,
> may this oath kill me.
>
> I solemnly swear to give myself to be a warrior of my country
> who will never go back even if blood will run like a flood; such
> blood being ours or that of the enemy. And should I ever falter in
> this respect, may this oath kill me.
>
> I solemnly swear that I shall never sell our soil to the white race
> or even let them take it from us, and should I ever do so, may this
> oath kill me.[2]

A candidate was supposed to bite the piece of meat which he was holding in his left hand in each and every part of the recital, and to eat it. The house in which the oath was being administrated was heavily guarded, and all present at the ceremony were well armed.

At this period, the fighting on both sides was bitter and intense, and the more severe it became, the more exciting and varied was the second Mau Mau oath. It was also at this time that the Kenyan government introduced a de-oathing system among the Kikuyu population, hoping thus to counteract the effect of the Mau Mau oath.

There were two systems of de-oathings; one for the Christian Kikuyu in which they confessed the oath in church, holding the Holy Bible in the presence of a priest. The other system was used for the non–Christian Kikuyu, who were cleansed by the Kikuyu medicine men, or "Ago."

The effect of the de-oathing system as administered by the Kikuyu medicine men was not very successful, for most of them, if not all, had taken the Mau Mau oath themselves, and the invocations used in their de-oathing ceremonies were not, in African opinion, reliable. As mentioned earlier, this concept of de-oathing was quite unknown in Kikuyu society, and the fact that it was then introduced by the colonial government did not make the innovation any more convincing. However, the de-oathing system must have had some effect on the Christian Kikuyu because it was largely from this group that the government was able to recruit the "Home Guards."

It should not be assumed, however, that all Kikuyu Christians were dissociated from the Mau Mau, or did not take the Mau Mau oath seriously. The fact of the matter is that, as in every other society throughout the world, there were people who regarded religion dogmatically, who believed that all human problems would ultimately be solved by God.

In other societies, some might have suggested that the best solution would have been to use persuasion—more and more persuasion. The difference here was that many Christian Kikuyu supported Mau Mau on patriotic grounds and recognized that the importance of the movement lay not in the oath itself (mainly a security measure) but in the nationalist struggle, which the oath existed only to protect and strengthen.

Such Christians were educated people who had read about the American Revolution and other anti-colonial struggles; ironically it was they who were best equipped among the Africans to judge the historical and ethical validity of the movement. They realized that no Kenyan African could claim to be more Christian than, say, the Irish. Yet the Irish had successfully reconciled their faith with their violent struggle for independence.

In context, it was justifiable for Christians to adopt violence when all other means had failed to change a system of government itself based on principles which were morally indefensible.

A ceremony for people who had not taken the oath, and who were not Christians, was to slaughter a goat. They took out the skull bone, and with a "mugere" stick would declare: "I truly swear before God and before the public that I will be loyal to this government and, if I fail, may this oath kill me. Also, I truly swear that I will never take the Mau Mau oath, and if I see Mau Mau hiding, taking an oath or carrying weapons, I will inform the government, and if I fail may this oath kill me."

The de-oathing ceremony for non–Christians who had taken the Mau Mau oath was administered by a witch-doctor. He cleansed them with water and the stomach contents of a goat, declaring, "I cleanse you of the Mau Mau oath which you took and of which you know and of which you don't know."[3]

As for the second Mau Mau oath, anyone who misbehaved or acted recklessly or disobeyed orders or made a careless mistake after taking his oath was punished very severely. This oath was not, therefore, applicable to every Kikuyu, nor was it administered indiscriminately.

It cannot be denied that some of the methods used by the Mau Mau leaders in their oathing ceremonies were in fact a perversion of traditional Kikuyu procedure. It would, however, be an over-simplification to assume that all the Africans' sufferings from 1895 to 1963 could be explained away in terms of these "horrible, filthy, and degrading oathing ceremonies."

It should be borne in mind that certain variations of the Mau Mau oath were introduced because of the behavior of the security forces, including, of course, the Home Guards.

In Muranga, for example, a government official was killed one afternoon, and the following morning the entire village was invaded by the security forces and destroyed. One hundred people were killed. The price of one government official was equal to the lives of one hundred villagers. Thus was collective punishment introduced.

In Muranga District particularly, it was usual for the security forces, after capturing the suspected individuals, to collect them in a circle, if they did not decide to shoot every one of them on the spot. The captives were then ordered to make a big fire in which a heavy iron was burnt to red heat. Then the suspects were tied up, their hands behind their backs, their legs tightly secured. Two members of the security forces would then take the hot iron and put it on the stomachs of the helpless Africans, an agonizing ordeal indeed.

In other verified cases, some of the Home Guard would knock on the door of a married man's house while he and his wife were asleep. Ordering the husband to get out of bed and to lie down on the floor on his stomach, they would then cover him with blankets as if he were dead. Then they would rape his wife while her husband was lying helpless on the ground, wondering if he were about to be shot. The raping over, the Home Guard would dash cold water over the husband and leave. "Sometimes a daughter may be raped while her parents were forced to watch."[4]

The unfortunate husband would sometimes be ordered to follow the Home Guard, and when his tormentors had gone a distance of a hundred yards he was told to run as though he were being chased. Running as ordered, he was then shot in the back. Many husbands who had beautiful wives endured this unspeakable practice.

To read of these things today may seem incredible, but the author has the best possible evidence: that given to him firsthand by one of his closest female relations, who had this frightful experience in the Rift Valley Province. She was raped by five men of the security forces while her husband was lying helpless on the ground.

One of the most notorious individuals associated with this business was a European district officer in the Muranga District nicknamed "Gachuhi" ("one who wears a small ring"). He used to lead a group of his security forces into the villages in the evening hours, and if they spotted a female they fancied they would then force her to submit, whether she was married or single. In the case of a stubborn husband who would rather have been killed than see his wife raped in his presence, "Gachuhi" would say: "I admire your courage, mate. You are a likeable brock, you know, and I know very well that every Kikuyu likes to have a piece of land. Now, you follow me and I will give you a piece of land, a very nice piece about 6 feet by 3 feet."

The Kenyan government's colonial security forces attracted some very strange recruits, as did the white mercenary forces in the Congo. Such sickness in the world is to be pitied wherever it is found.

Violence is an ambiguous weapon in human society. It is a tool either for good or for evil, depending on the context in which it is used. Down through the ages man has warred against man in an attempt to conquer or to liberate himself from an oppressor.

Franz Fanon[5] has developed a theory of violence which merits discussion. Specifically, we will attempt to interpret facts in respect of the Mau Mau rebellion in Kenya in order to find out whether these facts would fit Fanon's theory. Many writers have tried to explain the Mau Mau rebellion as simply a return to tribalism or a religious cult. Viewed within the context of the entire nationalistic movement, the Mau Mau rebellion has a legitimate place in the struggle for independence in Kenya.

In the colonial society, violence plays a number of roles, which will be elaborated upon in the following pages.

Violence as a Tension Reducer

Colonial society is one which is built on inequities. As such it can only be maintained through authoritarian rule. The human organism must have a release vent for the inner tensions which result from this condition of oppression. This release takes the form of violence.

Many of the grievances in Kenya centered around the question of land. Colonialism had its birth in violence. The pacification of the tribes in Kenya in the late 19th and early 20th centuries was affected over the barrel of a gun. This is true of:

1. The Nandi rebellions of 1895 and 1905
2. The Kipsigis rebellion of 1902–1905
3. The Luhya rebellion of 1895
4. The Kisii rebellion of 1904–1908
5. The Taita rebellion of 1890
6. The Giriama rebellion of 1914

Between 1901 and 1907, land was set aside in the fertile highlands for the white settlers. The Kikuyu, one of the largest tribes in Kenya, were greatly affected by this land alienation, and many, many African squatters working on the European farms were recruited from the Kikuyu. As L. S. B. Leakey pointed out, there was a great deal of misunderstanding on the part of the British during the initial land alienation, due to a lack of knowledge of Kikuyu law and culture. Native reserves were set aside for the major tribes, including the Kikuyu.

Colonial land policies never attained legitimacy in the eyes of the Kikuyu and remained a major issue in the nationalistic movement. The breakdown of Kikuyu culture began, followed by the restructuring of a compartmentalized society.

With the growth of an African urban population, the inequalities of the society became more evident. Forced to live in overcrowded, degrading circumstances, with no possibility of improvement, chaffed by the registration system called "Kipande" and the necessary carrying of passes, the frustration and hatred for the colonizer mounted. Prior to political wakening, this anger could only be released in the form of hatred toward the whites.

Violence as an Organizational Tool

Franz Fanon contends that a system which is built and maintained through violence can only be destroyed by the same means. Violence is the only tool that the oppressor can understand. The greater the interest of the group in power, the less likely they will relinquish this power without a struggle. Colonialism in Kenya was complicated by the presence of firmly entrenched white settlers.

For many years the Africans struggled peacefully to obtain redress of their grievances, economic, social and political. Early political organizations such as the East African Association, followed by the Kikuyu Central Association, founded in 1925, ended in failure. The colonial government's reaction to political agitators was to ban the organizations and jail the leaders when necessary. A colonial law could usually be found to support their actions.

In 1944, as it has already been mentioned, the Kenya African Union was founded. Its approach to the solution of problems was moderate. Faced with the intransigency of the colonial government, the Kenya African Union had difficulty holding to a moderate approach in the wake of a growing militancy. A secret organization, based on the "Oath of Unity" and dedicated to whatever force was necessary to effect decolonization, began to flourish. This was the movement which would eventually be called "Mau Mau" by the colonial government. The arrest of Jomo Kenyatta and other leaders of K.A.U., as leaders of this "evil, secret society" served only to sever the restraints on the militant forces at large.

The government instituted a State of Emergency which was to last almost until 1960. From 1952 to 1956, from bases in the Aberderes Mountains, the Land Freedom Army fought guerrilla warfare against the overwhelming strength of the forces of the colonial government supported by the British army. Estimates of the actual numbers of whites killed vary from 80 to 95, against over 2,000 Africans killed and over 80,000 Africans detained. The action itself ended in failure to the extent that there was a British military victory on the battlefields, but there were no economic, political, cultural or psychological victories. The Mau Mau Rebellion brought the situation in Kenya to the eyes of the world.

Violence as a Unifying Force

Once the decision is made in favor of militant methods of achieving goals, the transfer of violence from a state of mind to a state of action acts as a unifying force among the people. Various groups become united in search of a common goal.

In Kenya, as in most colonial countries, the policy of "divide and conquer" was used. The system of separation of tribes in different reserves and the fostering of tribal jealousies hampered unification of the African peoples. No colony-wide political association was permitted by the Kenyan government.

In the Mau Mau movement, the use of oaths was made to bind the members to the movement. Oaths had always been an essential part of Kikuyu culture and had a strong psychological effect on the recipient. The oath was irrevocable and as such assured the loyalty of the individual. Leaders excused the force sometimes used in administering oaths on the grounds that unity and secrecy were an absolute necessity. The guerrilla forces were highly dependent upon this base within the reserves. Pressures from the colonial government, however, were too great for the base to withstand, thus isolating the mountain forces.

Charges were made that the Mau Mau rebellion was strictly Kikuyu in character. However, support of the forces of the Land Freedom Fighters was given by members from the Kamba, Luo, Luhya and a few other tribes.

The Mau Mau rebellion never achieved the unity that brings strength to a cause. Pitted against British strength, the odds in the white man's favor were overwhelming. In addition, within the army, unity suffered from difficulty in communications and sometimes jealousy among various leaders.

Violence as a Stimulant to the Movement

The violent counter-reaction of the colonial oppressor to the political awakening of the native serves to reinforce his aggressiveness.

From the early days of the East African Association, the policy of the Kenyan government was the suppression of social and political agitation by jailing the leaders. Colonial show of force during political meetings antagonized the African people.

With the declaration of the Emergency in 1952, the British military were brought in to reinforce the Kenya colonial army and police. Drives to arrest members of Mau Mau led many young men to join the guerrilla forces in the Aberdares and Kenya Mountains. Such activities led to counter-reprisals against colonial institutions. The jailed leaders became heroes in the eyes of the African people.

The conditions under which over 80,000 people were detained and the brutal treatment which detainees often endured strengthened their resolve to be free from British domination. Reprisals led to counter-reprisals. The only difference lay in the magnitude of the government's action in comparison with any action of the freedom fighters.

Violence as a Catalyst

It is almost certain that wars of liberation must have some effect on neighboring countries still under colonial rule. One of these effects is to show a colonized people a method of freeing themselves. The second effect is to convince the colonizer to decolonize prior to violent revolution.

Where no white settlement was involved, decolonization was. This was true of Ghana, Tanzania, Uganda, and Nigeria. In Kenya, the situation was complicated by a white settler–dominated Kenyan government. Their goal was a "White Man's Land" in Kenya. To this end, they were willing to use any means to prevent "Black Rule" and to protect their interests. Independence was not destined to come easily to Kenya.

Violence was very much a part of the colonial system in Africa, a tool used by both the colonizer and the colonized. One must ask if violence was a necessary ingredient to the success of Kenya's nationalist movement. Many years of dependence on constitutional methods to effect reforms had ended in negligible results. Faced with the intransigence of the white-settler group, and in a state of extreme frustration, the movement took on a violent nature.

It would appear that the Mau Mau rebellion was the missing factor which turned the tide of victory for the Kenyan African. The British government was made to realize that the colonial situation in Kenya was not tenable. In 1963, the nationalist movement finally bore fruit in the granting of independence to Kenya by Britain.

The history of Kenya appears to lend validity to Fanon's theory that colonialism born of violence can only be destroyed by violence. While it is not necessary either to advocate or to condone violence, one must try to understand that, in certain situations, a people may be forced into the use of extreme methods. Perhaps, some Britons in Kenya and Great Britain may not appreciate this argument. However, as has been shown, the spirit of rebellion in Kenya did not spring from, but pre-existed the Mau Mau.

19

The Supremacy of
Settler Politics Ends

The arrest of Jomo Kenyatta and declaration of the Mau Mau Emergency in October of 1952 demonstrated the vulnerability of the settlers and their dependency upon the British government's military and economic power to protect them. The British government was committed to the destruction of the African nationalist movement. All leading African politicians were soon in prison or exile, some indefinitely. Lacking central direction, it was only a question of time before the forest fighters would be largely neutralized as the British army systematically tracked, arrested or killed the Mau Mau "Generals."

And yet, only eleven years later, an African majority government led by Kenyatta achieved full independence for Kenya with the blessing of the British and the acquiescence of most of the European settlers. What explanation can there be for this extraordinary and total reversal?

The extraordinary and total reversal had many causes in addition to those already stated. For example:

(a) The Mau Mau war had a shattering effect on Kenya's social and political fabric—no matter how this was denied by the authorities.

(b) British government constitutional proposals were an attempt to pacify moderate Africans and discredit "radical" nationalists. They failed for being half-hearted and seeking to protect "white minority" rights—leading to African nationalists' triumphant victory over white supremacy.

Tom Mboya, one of those Kenyan Africans who helped to accelerate the rate of African political dynamism in Kenya after Kenyatta's detention.

The story is complex and deserves a book of its own. Without wishing to glamorize the situation, the main credit must certainly go to the strength and courage of the African people. If their spirit had been broken, all individual effort would have counted for nothing. However, the story is also one of a lesson well-learned by the British government who, at the moment of conceding to the settlers their greatest triumph, lost patience and resolved that never again would they be caught and so embarrassed. Further, it is the story of the African trade unions and the coming of age of a new generation of African politicians, born in modern times and trained in modern ways, men who knew the British were weary of Empire and how to focus the will of the people on this key point.

The tide turned and, although far from being the only one, the man who most surely rode the wave was Tom Mboya. Twenty-two years of age and almost unknown when the Emergency was declared, he was not "tainted" as were the older men and the British could treat with him, uneasily, but with honor untarnished. With his charm, unfailing political sense, and flair for timely publicity, Mboya was able to put the "Kenya problem" into perspective for the British public and the outside world. Clearly, he was no wild man himself.

In addition to Tom Mboya, there was Joseph Murumbi in London with the Hon. Fenner Brockway, M.P., who were actively participating and organizing the movement for colonial freedom; Mr. Mbiyu Koinange who was exiled in England and was still actively voicing the Kenya African causes; and Argwings-Kodhek, first African lawyer, who defied the Kenya colonial government in December of 1955 and formed a country-wide political organization called the Kenya African National Congress. Prior to December of 1955, African political parties were allowed to be formed only on the basis of district level. Mr. Argwings-Kodhek challenged this policy. The contributions also made by the Hon. E. W. Mathu in the legislative council and Mr. James S. Gichuru of the Kenya African Union cannot be overlooked.

Eventually, public opinion began to accept that a genuine national movement might exist which could not be explained away in terms of a dissident Kikuyu minority (Mboya was a Luo) guilty of alleged inexcusable atrocities. Mboya spoke convincingly of atrocities also committed in the name of the colonial regime, arguing that the issue was the oppression of an entire people and not the suppression of a local disturbance. Perhaps Mboya lacked Kenyatta's national appeal, but there can be no question that his development was one of the most important political factors in Kenya in the 1950s.

On leaving school in 1951, Mboya went to work for the Nairobi City Council. A year later, the Emergency was declared and he left to become a full-time trade union official. His rise was rapid. His own union (Local Government Workers) was formally registered in 1953 with Mboya as General Secretary, and immediately joined the Kenya Federation of Registered Trade Unions which had been created (five unions) in 1950. The office having fallen vacant, in September of 1953, Mboya was elected General Secretary of the KFRTU, which then changed its name to the Kenya Federation of Labour. With all other leaders out of action, perforce the African political leadership fell now to the trade unionists in general, and Mboya in particular. Their new status was recognized in April 1954 when in one day (Operation "Anvil") the government security forces arrested 35,000 people for screening, including 39 trade union leaders of whom nearly half were permanently detained. Mboya escaped detention, however, as the colonial authorities were still convinced that they were fighting a Kikuyu rebellion and released members of other tribes, including Mboya. For the same reason, he had greater freedom than his fellows, in movement and also in print, for he was by now writing for the overseas press.

In 1954, at the height of the war, the first significant move came from the British government in London. The Colonial Secretary, Oliver Lyttleton, imposed a new constitution. This was unremarkable in its concessions to the Africans, which were meager to say the least. Lyttleton's constitution was an attempt to answer the African demands, and also a half-hearted answer to Kenya African Union and Mau Mau demands. Its importance lay in the fact that the British were prepared to make concessions at all, and in such circumstances. There was a clear warning to the settlers of more change to come. And more change there was—five colonial secretaries and five constitutions in the nine years still to go before independence.

Lyttleton introduced a council of ministers with six official, two nominated and six unofficial members, in addition to the governor and his deputy. Of the six unofficial members, one was to be African, two Asians and three European. This was hardly a solution to Kenya's problems but the establishment of a principle, it being also provided that there should be five parliamentary secretaries of whom one was to be Arab and two African. The real balance of power was unchanged, because the council of ministers had little to do apart from approving draft legislation. The authority of the executive council remained, although all ministers were to be members.

In October of 1955, Mboya flew to England for a year's study at Ruskin College in Oxford. The change from the atmosphere of Kenya and its state of war must have been as welcome as the opportunity to meet "home grown" Britons and exchange views with them. He was able to make friends with English politicians and, before his return to Kenya in November 1956, he traveled in Germany, Belgium, Canada and the United States, in each case taking every possible opportunity to publicize the African cause.

Mboya returned to face an election. Until Lyttleton, the legislative council had consisted of 54 members of whom six were Africans, all appointed by the governor, who also nominated one African to the executive council. In February of 1955, a commission was established to determine, within the limits of the Emergency, whether any changes should be made in African representation. Subject to serious qualification, it was decided to allow Africans to elect eight members out of 54 by direct but highly qualified vote. The election took place in March of 1956 under the most difficult circumstances. National parties were banned and each candidate had to organize his own local committees. The Kenya Federation of Labour was banned from direct political activity, but despite this Mboya was one of the successful candidates, standing in Nairobi.

The first act of the eight African members was to denounce the Lyttleton constitution. Supported by the Asian members, they demanded that African representation should be increased to 23, and would have nothing to do with the single ministerial post offered to them. They also demanded an end to the Emergency and the right to form a national political party, all denied.

The next Colonial Secretary, Alan Lennox-Boyd, arrived in Nairobi in October of 1957, and soon declared the Lyttleton constitution unworkable. His new constitution allowed for 14 Africans out of 36 elected members.

Of the 14 African members of the Kenya Legislative Council, one was brilliant: the first African Ph.D. holder, Dr. Julius Gikonyo Kiano, a graduate of the University of California at Berkeley. He had defeated an equally brilliant and authoritative speaker, Mr. Eliud W. Mathu, the first African member of the Kenya Legislative Council earlier on. Jeremiah Nyaggah, a longtime capable and likeable schoolteacher, was also in this group. Prior to this new arrangement, the Kikuyu-Embu-Meru were represented by only one representative who was also one of the first eight elected African members: Bernard Mate, an M.A. graduate from a British university.

It appeared at the time that the Kenyan colonial government would have liked to intimidate or "suffocate" the Kiano-Nyaggah-Mate combination as it represented the "undesired people" (the Kikuyu-Embu-Meru). Hence their position in the Kenyan legislative council was not always smooth-running, freedom of speech notwithstanding. Nevertheless, they were determined and remained steadfast decidedly. Effects of Emergency regulations on political development in Kikuyu-Embu-Meru areas—for example, "loyalty certificates" for voters, no "open air meetings" and movement passes—all were aimed at suppressing the Kikuyu-Embu-Meru politically.

In the legislature, there were additional elected members to be chosen by the whole legislative council sitting as an electoral college—four Africans, four Europeans and four Asians. The Africans were also offered another ministry. This constitution was no more acceptable to the Africans than before, as it still failed to concede the principle of majority rule in the future. However, on the basis that more cooks have a better chance of spoiling the broth, the existing members cooperated to the extent of grooming the best available candidates for election. Ministerial office was still refused.

In early 1958, Oginga Odinga made a dramatic visit to England for a few weeks. It was dramatic to the extent that while in London, he addressed a British audience attended by various influential members of Parliament, and stated quite clearly that Jomo Kenyatta, then in detention, was still being regarded as the real leader of the Kenyan Africans—notwithstanding the 14 African members of the Kenya Legislative Council!

His audience was shocked. No one in Great Britain or in East Africa generally at that time was ripe to make such a daring pronouncement openly. Indeed, from the point of view of the Kenyan colonial government at that time, Kenyatta's name and conduct were regarded as worse than those of Nazism in Hitler's Germany, and here was poor Odinga lecturing to the British audience that "Kenyatta was still our leader." Yet, the effect of the severe state of the Emergency was actively being felt all over Kenya.

On his return to Kenya, Odinga pressed his point that Kenyatta was still the undisputed leader of the Kenyan people. He said this repeatedly even in the Kenya Legislative Council, to the extent that even some of his colleagues among the 14 African members felt that he should tone down some of his utterances in respect to Kenyatta.

Nevertheless, Odinga was not the type of person who could be "kowtowed." He disagreed with these African colleagues who questioned his stand and challenged them to state flatly and publicly that they thought Kenyatta was not the African leader. Some were embarrassed.

Earlier on, in the Central Nyanza District of the Luo people in Western Kenya, near the shores of Lake Victoria, it was Oginga Odinga, a Luo leader from the area, who had popularized Kenyatta, a Kikuyu leader, as the true leader of the Kenyan Africans. Indeed, he used to refer to Kenyatta as the "father of African politics in Kenya."

Odinga was a fearless African politician who did not hesitate to speak the truth. He did not feel that his own financial security or that of his family and a good job in the government or that his position as an African member of the Kenya Legislative Council was a life insurance. To him, honesty and speaking the truth were virtues.

When Kenyatta and other members of the Kenya African Union were tried and convicted as members and managers of an "illegal society," the Kenya colonial government embarked steadfastly on a scheme of downsizing, degrading, denigrating and chiseling Kenyatta's reputation and achievements. His character was systematically assassinated. As a matter of fact, the British governor in Kenya at the time, Sir Patric Renison, kept on with his pressure against Kenyatta by telling the people of Kenya, Europeans, Asians and Africans, that Kenyatta was not the true African leader but rather a leader of "death and darkness."

To what extent did all these efforts at demeaning Kenyatta succeed? The efforts by the Kenya colonial government succeeded brilliantly among most Europeans, especially the European farmers in the "white highlands," among some few Asians, some few Africans working in the Kenya colonial establishment (the Kenyan colonial government was the main employer of the Africans), and among the African loyalists who supported the Kenya colonial government against the Mau Mau movement throughout the period of 1952–1960. Some African members of the Kenya Legislative Council were so highly intimidated that they were also afraid of mentioning Kenyatta's name, let alone speaking anything favorable about him.

Under these circumstances, it was Odinga who strenuously tried to restore Kenyatta's reputation, achievements and character to their proper place.

To the majority of the African population, the Kenyan colonial government propaganda against Kenyatta did not appear to have created a substantial dent in his popularity. Odinga might have known this already.

On matters concerning private companies or corporations in Kenya, Odinga felt that they should be nationalized and controlled by the Africans. He also felt that all government agencies or departments should be Africanized at once.

On international relations, Odinga felt that the Kenyan Africans should be friendly to all nations irrespective of their political and economic ideologies. He insisted particularly that some African members like Tom Mboya—a fellow Luo—should "put out feelers" in the West, meaning Western Europe and North America. Some other African leaders, himself included, should also try to "put out friendly feelers" to Eastern

Oginga Odinga, a fearless member of the Kenya Legislative Council who popularized Jomo Kenyatta in Central Nyanza, openly declaring that Kenyatta was "the father and teacher of politics" in Kenya.

Europe as a "bargaining card" with the British and the West generally, in order to gain some concession from the West.

Some people regarded this as an unwise political move, especially since Kenya was within the framework of the British Empire and it was a very dangerous period of the Cold War.

In analyzing the forging of Kenya during the period in our study, it is interesting to note how some people, especially in official capacities or government positions, tended to ignore or totally disregard previous historical events. History is full of examples of people struggling toward certain goals. Sometimes these goals have been the attainment of national independence from a foreign power, or the alleviation of a social injustice. In the first category we find such peoples as Britain against the Romans, Netherlands and Holland against Spain, American colonies against Britain, and, in the 1940s and 1950s, India, Indonesia, Tunisia against Britain, Holland and France respectively. The characteristic feature of these struggles had chiefly been a conflict of philosophies of the dominating and the dominated peoples.

The philosophy of the governing power has generally been that the governed people were either unready and unworthy of what they believed to be their own or that the domination of such people could have been justified on some self-righteous humanitarian sounding principles.

The philosophy of the dominated people has generally been based on the conviction that they had been legally or forcefully denied certain fundamental rights which they, as a particular group, believed they were either entitled to or were their own.

Quite often, such struggles have culminated in bloody wars. There are many such bloody wars in history. In all these struggles the heroes have been subjects of value judgments. For the dominating power the heroes have been those people who died in attempting successfully or otherwise to maintain conditions as were profitable to them. For the dominated people, the heroes have been those who died and those who led their own people either implicitly or explicitly in such struggles.

It is this ultimate right to die for one's beliefs that the British exercised when they fought the Spaniards in 1588 and made Sir Francis Drake a hero. It is the same right also exercised in 1939–1945 when Britain fought Nazi Germany.

In Kenya, by 1958, events were moving fast, amazingly so to those who had searched for years for a hair's crack in the wall of the dam. Not surprisingly, the more that was conceded, the more the Africans were confident of ultimate success.

The fourteen African members demanded universal suffrage and a constitutional conference. They were refused, being told to negotiate with the governor, and further that there would not be any more constitutional changes for ten years. However, a delegation of non–European members of the legislative council visited London on April 1959, and the Colonial Secretary at last agreed a conference should take place the next year. With this in view, the Kenyan government announced in July of 1959 that it would not oppose the formation of a multi-racial national party, a specifically African party of course still being banned. The Kenyan National Party was formed and had much to recommend it. Its policy was specifically non-racial, it asked for self-government by 1968, and it had the great asset of support from ten of the elected African members. It was, however, too late. Its practical proposals were necessarily vague on matters like the use of the White Highlands by all races and, in an impossible attempt to appeal to all, it failed really to inspire any.

Although in a minority of their fellows, the remaining four African elected members, Kiano, Gichuru, Odinga and Mboya, felt that they more truly represented the mainstream of African opinion in forming the rival Kenya Independent Movement, which as an African party was not officially recognized. KIM's policy included majority rule and immediate self-government.

It may occur to some at this stage that the founders of KIM were asking too much too soon, that they should have given the KNP a trial now that the end was in sight. But was it? Could the African politicians be sure? The settlers had not moved an inch from their earlier stand and their protests were being overruled by London for complex reasons which surely included a strong desire to see peace with, as a secondary consideration, as much salvaged for the settlers as reasonably possible in the circumstances. In seven years, the African politicians had experienced three constitutions and anticipated a fourth. Changes had come only with African demands, each was meant to be the last for many years. If the Africans rested now, one might well expect the colonial secretary thankfully to do the same, and perhaps shelve the "Kenya problem."

Finally, let us not forget the background against which this story is set. The Emergency continued, and with it the war on the forest fighters with whom by now most Africans had learned to identify themselves. In April 1959, while Lennox-Boyd was agreeing to the next round of constitutional talks, eleven Mau Mau detainees died in a concentration camp called Hola, a name not easily forgotten. At first, it was reported that the men had died from drinking poisoned water, but curiously no camp officials had been taken ill. At the inquest, it was revealed that they had been cruelly and senselessly beaten to death by camp warders and that violence to detainees was condoned by the camp officials. Public outcry was immense, nationally and internationally, and reforms introduced. But the men had died and the officer responsible for the Hola Camp was later honored by the British government for his distinguished service.

Was it any wonder that the African politicians decided that they could not rest until the battle had been fully won?

20

The Turning Point—
Enter MacLeod

The constitutional conference in February of 1960 was the most important of the series, and much of the credit must go to Mr. Iain MacLeod, who had replaced Lennox-Boyd as Colonial Secretary. MacLeod was a strong man, a realist, and his conduct of the conference as its chairman was a consummate political performance.

Representatives of all races came to London, each with their own ideas. The African politicians subordinated their personal differences to the greater power of unity and sent a joint delegation to London, with Ronald Ngala as leader and Mboya as secretary. As we shall see, this unity did not last. At the conference the delegates divided mainly on racial lines, European against African, with the Asians and Arabs ultimately siding with the Africans.

The most dramatic moment of the conference came with MacLeod's opening statement, in which he recognized the inevitability of Kenya's independence under African majority rule and intimated that the task of the delegates was to plan a wide measure of suffrage as an essential step towards this goal. The Africans were delighted—the end really was in sight! Equally, the Europeans were appalled. There was deadlock for over a month until MacLeod suggested or introduced his own formula—after which time he secured, after much deliberation, African, Asian, and Blundellite support for it. Most of the European die-hards rejected it, but without much success. MacLeod's formula, although it did not concede immediate complete suffrage or an overall African majority in the Council of Ministers, was at least vastly preferable to the only alternative: if his terms were not accepted, MacLeod proposed to scrap the conference decisions completely and appoint a British government commission which, he made quite clear, would take its time in making unilateral recommendations.

The delegates returned home to prepare for the general election to be held in February of 1961, by founding the first nationwide African party to be allowed since the Emergency was declared in October of 1952. The final split between the African leaders took place almost immediately. A conference was held at Kiambu near Nairobi in March of 1960 to form the Kenya African National Union, but much time also was taken up with personal recrimination. The smaller tribes, of whom Ngala was a member, complained of a Kikuyu/Luo alliance which threatened to destroy the national element essential to the new party's success. But the key issue was not in fact tribal at this stage but personal rivalry. The atmosphere was not helped by the fact that in London Mboya had abrogated to himself the right to make press statements on behalf of the delegation, something he should certainly have left to the leader, Ngala.

The obvious leader of KANU would have been Kenyatta but he was still in detention. Instead, James Gichuru, who had recently been released, was chosen as acting vice president on behalf of Kenyatta. He had been president of KAU, the last national party banned in 1952, and it was hoped that his prestige and experience would be sufficient to reconcile the various factions. Unfortunately, this was a forlorn hope, for in May of 1960, on adoption of KANU's constitution, Ngala, Moi and their allies refused office and the following month formed their own party, the Kenya African Democratic Union.

What were the reasons for this retrograde move and why then, in 1960? When considering splits among African leaders, the role played by the Kenya whites to split the African leaders should also be remembered, for example, the efforts employed by (a) The Kenya National Party (whites), (b) The Kenya New Party (whites), and (c) the Cafricorn Society (multiracial), and all other attempts on multiracialism as against African nationhood. Multiracial politics in Kenya meant in essence "white rule" through black puppets.

Quite simply, there were too many leaders. From October of 1952 to June of 1955 there was an absolute ban on all African political activity of any kind. In 1955, political parties were allowed again but only on a district-wide basis. Inevitably, members of each party tended to come from particular tribes, as district boundaries were largely drawn on tribal lines. The parties cooperated as far as possible, but restriction on movement and public assembly made the difficulties almost insuperable. The most that could be done was for the regional leaders to meet privately from time to time to decide the broad lines of common policy. As they could not even address public meetings in each other's regions, by the time a national party was once again possible in 1960, there was no basis for a national structure and only a few of the leaders were well-known outside the boundaries of their regions; the public expected their own men to be the new national leaders—and those leaders were used to power. The almost inevitable split was postponed until 1960 because it was not until the MacLeod Conference that the British admitted the inevitability of African majority rule. With this achieved, the need for unity lost much of its force.

In the event, the split was a healthy advance in the coming of age of African politics. KANU organized on a national basis, the regional parties supporting it dissolving to become branches subordinated to central direction and policy. This was clearly the only way to develop, and the process might have been slowed disastrously if instead a compromise had been made. On the other hand, the regional parties supporting KADU did not dissolve but formed a negative, defensive federation with only the minimum of sovereignty surrendered to the center. It was logical that the parties' policies should follow the same lines. KANU favored a strong united national government; KADU argued for a weak center and strong regional powers which implied the perpetuation of tribal division and would postpone, perhaps indefinitely, the golden prize of nationhood.

So the Africans fought each other in the election of February 1961, the European politicians being largely a spent force. Against all the odds, Kenya did not divide cleanly on a regional basis. In fact, KANU won the majority, but refused to form a government until Kenyatta had been released. Apart from regionalism, the main issue in the election had been Kenyatta's release, with both KANU and KADU claiming him for their own. It was not a policy that any politician could afford to dissociate himself from.

The governor, Sir Patrick Renison, flatly refused to consider Kenyatta's release—and after all, his main claim to fame may one day be his description of Kenyatta as "the leader to darkness and death." Instead, from April of 1961 to April of 1962, Kenya was ruled by a coalition of KADU and the New Kenya Party which had been formed by Sir Michael Blundell in April of 1960 as another experiment in multiracialism. To digress, a political party founded on the explicit concept of multiracialism is as doomed to failure as any other negative force.

The idea of multiracialism was particularly promoted or advanced by

Sir Philip Mitchell, the Colonial Governor of Kenya. On Sir Philip Mitchell and the concept of multiracialism, Fay Carter writes:

> Culturally and politically Mitchell believed that the African Colonies must aspire to the beliefs and values of Western Europe. The peoples of East and Central Africa had, he believed, no indigenous civilization of their own. The country had been an unexplored belt of anarchy and ignorance, their lives composed of sorcery, savagery, famine and tribal wars.... His beliefs in European civilization led logically to the conclusion that Kenya should be developed as a multi-racial society, an essentially European society, though composed of men of different races. Civilized men were Anglicized men. He never seemed to have worked out the place of East African Asians in his future Kenya. But he accepted that minority religions, by which he meant non–Christian religions, would have to be tolerated, and presumably the recipients of an English education would be acceptable.[1]

Multiracialism is backed by fear and mistrust and in fact perpetuates racialism as much as KADU threatened to perpetuate tribalism. The only kind of party that can succeed is one which is non-racial, which inevitably involves majority control and not the preservation of sectional interests. Everyone must work to the same national ends. This is not an African idea but a basic fact of political life. Both KADU and the NKP lacked this dynamic element—their main attraction for each other being that neither was KANU—and today they have both ceased to exist.

It was, of course, only a question of time before Kenyatta was released in 1962, but which party would he support? KADU claimed credit for his release but this could not be taken too seriously. Kenyatta was far too experienced politically to be attracted by KADU—if he had joined, there might well have been an end to all hope of a Kenya nation. His real choice was between KANU and the formation of an entirely new party in an attempt to draw support from both KANU and KADU. He realized that the breach was too deep to attempt a reconciliation at that time and opted inevitably for KANU. Gichuru resigned as party president to make way for the Old Man, as he had done once before in 1947, when Kenyatta had taken over as president of the Kenya African Union. Kariuki Karanja Njiiri, who represented one of the constituencies in Muranga in the Legislative Council, resigned also to allow Kenyatta to be returned to the legislative council as member for Muranga. This made it possible for Kenyatta to become technically a member of the Kenya Legislative Council.

Kariuki Karanja Njiiri, who made the move on behalf of Jomo Kenyatta, obtained his elementary school education from the Africa Inland

Kariuki Karanja Njiiri, who received his M.A. from the New School for Social Research in New York in 1958, resigned his position as a member of the Kenya Legislative Council in favor of Kenyatta.

Mission Preliminary School at Kinyona, run by the American missionaries, his primary school education at Kahuhia Primary School, run by the Church Missionary Society in Fort Hall (Muranga), Kenya Teachers' College, Githunguri, in Kiambu District in Kenya. He attended St. Joseph's High School in India, received his B.A. degree at Lincoln University in Pennsylvania, and an M.A. degree from the New School for Social Research in New York in 1958. He had a beautiful American wife.

KADU had one triumph left to come. Kenyatta's first decision was to press for yet another constitutional conference with a view to full majority self-government and ultimately independence. At first, Reginald Maudling, the new Colonial Secretary, was reluctant. He would have liked more time to try the MacLeod constitution. But a conference was agreed to and was, if anything, more testing for Maudling than anything MacLeod had had to face.

Unfortunately, where MacLeod had been strong, Maudling was weak, or at the least imperfectly understood the needs of the new African countries. He entrenched the concept of regionalism in his new constitution, making almost impossible the kind of national control and planning vital to the progress of developing countries. Further, he wanted a short period of government by the main parties in coalition before another election and final constitutional conference before independence. Politics being the art of the possible, KANU agreed (KADU of course being delighted) and Kenyatta and Ngala were given equal status in the government, an extraordinary solution by any standard.

But this was just a phase. In the 1963 election, KANU won a landslide victory and Kenyatta was sworn in as Prime Minister on June 1. The people had doomed KADU and chosen progress. The date for independence was fixed as December 12, 1963, and the final constitutional conference was convened in London in September. Duncan Sandys, the new Colonial Secretary, presided.

Again, there was trouble. KADU's delegation was much weaker than before, but they had the advantage of supporting an existing constitution. Further, now they were perhaps permanently in opposition, they argued for the consolidation of the constitution by strengthening still more the powers of the regional governments, particularly in the vital control of police and the civil service. KANU argued, as was the case, that the constitution was too rigid and basically unworkable.

At last, Kenyatta threatened to return home and declare Kenya an independent republic on the 20th of October. Sandys already knew that the Maudling constitution was a failure, and opted for central control of both police and the civil service, the regional authorities being represented in the central bodies. He also eased the procedure for future constitutional amendment, taking the realistic view that it was his duty to "consider not merely the formula agreed in 1962, but also the purpose which it was intended to serve, namely to make the constitution more durable." If change was virtually impossible, the constitution would fall into disrepute. KADU in turn threatened to declare an independent republic inside Kenya of the areas which they controlled, but this was no more than a gesture. There was no civil war nor ever any real likelihood of one, and time has proved Sandys right entirely.

On his return to Kenya, Kenyatta was widely acclaimed. He addressed a rally of 150,000 people in Nairobi Stadium, assuring them that the victory was theirs and that they must be prepared to work hard to fulfill the promise of that victory. His new slogan of "Harambee" (pull together) was cheered to the echo.

On December 12, 1963, Kenya became an independent nation within the Commonwealth, Kenyatta being the first Prime Minister, and the Right Honourable Malcolm MacDonald "the Good" became Governor-General. He is referred to as "Mac the Good" because he was an extraordinarily good Briton who was also extraordinarily good to the Africans in Kenya.

The rains were late that year and there was mud in the stadium where dancers from every tribe in Kenya swirled and danced and sang under the arc lights. The immense crowd rose and roared their goodwill to Kenyatta and the Duke of Edinburgh both. As the hour approached, it seemed as if the sky would burst with the color and the pride of Kenya. The noise, as if by miracle, died away with the lights until there was just one spotlight on the Union Jack, slowly falling from the flagstaff. Silence. Darkness. And then, a light again, the flag of Kenya rising high and the plaintive sweetness of the new Anthem. The races and the tribes, the wars and injustice, collided and collapsed like dreams or penny balloons. Kenya was born that beautiful morning and was not ashamed.

21

Education as a Necessary Tool for Independence

It is beyond the scope of this book to write about all the methods, means, and men and women in all walks of life who contributed from 1888 to 1970 in the forging of Kenya. It is also beyond the scope of this book to write biographies of all those individuals who were involved in the process of forging Kenya.

Specifically, it would be fair to say that among those peoples involved, whether individually or as a group, the European and the American missionaries of all denominations were remarkable.

The missionaries who went to Kenya to preach to the non–Christian peoples of Kenya intended to spread the Gospel of Christianity to the African societies, who were regarded as "clean slates" on which one could write anything. It was almost taken for granted that the African societies, prior to European arrival, did not possess well organized religious institutions of their own.

It would be pointless to go on writing about pros and cons of the Christian teachings in Kenya, but is true to say that this process had a very important side effect—education. Although the education which was introduced by the missionaries was not intended to educate all the African children en mass, the very few who obtained it were beneficial to their societies in many varied ways.

174

It is also true to say that most of the African leaders who emerged in the 1920s, 1930s, 1940s and even the 1950s—including, of course, those educated Africans who were absorbed in the colonial agencies or departments—were all products of missionary education.

Roger Bacon, an English philosopher who lived in the thirteenth century, wrote many scientific and philosophical studies. He himself did not make any profound discovery or important invention. However, he made a very important statement which is very relevant to the Kenyan situation and to Kenyan societies—that "knowledge is power." The importance of knowledge via education cannot be underestimated. This knowledge has no color, and when transmitted through a process of cultural diffusion can empower any society regardless of color, creed, religion, or nationality.

The school system which independent Kenya inherited from the British colonial rule was not meant to meet the goals of the Kenyan Africans. It was meant to educate a few African clerical workers who would be working under European or Asian professional establishment, always under supervision by other races. Their pay was very low.

The ideal goals would have been:

(a) Increased agricultural and industrial production so that all the people can have adequate food, clothing, housing, and health services

(b) Constantly developing pool of indigenous trained manpower

(c) Abolishing the inequities

(d) Lessening the dominance of towns over the countryside

(e) Substitution of values of egalitarianism for elitism.

All of these needs existed in Kenya during the colonial period and were not considered very seriously. In both Great Britain and Kenya, education was based on what may be described as social stratification. In case of colonial Kenya, this stratification was much more compounded than it was in Great Britain. The reason for this was that in colonial Kenya at least four different races co-existed, but were not integrated socially, economically or politically. For instance, there were different social services for the Europeans, the Asians, the Arabs, and the Africans.

In this pattern, social services for the Africans were always inadequate in comparison to those of other races. From about 1921 to the 1950s, there was unspeakable waste of human resources in all African schools. For example, if, say, 42,000 African children entered elementary school at the ages of seven to ten, it would not be exaggerating to suggest that only less than fifteen African students would ever see the university doors.

The situation was made particularly difficult by a process of eliminating most African students from school in the name of "quality education" through "public examinations." In this case, say 80 percent of the 42,000 African children had to be eliminated at the end of fourth year by an examination called "The Common Entrance Examination," and only the remainder would be able to go to the primary schools. The students who were eliminated by this process could not be described as "dropouts." Opportunities for those who were eliminated were very limited.

Those lucky remainders, who would go to the primary schools for three years, faced another difficult examination at the end of their third year called "The Primary School Examination"—at which time another 80 percent were eliminated before they entered the Junior High Schools or the secondary schools. Those students who were eliminated at the primary school level but were able to pass the examination with fewer points could be absorbed in the colonial establishment as cheap clerical workers. Their economic mobility was extremely limited.

The survivors of the Junior High School examination then went to forms III and IV, only to be faced at the end of their form IV education by another public examination called "The Cambridge Senior School Certificate Examination," at which time another 80 percent were eliminated.

The survivors would then be placed in forms V and VI and at the end of their training, they were faced by another public examination called "Cambridge Higher School Certificate"—whereby another 80 percent were eliminated. It is not surprising that perhaps only 15 to 20 African students would be able to go to the only one college in all East Africa—the Makerere College—which was regarded, in those days, as the "Oxford University of East Africa" in Uganda. It catered to Kenya, Uganda, and Tanganyika (now Tanzania).

It is also worth noting that the English language was not taught or introduced in the African elementary schools and only taught as a separate subject, not as a medium of instructions, in the African primary schools. Every African child had to learn three languages—Swahili, English, and his/her related mother tongue; i.e.; Kikuyu, Luo, Maasai, Kepsigis, Nandi, Kisii, Luhya, Rabai, or Kikamba.

At this juncture, the Africans were frustrated, dejected and depressed. There were certainly individual and collective efforts on the part of the Africans to deal with all these problems, but the odds and adversities were overwhelming.

As mentioned earlier on, the Kikuyu Karing'a Independent Schools and the Kikuyu Independent Schools—even though the main reasons for establishment were cultural conflict, and they probably did not always maintain a high standard or quality of education—very definitely helped to promote and spread mass education, especially in the central province of Kenya.

In the midst of the above, an individual with the name of Peter Mbiyu Koinange, son of Senior Chief Koinange—appeared on the scene.

Mbiyu did not emerge to solve all the Kenya African educational problems. However, he tried his best to at least alleviate them.

Mbiyu was born in 1907 in Kiambu District. At the age of seven he attended CMS School at Kiamba and also Alliance High School in 1926. In 1927, he left Kenya for the United States and attended Hampton Institute in Virginia, and Ohio Wesleyan University, from which he obtained the B.A. degree. In 1936 he entered Columbia University in New York, from which he obtained the M.A. degree. He then proceeded to St. John's College of Cambridge University for further studies in England. On returning to Kenya in 1938 and in 1939, he established the Kenya Teachers' College at Githunguri in Kiambu District, which was capable of accommo-

Peter Mbiyu Koinange, the first Kenyan African to obtain an M.A. degree. Founder of the Kenya Teachers' College, Githunguri, in 1939, the principal of the same institution.

dating over 1,000 future trainees as schoolteachers. He also helped the African farmers in his area to form the first African cooperative societies.

Mbiyu Koinange was not a good friend of the Kenyan colonial authorities. They resented him to the core. However, they offered him a job with a salary much, much lower than that which would be offered to a European with the same qualifications. Naturally, Mbiyu Koinange refused the offer, and decided to concentrate on raising money for the Kenya Teachers' College—the school he had already established at Githunguri.

Mbiyu Koinange, besides managing the new college, was also deeply involved in the affairs of the Kenya African Union. It is common knowledge that raising money for public causes is not always an easy thing, and Mbiyu Koinange experienced this problem in the course of raising money for the Kenya Teachers' College, Githunguri.

As a good educator and social anthropologist, Mbiyu Koinange realized that the traditional custom of the Kikuyu circumcision meant more than a physical operation. It meant social and psychological maturity. It had economic, political, and civic implications. On the economic side, the idea of the Kikuyu age-grade system had a sense of competition. Essentially, competition is not always a bad thing. It does stimulate and encourage progress.

To the Kikuyu, the idea of working hard is a virtue. One has to work hard for his or her survival, and working hard will result in progress and change. Competition among the age-grades did help Mbiyu Koinange to raise money for the Kenya Teachers' College.

The use of age-grade to raise money for the college or any other cause was an illustration of the way customary features of some African societies have conditioned the development of modern educational institutions. Such linkages require much more intensive historical investigation.

How did Mbiyu Koinange use the age-groups? Each age-group had a name associated with the time or year in which that age-group went through the ritual of circumcision. For example, the age-grade of small pox was so named because a small pox epidemic took place in Kikuyu country. The age-grade of earthquake meant the age-grade which circumcised during the time of great earthquake; the age-grade of famine, when a great famine occurred.

In practical terms, the age-grade of small pox may say that those numbers who belonged to that age-group will build a library at Kenya Teachers' College. On the same token, the age-group of earthquake may respond by raising enough money to help build the dormitories. Similarly, the age-group of "Kiendano" ("Love") which occurred in 1928 will raise enough money to pay for the teachers for the next five years, and so on.

In Kikuyu society, as in Japanese society, religion was not supposed to interfere with progress. Mbiyu Koinange knew this; and he took full advantage on behalf of the Kenya Teachers' College, Githunguri.

In 1951, Mbiyu Koinange and Achieng Oneko went to England to press the African case on the land issue to the Colonial Secretary and among the British members of Parliament. In addition, they also sent a petition to the U.N. Secretary-General in Paris.

Unfortunately for Mbiyu Koinange, the Kenyan colonial government refused to let Mbiyu return to Kenya. However, Achieng Oneko was allowed to return. Mbiyu was to be stranded in London as a persona non grata.

Mbiyu Koinange had an apartment in Hampstead, London. Sometimes he was financially embarrassed. Since the Kenya African Union was banned after the State of Emergency was declared in Kenya in 1952, Mbiyu Koinange's source of money was exhausted. Consequently, Mbiyu Koinange obtained a job as a machine-minder with a London co-op dairy, which paid him 10 pounds a week.

In 1959, Mbiyu Koinange was invited to go to Ghana to manage the Pan-African bureau dealing with the freedom movement of Eastern, Central and Southern African. Mbiyu Koinange was not always happy in Ghana.

During the Lancaster House Conference in London on the issue of Kenyan independence, the African leaders attending the conference asked Mbiyu Koinange to join them in London and act as their second adviser. Immediately, Mbiyu Koinange left Ghana for England. On his arrival in London, he joined the Kenyan African delegation.

The African delegates made it known to the British Colonial Secretary, Mr. Ian MacLeod, that they wanted Mbiyu Koinange to be their second adviser. To this demand Mr. MacLeod replied that Mr. Mbiyu Koinange was not acceptable as a second adviser to the African delegation as he was persona non grata in Kenya, and was involved in the Mau Mau conspiracy. The African delegates insisted on their demand consistently. Mr. MacLeod refused to yield. In return, the African delegates also refused to yield. Hence, a deadlock occurred which lasted about a week. Frustration on both sides was inevitable.

In its editorial, the *London Times* on January 19, 1960, commented:

> Complete confidence obviously requires that the delegations
> have the advisers of their own choice: and if, like the African
> elected members, they ask for two, there is no serious objection
> to indulging them.... Was this deadlock necessary?

In Kenya on January 24, 1960, a group of the Kikuyu loyalists, who had been collaborating with the Kenya colonial government in the course of the Mau Mau crisis, sent a telegraph to Mr. MacLeod stating their dislike of Mr. Koinange's presence at the Lancaster House Conference. They were led by Harry Thuku. It was too late. To this end, the *London Daily Mail* of January 24, 1960, reported:

> Enter Koinange—with a blank pass Kenya Deadlock Ends: Peter
> Mbiyu Koinange, the 53 year old Kikuyu over whom the London
> talks on Kenya have been deadlocked for a week is to be admitted
> to Lancaster House after all....

Immediately, Mr. Koinange became the second adviser to the Kenya African delegates. The European delegates were extremely unhappy—but to no avail. Mr. Koinange returned to Kenya in 1961 and in 1963 was elected as a member of the independent Kenya Parliament.

Mr. Koinange, besides his involvement in politics, was a great inspiration to the African generations of the 1930s, 1940s and even 1950s. He made a hallmark on African education in Kenya. He was the first African to obtain a B.A. degree. He was the first African to obtain the M.A. degree. He was a symbolic figure in African educational advancement.

To this end, we can join with Roger Bacon, the English philosopher, once again and repeat, "Knowledge is power!" Independence cannot be meaningful without educated men and women who manage and maintain the government bureaucracy or the government agencies efficiently.

As for the Kenya Teachers' College, which Mbiyu Koinange established in January of 1939, Mbiyu and his father Senior Chief Koinange had a big, long range plan for it. They intended to make it one of the most important institutions of higher learning in Kenya, if not in all of East Africa.

Mbiyu intended originally to recruit many American educators, especially American Negro educators, as they were referred to in those days. Perhaps this was due to his higher educational background in America, and his early contact with Negro scholars and educators. He was very fond of Negro athletes, professional boxers and singers. He kept on talking about the famous Marian Anderson and her beautiful voice, Paul Robeson and others. In one of his classes at Githunguri, he would digress and talk about Jesse Owens of Ohio and his extraordinary performance during the Olympic Games in Berlin in 1936. Mbiyu was particularly fond of Dr. Ralph Bunche, who became the Secretary General of the Trustee Council of the United Nations. They were very close friends. As a matter of fact, Mbiyu used Dr. Bunche as a contact man when he sent a complaint to the United Nations about the African conditions in Kenya.

It appears to be true, however, that the Kenya Teachers' College, Githunguri, did not become the reservoir of teachers that it was intended to be. There appear to be three main reasons for this. The first one was the outbreak of World War II, whereby many men were recruited or enlisted for the war efforts. The second reason was that after the war was over, there were new political changes in Kenya, and Mbiyu became more and more involved in political, economic and social matters at the expense of educational considerations. The third reason is the outbreak of the Mau Mau rebellion in 1952, whereby Mbiyu found himself as an exile from Kenya from 1952 to 1960.

22

Independence

The final stages of Kenya's constitutional development followed quietly and inevitably. Those in KADU and their supporters found that the fears which had driven them to opposition were not fulfilled. KADU could not continue to exist in this vacuum and gradually of their own accord KADU members in the National Assembly began to cross the floor to join the Government party, where they were welcomed without recrimination.

In the National Assembly on August 14, 1964, Kenyatta told of his plans to make Kenya a republic on December 12, the first anniversary of independence. There would be a president as head of state whose term of office would be commensurate with that of the Assembly from which he would choose his ministers. He did not propose the abolition of the regional assemblies but made it clear that they would "have no exclusive authority or legislative competence in any matter which should be planned and directed on a national scale; education, agriculture, health, economic and social development, and utilization of land." Local authorities and the taxes they could levy and services they should provide were to be controlled by the central government. The civil service and police would be a central government responsibility, as would be the utilization of land and the exploitation of minerals.

In November of 1964, Ronald Ngala, leader of KADU, announced that his party was to dissolve voluntarily in favor of the one-party system. No pressure forced this decision, which was greeted with tumultuous applause in the Assembly. So, on December 12, 1964, Kenya became a republic inside the commonwealth, a strong united state, with the full approval of all her ten million inhabitants, and Jomo Kenyatta was inaugurated as the nation's first president.

According to the constitution that came into force on June 1, 1963, the government of Kenya was headed by a prime minister, who was the leader of the majority party in the National Assembly. When Kenya became a republic in December of 1964, the title of prime minister was changed to president. The president and the ministers he appointed, who might be members of either house, were collectively responsible to the National Assembly. This body consisted of the Senate of 41 members, including one for each of the seven provinces and one for the Nairobi area, and the House of Representatives of 158 members elected by universal adult suffrage and based on single-member constituencies. In addition, 12 members elected by the House sat as an electoral college and the attorney-general participated in the House as an ex-officio member. Elections for the Senate were to be staggered over a six-year period, so that one-third of the seats were contested every two years. The Senate was later abolished so the legislature became unicameral. A state of emergency might be declared if a resolution was passed by 65 percent of the members of one house and endorsed by the other house within seven days.

The principle of maximum possible decentralization of governmental powers to local authorities was recognized by the constitution, and provision was made for the establishment of provincial assemblies with local administrative powers. The central government could abridge or extend the powers of local governments in the national interest.

The Kenya Development Plan 1964–1970

In the Sessional Paper Number 10 titled "African Socialism and its Applications to Planning," the following is set forth: an attempt to explain to the world what the Kenyan government was trying to do, that being defined as African socialism. What was sought was a welfare state in which equal opportunity was available for all people without discrimination, and where free enterprise was not discouraged. In order to achieve this rapid economic growth had to be attained, and this could only happen through planning and selective state participation. The paper rejected communism and capitalism both as irrelevant to the Kenyan scene, and hence the question was not that of the ownership of the means of production, but of the equitable distribution of the country's wealth, particularly the new wealth that was being created.[1]

Much has been written on African socialism—and many theories have been advanced on this subject by Julius Nyerere (*Freedom and Unity*), Jomo Kenyatta (*Suffering Without Bitterness*), Tom Mboya (*Freedom and After*), and Oginga Odinga (*Not Yet Uhuru*).

In analyzing the respective development plans it would be better to pinpoint the goals aimed at, and then see if such goals were achieved, and also to compare the growth of the various sectors—for example, agricultural industry and land use. That would be the way to know whether the plans have been successful.

Unproven theories are interesting to read about, but pragmatic ideas and plans appeared to have worked in Kenya during the period of 1964–1970.

To put these ideas into practical application, the "Kenyan Development Plan 1964–1970" was inaugurated, the characteristics of which were: first, the total development expenditure sought was 325 million pounds, of which 145 million pounds was to be contributed by the public sector,[2] that is, the central government plus public bodies, with the central government accounting for 80.6 million pounds.[3] The private sector was expected to contribute the rest, that is, about 60 percent of the total development expenditure. This expenditure was expected to enable the economy to grow by 6.3 percent each year, and although this was partly offset by the fact that the population was increasing by about 3.5 percent per year the per capita income would increase by over 3 percent per year. It was immediately obvious that the contribution of the private sector was crucial if the overall target rate of growth was to be achieved. It is important to remember, too, that Kenya's was a mixed economy, and the cooperation between the government and the private sector was very vital. To ensure that the private sector came forward in the right magnitude and direction, the government instituted certain policies. These included the establishment of investment priorities, so that private investors could know in which industries they could expect maximum government assistance; the provision of basic service and related facilities by the government; guarantees on security of investment and return of profits, protection against competing imports, investment allowances, etc. It has often been said, and this criticism is leveled against many African governments, that Kenya expected too much from the private sector, but what they were asking the private sector to invest was just over 31 million pounds[4] a year during the planning period, a figure which the sector had more or less achieved between 1956 and 1957. The total planned capital formation is summarized below:

Capital Formation in the Private Sector	1965–66 to 1967–70[5] Millions
Agriculture	48.2
Manufacturing Industries	61.5
Electricity	24.0
Transport	15.0
Housing	11.1
Private Cars	25.0
Others	20.9
TOTAL	205.7
of which: privately financed government financial contribution	180.0

Capital Formation in the Public Sector	
Central government development estimates	64.5
Central government, other	7.5
Local Authorities	20.0
East African community	22.0
University College, Nairobi	4.1
TOTAL	119.0
Grand total all capital formation	325.0
of which: financed by the public sector	145.0

Another criticism was that they relied too heavily on foreign capital. The cost of servicing foreign loans was a thing to watch, and pressure was building to turn such loans into grants. (United Kingdom, Sweden and Japan did turn some of their loans into grants.) The truth, as government officials saw it, was that at this stage of development, to give up foreign capital was equal to giving up development itself. Their aim was to use foreign capital in building up their own resources so that eventually the role of foreign capital would be marginal in attaining higher rates of growth. In other words, it was only in the beginning that they would need foreign capital, but subsequently would have to rely entirely on their own resources. In the meantime, foreign capital was needed to supplement their meager domestic resources. It must be noted that the more they used their own resources, the more likely they were to obtain additional foreign capital including aid, for many donor countries were more likely to help those who were helping themselves. There was, however, one major problem with foreign capital. In most cases foreign loans take a very long time to materialize, often over a year between the application for one of these loans and its being given. This, of course, slowed down plan implementation because some of the major projects could not be undertaken until the promised foreign loans were actually given. It is also true that until quite recently (and the British were the first to introduce this new deviation from the norm), most of the loans given for development have actually been too expensive to accept. Now there is a trend of interest-free loans, which, of course, is quite welcome.

The most important feature of the plan was that it stressed vigorously the importance of agriculture. Of the total development expenditure by the central government and public bodies the share of agriculture and irrigation was over 32 percent including transfer payments, while those of commerce and industry, basic services, and associated services were 3.9 percent, 41 percent and 12.5 percent respectively.[6] The rest of the public expenditure went to natural resources, tourism, security and defense.

Their policy was to emphasize agriculture in the first plan (this is the first 6-year plan), which was based on several considerations. The first one was that they felt that it was in agriculture that they could make the most immediate impact on the development of the entire country. This was not only because this sector involves over 90 percent of the population, but also because it was in agriculture that they were most competitive. There was, in any case, the political and economic need to Africanize the agricultural sector of the Kenyan economy. Secondly, it was in the expansion of agriculture that they could remove quickly the unemployment at that time plaguing the country, if only because agriculture is more labor intensive than industry.

Also, the Kenyan manpower problem involved a scarcity of high level manpower and an increasing surplus of unskilled workers. The latter category demanded immediate action, and Kenya must provide employment for these people. Most of the future industries would depend on agriculture for raw materials; since there are no large deposits of minerals such as iron, coal or oil, a large part of the industries in the first few years would be those of processing agricultural livestock and forest products. Already these industries contributed over 50 percent of the manufacturing activities in Kenya.

And finally, since they had to develop through import substitutions, local incomes had to increase rapidly, and it was through agricultural development that the government could most easily raise the incomes of the rural population. The impact of the Development Plan on the economy is measured by the planned growth of the Gross Domestic Product:

Gross Domestic Product at Constant Prices (Millions)

Monetary Sector	1964	1970[7] (planned)
Agriculture and Livestock	46.22	66.25
Manufacturing	29.38	46.60
Construction	4.38	12.00
Transport, Communications	26.30	39.50
Wholesale and retail trade	34.06	48.30
General government	34.11	51.20
Other Activities	38.34	57.90
Monetary Gross Domestic Product	212.79	321.75
Subsistence Product	68.53	83.10
Total Gross Domestic Product per capita	31	37

Saying that in this first plan they were emphasizing agricultural development is not to say that they were doing nothing about industry. On the contrary, they established certain bodies, specifically the Development Finance Corporation of Kenya and the Industrial and Commercial Development Corporation, to foster industrialization; the former body for large-scale and the latter for small-scale industry. Rate of growth of the manufacturing sector of the Kenyan economy between 1964 and 1970 was far ahead of the other East African territories, averaging over 10 percent per annum during the first seven years of independence. Proper examination of the plan will reveal that great attention was being paid to the processing of agricultural livestock and forest products, and such activities are aspects of industrialization. In short, the first plan was a program of development which, while working toward ultimate industrialization, recognized the tremendous importance of agricultural development in the economy in the next few years. It is important to keep in mind that industry cannot flourish in a country with a stagnating agricultural sector. They were attempting to stimulate agricultural development through the reorganization of the agriculture itself by stepping up land consolidation and registration, irrigation, and settlement schemes, all accompanied by extension services, provisions of credit and improvement of marketing systems for the farmers. This was their form of agrarian revolution. They wanted to transform the land; to make it much more productive on an economic basis rather than on subsistence. Many felt that unless they could reorganize and improve and develop agriculture they would be simply scratching the surface of the problem.

Purchase of formerly European owned farms by the government for

African settlement was a bigger step in land reform. Their intention was that this kind of reconstruction would be followed in the next plan by a very vigorous program of industrialization; they must lay down the foundations for it and the prospective industrial survey. They had basically to provide food for the people, and later to industrialize the country.

Another industry which was to be expanded vigorously was tourism. Perhaps it was only in this industry that they could favorably compete with other countries. The importance of the tourist trade lies in its ability to "earn relatively easily additional foreign exchange for the country."[8] In the plan they intended to make it possible, through the construction of new game lodges, new roads, national parks, etc., to increase the number of tourists visiting Kenya. The point being made is that they wanted to raise the number of tourists going to the country and therefore increase the percentage of the earnings to about 12 million pounds[9] by the end of the plan period. Looking at the economy as a whole, it may be only the tourist industry which could be relied on to meet quickly the foreign exchange problem created by the demands that had come about as a result of independence. Agricultural exports still lead in this field.

Income

The gross domestic product for Kenya in 1964 was 277.70 million pounds and the total recorded monetary economy was 209.21 million pounds as compared with 192.43 pounds for 1963 and 180.87 million pounds for 1962, 178.0 million pounds in 1961, 175.32 million pounds for 1960 and 161.76 million pounds for 1959. This equals a 50 percent increase from 1959 to 1964. Of the 1964 total, wages amounted to 103.1 million pounds, of which Africans received 58.9 million pounds, Asians, 21.1 million pounds; and Europeans, 24.1 million. Operating surplus was 84.03 million for private enterprises and 3.59 million for public enterprises. In 1961, the operating surplus of private enterprises was 67.15 million pounds and 2.99 million for public enterprises.[10]

Labor

In 1964, there were 589,600 persons in paid employment, of whom 536,900 were African, 36,700 were Asians, and 16,000 Europeans.[11] The total represented an increase of more than 56,000 over the 1963 figure.[12] In 1961, there were 589,391 persons of all races in paid employment of

Julius Gikonyo Kiano, the first Kenyan African to obtain a Ph.D. degree, in 1955. (Photograph courtesy of Julius Gikonyo Kiano.)

whom 529,386 were African, 37,820 were Asian and 22,184 Europeans.[13] These figures represent a decline by more than 5 percent over the previous year and were at their lowest level since 1954.[14]

Large scale agriculture and forestry continued to be the largest employer of African labor in 1964, with over 35 percent of the total, or 208,300.[15] There were 6,000 Asians and 1,200 Europeans also employed in this area, which had been in steady decline since 1960, when a total of 271,800 were employed. Private industry and commerce employed 169,500 Africans, 28,000 Asians, and 10,100 Europeans; while the public sector employed 160,000 Africans, 28,000 Asians and 4,700 Europeans. In 1965, it was reported that Africans held 44,000 of the nation's 51,000 civil service posts. The minimum wage in Nairobi for males over 21 in 1965 was 115 shillings per month, with a 35 shillings housing allowance. Minimum wages were tied to a cost of living index and were set by the Statutory Minimum Wage Board.

The trade union movement in Kenya was completely reorganized in September of 1965, following severe riots in Mombasa on August 2. President Kenyatta ordered the deregistration of the two existing organizations, the Kenya African Workers' Congress and the Kenya Federation of Labor (KFL), formerly led by Tom Mboya. The government also froze the assets of these two groups, canceled their existing affiliations outside of Africa, and provided for a Central Organization of Trade Unions with a General Secretary appointed by the president and elections supervised by the government. In addition to the Mombasa riots, 267 labor disputes involving 56,011 workers were recorded in 1964. (In 1959, there were only 67 such disputes.) It was estimated about 20 percent of eligible Africans were members of the 26 trade unions, the strongest of which were the Dock Workers' Union in Mombasa, the Transport Workers' Union, and the Agricultural Workers' Union.

Following a series of severe strikes in 1962, an Industrial Relations Charter pioneered by Tom Mboya, the Minister for Labor, was signed by the Kenyan Federation of Labor and the Federation of Kenya Employers in October. This charter set out the agreed responsibilities of management and unions, the policies to be applied when staff became redundant, operations of dispute commissions, joint consultations at regular intervals, and protection for both management and unions from intimidation.

Stating that the government was determined to pursue "a clearly defined program of Kenyanization of jobs, particularly in the private sector of the economy,"[16] the then Minister of Labor, Dr. Gikonyo Kiano, announced at a press conference in Nairobi on April 7, 1967, that a Kenyanization of Personnel Bureau would be set up to keep a record of all citizens who had acquired a skill or received training locally or overseas for posts in any of the categories of jobs available in the private and public sectors; this bureau would in turn supply companies with names of qualified local personnel. Employers would be required to provide statistics regarding non-citizens in their employment to enable the government to judge each company's progress toward Kenyanization. "This employment policy will not be allowed to impair the overriding objective of reaching the development targets set out in the Development Plan (1964–70),"[17] Kiano said. All government departments making outside purchases were instructed by the Treasury to give a 5 percent advantage to firms within East Africa, other things being equal over firms from outside the area. A further 5 percent was to be given to Kenyan Africans over non–African forwarding firms, and contracts were not to be awarded to companies tendering from a neighboring country which imposed trade restrictions against Kenya on that particular firm's item.[18]

Agriculture

With improvement in farming methods and the spread of land consolidation and enclosure, more and more African farmers began selling part of their annual production for cash. The effect was a rising level of agricultural exports of which African farmers produced 28 percent in 1964. While the expansion of agricultural export crops was the most important factor in stimulating economic development, much agricultural activity also was directed toward providing food for domestic consumption. Kenya's agriculture was sufficiently diversified to be able to produce virtually every basic agricultural foodstuff. Not only was Kenya able to produce foodstuffs to meet its own needs, but it helped to a considerable extent to feed neighboring territories and played an important role in insuring the self-sufficiency of the East African Common Market.

Coffee was Kenya's largest cash crop in 1964, with a gross revenue of 14,991,000 pounds (9,482,000 pounds in 1962).[19] The production of pyrethrum, with 985,000 pounds in sales, was down to less than half of the 1962 total.[20] Tea production, however, had rapidly developed with 19,000 tons produced in 1965.[21] The Tea Development Authority predicted that Kenya would be Africa's largest single tea planter by 1970, when 25,500 acres would be in production; in 1965, wheat was the largest crop in tonnage, with 281,200 acres producing 141,000 tons.[22] Wheat sales were 3,683,000 in 1964, and 2,136,000 in 1962.[23] Although African small-farm agriculture was still predominantly of a subsistence character, its contribution of marketed products continued to grow rapidly as the new political situation resulted in land consolidation and resettlement schemes in formerly European areas. European agriculture in Kenya was generally large-scale and almost entirely commercial. In 1964, the number of holdings of large farms (20 or more acres) was 2,958—down 666 from 1961—with a total acreage of 6,797,000 (small farm holdings were 7,216,000 acres).[24] Some 500,000 acres on the large farms were under permanent crops such as coffee, tea, sisal, and wattle and a rather smaller acreage was under cereals. It was estimated that gross farm revenue would increase from 55 million pounds in 1964 to 90 million in 1970, with exports earning 61 million pounds.[25]

The political uncertainty and definite government policy to buy out the Highlands caused considerable uneasiness among the European farmers, and development capital in this field was not forthcoming in these years. It was estimated, however, that resettlement schemes for African farmers in the Highlands, who had thus far replaced the European owners of 600 large farms, would increase productivity in commercial agriculture and that the European farmers who remained would be those who were most efficient and productive. Most European farmers who left Kenya received compensation from the British government.

In 1964, some 900 harvesters and 5,800 tractors were in use, and the government announced that 21 percent of the national budget in 1965 would be spent on farm improvements.[26] Large-scale irrigation projects had begun and the United Nations Special Fund was helping to finance a survey of the irrigation possibilities of the Tana River Basin.

Industry

Net output of manufacturing in 1964 was 22,782,000 pounds as against 14,140,000 pounds in 1954.[27] The 1963 total industrial output, which included building and construction, was 32,531,000 pounds.[28] Flour milling, brewing, and cement manufacturing were among the most important of the 100 or more main types of industries. Products manufactured in Kenya included aluminum hollowware, fertilizers, glassware, footwear, metal containers, metal furniture, preserved fruits and vegetables, paper products, sisal products, and tanned leather. In 1964, 4,900 companies were registered, of which 636 were foreign owned. In 1961, there were slightly over 4,000 companies and 580 were foreign owned. How does the rate of growth in industry compare with agriculture? The rate is faster! The policies to promote Africans therein were encouraging.

Foreign Trade

The value of domestic exports in 1965 amounted to 47,173,000 pounds, as compared with 47,114,000 in 1964 and 35,175,000 in 1961.[29] Coffee, tea, and sisal accounted for about 58 percent of the value of domestic exports, only 50 percent in 1961; and coffee earned 14.1 million for more than twice the total of tea and sisal combined.[30] Production of coffee, however, stabilized at the quota allocated to Kenya under the International Coffee Agreement. Tea has in recent years replaced sisal as the second commodity and pyrethrum extracts were exceeded for the first time by meat and meat preparations which continued to expand. Petroleum products appeared on Kenya's list of exports for the first time in 1963 and 1964, accounting for 4.6 percent of total exports. The United Kingdom continued to be Kenya's principal trading partner and purchased 24 percent of her exports in 1965. Other important export markets in 1965 were the European Economic Community (23 percent), West Germany (13 percent) and the United States and Canada (10 percent). In December of 1965, Kenya effected a complete ban on trade with Rhodesia (imports in January–July of 1965 were 185,362; exports were 170,877). In February of 1966, restrictions on imports from Japan were announced to help restore a favorable trade balance.[31]

Principal Exports (by value, in thousands of pounds)[32]

	1961	1964	1965
Coffee	10,609	15,395	14,095
Tea	4,004	6,055	6,084
Sisal	4,192	6,082	3,851
Meat & Meat Preparations	2,281	2,166	2,468

Principal Imports (by value, in thousands of pounds)[33]

	1961	1964	1965
Crude Petroleum	0	7,273	9,070
Machinery (non-electrical)	0	6,732	5,672
Paper & Paperboard	1,778	3,197	3,873

Principal Trade Partners: 1961[34]

	Imports	Exports	Balance
United Kingdom	8,505	30,508	-22,003
West Germany	5,860	4,293	+ 1,567
United States	5,018	5,041	- 23
Japan	1,404	8,469	- 7,065
Netherlands	1,287	1,976	- 698

Principal Trade Partners: 1965 [34]

	Imports	Exports	Balance
United Kingdom	10,137	25,136	-14,999
West Germany	7,373	8,511	- 1,138
United States	2,942	8,511	- 5,869
Japan	1,723	9,050	- 7,327
Netherlands	2,037	2,396	- 359

Foreign Investments

The overall policy for industrialization was designed to help raise the standard of living, skills and experience of the people by providing employment and training opportunities. In that process industrialization was designed to provide consumers with goods and services, as well as with the means by which the value of the country's annual resources was raised by way of processing. The government realized that it had limited resources, and therefore welcomed private and foreign capital. The sector depended overwhelmingly on private investment in the form of equity or loan capital, bank credits and supplier credits, both from within and outside the country.

Kenyan policy was, therefore, basically positive and nonrestrictive, characterized by encouragement and support where needed in order to secure a maximum rate of economic growth and structure which would benefit the country most. Investment was greatly welcome where citizens or foreigners were willing to risk their own money and effort to increase production and employment. Kenyans realized that the government's support and protection of these industries was necessary, and in the fulfillment of this requirement the government looked for industrial projects which satisfied the following criteria:

(1) the saving of foreign exchange

(2) projects which were labor intensive so as to make the limited capital available provide maximum employment opportunities

(3) degrees of integration—the industries which processes output of agriculture, forestry and other natural resources were specially favored, and firms were expected to substitute domestic imports for material which was then being imported

(4) wider geographical distribution—the government would assign a higher priority to a project which could be economically located in places other than Nairobi and Mombasa.

The overriding consideration in allocating industrial priorities was the actual or potential efficiency of the proposed industry.[35]

The government realized that the country was among those which were in need of foreign investment. Their market was also small by world standards. To ensure that planned industrial development took place, investment incentives were devised. Rights of ownership were guaranteed in the constitution, which stated that "no property shall be compulsorily acquired for public purposes, except on prompt payment of full compensation, and that every person having an interest or gith in property which is compulsorily taken possession of shall have a right of direct access to the Court."[36]

In addition to this, and in accordance with the Foreign Investment Protection Act, any foreign investment that contributed significantly to development would be granted an Approved Status Certificate which entitled the owner to repatriate guaranteed earnings and capital.

Kenya's New Five Year Development Plan (1970-1974)

President Jomo Kenyatta, addressing the Kenyan nation on Jamhuri Day, December 12, 1969, launched the new development plan in the following words:

> It is fitting that this anniversary should also coincide with the launching of our Development Plan for the period up to 1974. A popular version of this Plan has also been published. All our people must understand the way in which our Republic as a reward for stability and effort, can now move into a more prosperous future within modern world society.[37]

Kenyatta went on to outline the main points of the plan. He said that during the plan period, the total central government budget would amount to 720 million pounds. This would be more than was provided in the previous development plan. "Such fact is an impressive symbol of the national strength already gathered, from the people's own productive capacity, and domestic savings. Moreover, taking developing and recurrent outlay together, overseas finance will have to be sought for only 12 percent of the total program."[38]

The new plan, the president said, was far more ambitious than anything Kenya had attempted before. All the "early years of survey and experiment, weighing up material and human capacities, and getting things moving in directions dictated by our own political philosophies and social aims, are now behind us."[39]

Early in the plan, the government recognized that higher incomes resulted from increased production and increased production came from increased investment. The plan envisaged government expenditure over the five years of 720 million pounds, compared with 430 million pounds in the first plan. It set out numbers of capital programs aimed at creating more production and income.

One of these dealt with the pattern of investment, the plan revealing that in 1970 investments in Kenya were about 100 million, expected to reach nearly 160 million by 1974. Of this, one-third would be undertaken directly by the government and other public institutions, and the remaining two-thirds would come from private companies and individuals.

Public expenditures were largely reserved for basic investment, such as the improvement of the transport network (particularly the road system), and the extension of basic utilities such as water, education and staff housing, which do not lend themselves readily to private investment.

Private investment was encouraged in agriculture manufacturing, commerce and other areas which attracted it, both locally and from abroad. "The major role of Government," the plan stated, "is to guide, to assist, is to maintain a favourable climate for investment, and to supply basic facilities."[40]

It added that in large projects, the government was also prepared to participate financially, as a shareholder or in other ways.

In education, the government planned an increase in primary school enrollments from 1.3 million in 1969 to more than 1.8 million in 1974, and an increase in secondary school enrollments from 103,000 to over 144,000. University students were expected to increase over the same period from 1,700 to more than 3,400.[41]

To support this rapid rise in enrollments the government programmed the output of primary schoolteachers to rise from 2,500 in 1969 to 3,700 in 1974, and of secondary schoolteachers to rise from 380 to 670.[42]

Because of national manpower needs, high priority would be given to the rapid development of technical, vocational, and commercial education. On the basis of projections of population, the labor force would increase by about 850,000 persons during the period of 1968–1974.

The government warned that although the plan aimed to expand the economy fast enough to provide livelihood for these additions to the labor force, and also create job opportunities for those then without any means of livelihood, this did not mean that wage-paid jobs could be created for all these people.

The government aimed to increase wage-paid jobs by about 275,000, and the larger portion of opportunities would result from the emphasis on rural development, the stimulation of economic growth in the rural areas being designed to create more self-employment in commerce, small-scale rural industries and agriculture.

It was estimated that about 3.7 million adult men and women were employed on the land in 1968. If the targets for the non-agricultural employment in the plan were achieved, about 4.3 million adults would gain their livelihood from the land in 1974.

During the plan period, about 2,000 new hospital beds were provided under a program planned to achieve a better balance in the health service, and aimed at providing one bed for every 1,250 people in each district by 1974.[43] There was also a long-term aim of providing one health center for every 20,000 people, although this goal was not reached by 1974 due to the shortage of trained staff and finance.

Kenyatta in 1968 made an annual address to the nation from which the following was taken: "We have thus set the pattern for future progress. Let us, therefore, redouble our efforts that the next five years will be a further milestone in our endeavor to raise the living standards of our people."[44]

There has been much argument, notably in the Western world, as to why Africans should prefer a one-party system to the Westminster model. Some consider that a one-party system will inevitably lead to dictatorship. To others, a single party is a logical step from the tribal structure, which has elements of paternalism.

In fact, the single party is attractive to Africans mainly because the proliferation of parties tends to perpetuate traditional tribal conflict. Tribalism in this sense, complicated at times by religious partisanship, is disruptive and cannot be allowed any place in the modern state. In addition, personalities often play a disproportionate part in African politics at the expense of more important economic, educational and social issues.

The combination of tribal issues and personal rivalries can prevent the proper implementation of a clear-cut program for a country's development. Similarly, African politicians are not usually very well-to-do, and when in opposition tend to seek external financial aid to help them fight against the ruling party, not to promote an effective policy but to attain for themselves the privileges of government office. This inevitably leads to interference from other countries and the introduction of disputes and ideologies alien to the national interest. A one-party system does not do away with the threat of outside intervention completely, but at least minimizes the risk.

Some find a one-party system distasteful because they fear it cannot do justice to the interests of racial minorities. However, the subordination of racial interests, like those of individual tribes, to that of the nation as a whole is essential. Not all can hope to be satisfied, but this does not inevitably involve discrimination and, to be a nation, the people must learn to think nationally. The Africans were not consulted when different ethnic groups were introduced by the colonial powers to assist their government but are quite content that they should remain, provided they abandon their traditional loyalties and accept their new identity. This is not more than the Africans ask of themselves: the Masai, the Kikuyu, and the Luo must learn foremost to be Kenyan, if Kenya is to survive.

The division of Africans amongst themselves was not, unfortunately, discouraged by the colonial powers. A territory was ruled as a whole but administered at the lowest levels through the existing tribal mechanism. Naturally, each tribe remained weaker than the whole, knowing of each other only through the government information services. Trade between the African tribes was not possible. Schools were run separately. Suspicions remained and traditional rivalries were not forgotten. The most important factors which had brought the African tribes closer together were common suffering under the colonial power, the development of townships and cities in which different groups of people could meet and exchange ideas, and the growth of senior high schools often situated in one province but attended by students from all parts of the country. In Kenya, this was especially true of the Alliance High School, the Mangu High School, Maseno High School and Kagumo High School, and there are now others.

In essence the two party system seemed to Africans expensive and irrelevant at this stage of development; the basic issues were common to all, and the one party was a positive unifying force for nationhood and a protection of national security. Africa accepts its responsibilities in world affairs but should not be the battlefield for the quarrels of others.

It follows, of course, that the rulers of a one-party state must accept that they have perhaps a greater responsibility than other rulers.

Kenya was to advance, and there was not reason to believe that true democracy, government by consent with the active participation of the people, would not continue to flourish. Kenya was determined to be constructive and should be receptive to ideas and suggestions from all. Mzee Jomo Kenyatta created the firm foundation upon which her destinies could be planned. If her future leaders abuse his trust, they will have only themselves to blame. The tragedy will not be whom to blame but who will suffer as a consequence of failure.

23

Kenya and East African Economic Integration

The East African experience in economic integration was an often cited example of the successes and the inherent problems of economic union. Peter Robson, William A. Hance and Arthur Hazelwood among others examined the East African example at length, and this along with the several official bodies such as the Raisman Commission and the Blumenthal Report produced a substantial amount of data relevant to emergent states.

The East African states, Kenya, Uganda and Tanzania retained several factors which made the integration attempt more established but were also illustrative of the potential problems. Like many former colonies, the French-speaking UDEAC stated as an example, the East African States had a history of attempts at unification, or at least non-duplication of services. The earliest institution was a customs union between Kenya and Uganda in 1917.[1] Other unified institutions and services arose from the needs of the developing areas. Joint administration of Kenya, Uganda, and Tanganyika was established in matters of revenue, transport, and tariffs. These services in turn came under interterritorial administration in 1948 with the formation of the East Africa High Commission, later to be replaced by the East African Common Services Organization (EACSO) in 1961. The services administered included the railways and harbors (EAR&H), the East African Airways and various communication, statistical, technical and revenue-collecting agencies. Equally important was the fact that all three nations operated under a single currency until 1966. The services of EACSO were administered first by the East African High Commission and later by EACSO itself, and were divided into those that were self-contained operationally and financially, and those that received aid from the participating states as financial and technical aid from the United Kingdom.

Resources

East Africa covers some 680,000 square miles with a population of some 28 million (1966).[2] Agriculture was the primary activity broken down according to William A. Hance as follows: Uganda 57 percent of the gross domestic product (GDP) or 80 percent of total exports, Kenya 39.3 percent of the GDP, 75 percent of the exports, Tanganyika (Tanzania) 58 percent of the GDP and 81 percent of the exports.[3] Mineral assets include copper (Uganda), diamonds and gold (Tanganyika/Tanzania), and soda (Kenya) as well as some limestone, mica, phosphate, and tin.

In terms of industry, the three nations included the processing of the agricultural and mineral outputs, manufacturing of textiles, shoes, clothing, beer, cement, furniture, bricks, and containers, and services such as printing and vehicle repair.

Movement of these goods was accomplished by rail and road transport to the interior and to the coastal ports.[4] Primary movement of goods was by rail.[5] In comparison with the rest of Africa the rail and road network of East Africa was very good, but improvement both in quantity and quality was required. In particular need were both the primary and secondary road systems of Tanzania and the area around Lake Victoria.[6]

Trade, Organization and Expenses

Despite the assets listed above, Kenya, Uganda and Tanzania had to import much of their goods. In 1966, this difference amounted to roughly 16 million pounds deficit incurred primarily by Kenya. While the need for such integrated institutions as EACSO was obvious, the East African Common Market was less obvious, and at the same time involved more policy decisions that were open to debate. The criticisms arising from the operation of EACSO and EAR&H included charges that the organization had Kenyan orientation due to the location of its headquarters and workshops at Nairobi, less than equal benefits for the inputs involved for certain services, and that territorial viewpoints often superseded those of the organization.

With these criticisms applied to the Common Services, it was not difficult to imagine the escalation of such problems with regard to the Common Market. One result was the formation of the Raisman Commission (1961–62) to state recommendations for the improved operations of both the Common Services and the Common Market. One key recommendation was the modification of revenue distribution with the introduction of the distribution pool, which as an independent source of revenue could have enabled the non self-contained services to function "with greater certainty" and to "promote a more efficient use of funds between services by enabling the High Commission to function as a single authority, able ... to administer its services from the point of view of the whole of East Africa rather than as an agency of territorial governments."[7] The Distributable Pool, using combined revenues of the three territories, allotted half to a General Fund and the other half was to be divided equally among the participants.

However, by 1964, not only the Common Market but the Common Services as well were threatened. The monetary system under the East African Currency Board had used a single currency from 1919, yet despite the outside recommendations of the 1963 Blumenthal Report not to establish a separate currency and banking system (referring specifically to Tanganyika), by 1965, all three territories chose to establish separate Central Banks. Kenya did not choose to do so. It had no choice! Tanzania was first in establishing new currency and breaking the East African Currency Board.

On the issue of the Common Market as a whole, the adjustment problems seen by the Raisman Commission did not, in the government's view, offset the advantages of integration. Arthur Hazelwood points out that there was no synchronization of policy, and specifically no attempt to control the market mechanism. In addition, it was argued that the operation of the market worked in favor of Kenya, particularly in the area of industrial development, affecting not only Kenya but Uganda and Tanzania by virtue of location and shipping costs.[8]

In order to rectify this, a conference was held at Kampala in Uganda. Drawn up in April of 1964 (Kenya did not ratify because of the currency issues), the Kampala Agreements presented five points which enabled a more equitable distribution of economic goals and profits. Included was, (1) a shift in the distribution of production by those firms operating in two or more of the countries, (2) the reallocation of certain major industries between the countries, (3) the establishment of quotas on interterritorial trade, (4) the increase of sales to turn trade deficits into surpluses, and (5) the establishment of inducements and allocation of industry in order to obtain an equal distribution of industrial development.

Such were the Kampala Agreements, and, as argued by both Robson and Hazelwood, if they had been implemented with the goal of integration in mind they would have enabled continued operation. The reality, however, differed from theory. Post-Kampala actions included the establishment of three separate currencies and central banks, a unilateral Tanzanian restriction on Kenyan and Ugandan products, and the threat of dissolving not only the Common Market arrangements but the long-established Common Services Organization as well.

As a result, a Ministerial Commission was formed in late 1965 under Professor Kjeld Philip of Denmark. Its framework and tasks were designated as follows:

> To examine existing arrangements in East Africa between Kenya, Tanzania, and Uganda on matters of mutual interest and having due regard to the views of the respective governments to make agreed recommendations on the following matters:
>
> (a) How the East African Common Market can be maintained and strengthened and principles on which and the manner in which the Common Market can in the future be controlled and regulated.
>
> (b) The arrangements necessary for effective operation of the Common Market consequential upon the establishment of separate currencies.
>
> (c) The extent to which services at present maintained in common between the three countries can be continued and the form which such services should take.
>
> (d) The extent to which (if at all) new services can be provided in common between the three countries and the form which such services should take.
>
> (e) The manner in which the common services should be financed.
>
> (f) The extent to which the management of different services can be located in different parts of East Africa.
>
> (g) The legal, administrative and constitutional arrangements most likely to promote effective cooperation between the East African countries in the light of the recommendations made under paragraphs (a), (b), (c), (d), (e) and (f).[9]

The recommendations of the Philip Commission, which were adopted and signed by the three states in June of 1967, provided comprehensive changes in the economic structures and operations between the countries. With a legal foundation in the Treaty for East African Cooperation, the recommendations established an East African Economic Community including a Common Market. Both Hazelwood and Robson point to this

Treaty as "an impressive witness of its sponsors' dedication to East African unity."[10]

Among the provisions of the Treaty was the decentralization of the Common Services headquarters at Nairobi, the supplementing of the East African Authority with ministers of each state, the reorganization of Common Services into public corporations and the establishment of Councils to assist the Authority in the areas of the Common Market, Finance, Planning and Research. In economic terms international trade of indigenous goods is to be non-restrictive with the exceptions of basic food staples, a transfer tax was to be imposed, as well as a gradual phasing out of the Distributable Pool, the use of the General Funds only for specific expenditures without the establishment of surpluses, and the establishment of an East African Development Bank. This last institution was of particular importance to Tanzania and Uganda in terms of financing industrial development.

Despite the comprehensive recommendations there was still the problem that plagued the member states since the inception of integration, and noted by Peter Robson as a possible obstacle; that was the diversion of additional industry to Tanzania and Uganda in order to be on an equal footing with Kenya, which despite deficits in contributing to the operation of EACM still had both more and more diversified industry than the other two states.[11] Finally the ever-present influence of politics might have created new strains on the political reasons for economic integration if the economic terms were less and less equitable to the member states.[12]

The East African integration experience was notable for several reasons. While other African states, particularly the former French colonies, have had experience with common administration, none has had the degree of the East African Common Services, particularly in the post-independence stage. The institutions and operations of EASCO and EACM by the physical location of the administrative centers contributed debate on continued operation. The disproportionate financing of services in relation to benefits received constituted another factor (Uganda contributing to the Desert Locust Control was not a relevant problem in Uganda's case), as well as the fact that the union was threatened with dissolution due to the inability of the existing structures to respond to change. The East African Economic Community was an example of the high degree of effective operation of economic integration as well as those factors which could have promoted its downfall or minimize its effectiveness. In both areas there were valuable insights to be gained by other developing nations considering economic unions.

In the end, the East African Community collapsed because there was no will to make it succeed—particularly in Tanzania and less so in Uganda.

In this period of globalization and its challenges, the well-being of single nation's political and economic stability within increasingly complex interdependence will require regional economic and political fusion. Europe, after so many centuries of independent nation-states, is moving closer and closer to some form of political and economic fusion.

Perhaps, the East African leaders may learn from the European experiences that no country or nation can claim to be self-sufficient, in almost any circumstances.

24

Postscript

What then was to be the future of Kenya?

First in the broadest sense, there was to be development. The attainment of independence, though crucial, was in the long run but the initial step in the achievement of nationhood and the realization of that prosperity for which all nations, individually and collectively, must strive. Kenya was still essentially a land of tribal society, whether African, European or Asian, and the mass of the people had yet to discover a true sense of national identity and purpose. The problem was one of immense complexity, but overcoming it was essential.

All Kenyans appreciated the advantages of a communal life. The Africans especially accepted completely the responsibilities and comforts of a well-run society in which each man and woman had an essential part to play. However, at the beginning this was on the basis of the tribal unit, and the problem was to demonstrate that the idea could be worked on a national scale, without in any way lessening the commitment of the individual. It was in some ways easy to achieve that national identity when organizing the struggle for independence (the advantages were self-evident and universal), but how do you persuade a man in Kisumu that it is in his and his country's long-term interest to build a tea processing factory at Muranga, and that Muranga is sufficiently secure as a location?

However, Kenya was not the first country to encounter such problems and she was fortunate in her leaders, who were not prepared to ride roughshod over individuals in the interests of a magnificent five-year plan. For example, methods of farming in Kenya had to undergo radical alteration. The standard of living of millions could not be raised if each acre was cultivated in isolation. However, although there was to be cooperation in marketing, the supply of implements, processing, bulk buying, etc., there could at least be no nationwide nationalization of the land. To take an African's land from him, even to return it to him as a member of a community, was unthinkable, and might have done more than anything else to destroy his sense of purpose.

This is not to say that there could not be in time any direction of industry or control of development, or even nationalization. At the beginning, the idea of national planning was quite acceptable, even in the most sophisticated societies, whether West or East. What had to be understood by potential investors in Kenya was that there was no doctrinaire policy on matters such as nationalization and the flow of currency. Kenya reserved the right to make the best use of her resources in the interests of her people, who should have, inevitably, been offered first priority. It stood to reason that it served those interests to encourage foreign investment and to offer substantial inducements to investors, provided the bargain favored Kenya and was a purely commercial transaction. Having fought for the right to do so, Kenyans were to rule Kenya.

Who are Kenyans? Anyone who will commit himself mind and body to Kenya, whatever his race or creed. This was the avowed policy of the Kenyan government but, perhaps understandably in view of recent history, there were those among the minority races who found the policy difficult to accept. Nevertheless, it was true. At that time, Kenya was undergoing a crash program of "Africanization," and this was essential in many respects. Very simply, apart from reasons of national pride, the balance was all wrong. Key positions in government should at that stage have been held by Africans, or at least by those who had proved themselves committed to Kenya. Under the former colonial administration, very roughly the top third of government was kept for European expatriates who reserved the right, which they in many cases exercised, to return to England on retirement. The middle third was basically, though not so exclusively, Asian. The Africans took the lowest place. This state of affairs was now reversed; the best qualified Africans assumed the higher posts, and for the time being the other races had lower priority. At the most, this could not last more than a few years. Once the balance between the races became more realistic, then the usual criteria was to apply. In the long run, proven loyalty to Kenya was to be the only relevant virtue. At the independence celebrations in Nairobi in December of 1963, some of the loudest cheers were reserved for Briton Bruce Mackenzie when he took the oath of office (in Swahili) as Minister for Agriculture!

On Africanization, Senior Lecturer in Economics at Makerere and Yale Gharam Ghai observes:

> The progress made in Africanization of civil services in the last few years is remarkable by any standards. In Kenya for example, or at the time of independence, only one post in seven of the higher ranks of the civil service was held by an African. Even in the lower executive and technical grades less than half of the staff were Africans. By the end of 1966, well over half of the higher ranks, and an average of three-quarters of the executive and technical grades had been Africanized....[1]

Apart from the challenge of nationhood, perhaps the greatest problem facing the Kenyan government was the proper exploitation of the country's resources, most obviously by a degree of industrialization, and the additional problems which this brought in its wake. One particularly difficult problem was the right balance between industry and agriculture, town and country.

At all costs, Kenya tried to avoid the historical fate of the Eastern European countries where all wealth and privilege were concentrated in the towns and the lot of the countrymen changed barely with the centuries—India, perhaps, although for vastly different reasons. In Kenya, the balance of development was to be planned carefully, and, as Kenyans were largely an agricultural people, they must start in the country where often the return for modest expenditure could be staggeringly greater than, for example, the cost of a new steel mill. It was a question of priorities, and the problem was not only economic but also political as the people very rightly wanted results.

Kenya had inherited some enormous problems. Already the land of some tribes, notably the Kikuyu, would not support the increasing population. The result was a drift of unskilled labor and young people to the towns and a consequent unemployment problem. These people were demoralized, in many cases unfitted to return to their homelands (where there was no room for them), and not unnaturally they looked to the government to give them work and restore their self-respect. The government and employers of all races took on supernumerary staff, but the saturation point was soon reached.

There were vast tracts of Kenya, potentially productive, but at that time unused. No nation can afford such extravagance; resettlement of some areas was essential. This included the expropriation of some land on European farms but, it should be emphasized, not the farms as such. All land at that time under useful cultivation was left undisturbed—those

European settlers who had decided to stay, and had confidence in the government's word, were welcome. Indeed, it would have been incredible if a responsible government would have countenanced any other policy when the economy of the country depended so much on the efforts of all who had committed themselves as Kenyans.

The introduction of modern farming methods, quite apart from industrialization, had special problems in Kenya. After the disastrous floods in the Western Region, those Luo who were finding a bare subsistence from farming (in some cases relying on only one cow) were given higher land to plant with tea. At least half returned when the water subsided, unconvinced of the long-term value of a cash crop against an immediate return from their cattle. However, those who stayed harvested their tea and proved to their more cautious brethren that new ways could compete with the old. But the process was delicate and the only lasting solution was proper education on a national scale. Kenya was committed to free primary education for all and is set fair to achieve this goal.

But what could she do when all have had their primary education? Again, industrialization and modernizing agriculture were planned and technical schools were established to train for industrial jobs. There were special problems in teaching, not only the mechanics of such jobs, but also their essential value. A part of the population had to discard the traditional values, entirely related to land and the security it provided, and obviously social services must be developed for them.

The magnitude of these tasks was apparent even to those long used to modern European society; to reorient the economy of a country and not only maintain the basic values of the people, but forge a national loyalty in the process. But the tasks were real and Kenya was ready for them. Little wonder that Africa is a continent of revolution—there will be more surprises yet.

When Kenya attained her independence in 1963, the national slogan which Mzee Jomo Kenyatta initiated was "Harambee," meaning "Let us pull together." This national slogan was meant to be a total commitment by the politicians, intellectuals or elites, professors teaching at the universities and colleges, the school teachers, and church leaders and their congregations, and all those who were managing various government agencies or bureaucracies. It was also meant to create a sense of unity or nation-building.

Before independence, that is, when Kenya was still a British colony, there were numerous finger-pointings against the British colonial administration. There were, no doubt, legitimate reasons for all these finger-pointings. They were, however, over after independence. The only finger-pointings which remained were against neo-colonialism—but this was not a Kenyan problem alone. It was a continental problem, and indeed a big problem for the Third World countries. The Africans should now look themselves in the mirror.

As the first finger-pointings against the British ended in 1963, the second finger-pointings were now directed against their African leaders who did not seem to subscribe to the ideal goals, aims and objectives of the national slogan, "Harambee." This problem was real, and it was not limited to Kenya.

The African leaders had (and still have) good opportunities to learn about their developments from two important countries, who have a long history of economic, political, cultural and scientific development—the United Kingdom, one of the industrial powers in Europe, and Japan, an industrial power in Asia. How could a small country like England, from the time of the Spanish Armada, with a population of about 10 million people at that time, be able to challenge the entire world? What was the secret behind this? A sense of unity and grim determination? How could a small country like Japan, with only 145,869 square miles, be able to withstand and compete with giant industrialized Europe and North Americas? Perhaps unity of purpose, determination to achieve progress, and a sense of "go-ahead" appeared to have been the keys to these two countries' progress. It is also true to say that the religions which their institutions had adopted—Christianity and Shintoism—were compatible with progress.

The African leaders, after independence, were faced with monumental problems and responsibilities. However, some of them became susceptible to human failing and practiced corruption in its various forms. Generally, corruption is a process of accepting bribes, playing favor for monetary or political influence, nepotism, or ethnic favor at the expense of national interests.

Did Kenyatta's government eliminate corruption from 1963 to 1970? It would be ill-advised to think or suggest that Kenya was corruption-proof between 1963 and 1970. However, corruption was curtailed considerably. It was not allowed, at the time in question, to become a part of Kenyan culture.

After independence, did Kenyatta's government deal with the long-term goals of the nationalists, which included complete Africanization of the country's politics, economics and culture? The answer appears to be a "qualified yes," qualified because to expect a complete accomplishment of the above nationalist expectations from 1963 to 1970 appears to be unreasonable, considering the multiple problems which the Kenyatta government inherited as of 1963.

African intellectuals, professors, and school teachers had a special responsibility for advising, guiding and advancing the cause of "Harambee" rather than becoming armchair critics of Kenyatta's government. In addition, the country was mortally wounded, damaged and hurt by some of those who were engaging in corruption in all its forms.

The aim here is to tell the truth, and the truth is that the Africans are far, far behind in world history. It appears as if they will not catch up easily or quickly. Indeed, one could go so far as to say that maybe the mentality of some of the African leaders who have emerged requires another as yet undiscovered mental discipline besides psychology. Broadly, this has been true not of Kenya alone but continentally.

As a matter of overview, the Africans appear to have lost their pride, dignity, reputation and respect internationally.

Fostering tribalism and disunity did not end in 1963 after the British transferred political power to the Africans. However, it is true to say that the Kenyatta government appeared to have tried very hard to alleviate these problems, for example, picking Daniel Arap Moi, a Masai, as his vice-president, appointing a non–Kikuyu as minister of defense, and distributing the appointment of ambassadorships abroad among the different ethnic groups. This was also true of the government's departments and agencies. The speaker of the Parliament was a non–Kikuyu. The senior judge of the Supreme Court was a non–Kikuyu—and the list went on.

Basically, Kenyatta was very concerned about other peoples' sensitivities and he was always cautious not to hurt other people, especially non–Kikuyu, even Europeans and Asians. For example, after Kenya's independence, there was a kind of festival at Gatundu in Kiambu District. Jomo Kenyatta, at that time the prime minister of Kenya, and Malcolm Macdonald (Macdonald the Good) attended this festival. As the festivities were going on, a "muthirigu" song and dance were performed. It should be recalled "muthirigu" was initiated in 1929–1930 against the missionary churches who were vehemently against some of the Kikuyu customs, especially the idea of female circumcision. Both Kenyatta and Malcolm Macdonald—the last of the British governors in Kenya—danced to the "muthirigu" song. Ordinarily, "muthirigu" songs invoked very offensive and emotional ballads.

At the end of the festivities, the performers asked Jomo Kenyatta's permission to revive "muthirigu" now that Kenya was independent. Jomo Kenyatta said emphatically "No." He advised that the wording of "muthirigu" songs was offensive and that it was not the appropriate time for it—there was no need for it now. He emphasized the fact that he did not want the idea of "raking the past."

It would appear difficult to have put the idea of "Harambee" in actual application if the government ministers, under-secretaries, and individuals kept on fostering tribal strife or raking the past tribal discords.

This does not mean that scholars and other social scientists should refrain from criticizing the government and pointing out its shortcomings. Constructive suggestions and criticisms are essential, but being cynical in one's analysis of the working of the government and asking that government to perform things which have taken other governments in other countries many years or centuries to achieve appears to be unreasonable.

Kenyatta's government did not create a utopian society in Kenya, nor try to create one, but it appeared to have gone a long way in a short time after 1963 to alleviate the Kenyan's economic, social, political, cultural and agrarian difficulties. In the process, some mistakes were made. The government tried to do everything at once with limited resources. Some government ministers tried—and succeeded—to enrich themselves at the expense of the government. Perhaps the president did not know what some of his greedy and corrupt ministers were doing behind closed doors. This is especially true from 1970 to 1978 when he was frequently sick and had a series of heart attacks. Those around him during his period of sickness were doing things in the name of Mzee Jomo Kenyatta, yet some of these things were not in the interests of Kenya and the Kenyan people.

Was Kenyatta involved in the Mau Mau movement?

In order to answer this question, one should not expect a clear-cut "yes" or "no." If the answer is "yes" one may be accused of being speculative, simply because Kenyatta himself denied at his trial very vigorously that he was not a member or the manager of the Mau Mau movement. If one says "no," again one may be accused of being speculative, but there are instances which tend to indicate that the answer to this question is "yes"—that Kenyatta was involved in the Mau Mau movement, though it would be untrue that he was a manager of the movement.

Kenyatta was a very good speaker. His voice as he spoke resonated like the voice of a lion in the field roaring loudly before he or she is ready to go hunting. He was also a master of figurative speeches—and he did use figurative speeches very often in his public speeches and meetings.

By way of illustration, at a general public meeting in Kaloleni Hall in 1952, just before the State of Emergency was declared, Kenyatta stressed very strongly and enthusiastically that "the tree of liberty is watered by blood." He said this repeatedly. He also posed a question to the audience and asked, "If I hold a lion by the head, will you be able to withstand its scratches? Scratches will cause some blood," he added.

How would one interpret this figurative speech? In his autobiography,

Harry Thuku said that George Ndegwa, one of the old Kenyatta colleagues and one of the founders of the Kikuyu Central Association, claimed that Kenyatta, while in detention, sent a letter or message to the freedom fighters in the forest that Harry Thuku should not be harmed or killed because of his past struggle for the African people of Kenya. Rumor or not, did Kenyatta ever deny or contradict Harry Thuku's hearsay?

Commenting on what he thought was a clarion call by Kenyatta to arms, Gucu Gikonyo writes:

> I remember a meeting at Thika just before the outbreak of hostilities, when Mzee Kenyatta asked us whether we wanted to fight for our land. We replied "Yes." "Are you waiting then until the white man has bred in this country like rabbits?" "No," we replied, "We want to fight now!" "Then realize that the tree of freedom is watered not with water but with blood!"[2]

If one opposed Mau Mau, he or she would be stigmatized as "unpatriotic." If one supported the Mau Mau, he or she would be equally stigmatized as being "unpatriotic." Can under these circumstances and for the sake of scholarship, academic freedom, and freedom of speech, one be given a chance to ask and answer the above question?

Historically speaking, no one has ever claimed to be a custodian of "truth," and those who attempted the claim did not succeed—even the Popes during the period of the Reformation. There should be an open society.

One does not have to mitigate methods and techniques used by the Mau Mau rebellion against the Europeans in Kenya. However, there has been a tendency to be preoccupied with these methods and techniques, quite disregarding the facts as to why the techniques were used. Describing them as "horrible" or "filthy and barbaric" tends to obscure the causes. Condemning them in whatever negative adjective we have in our languages is almost like mitigating the causes and reasons. "Why Mau Mau?"

Civilized Europeans before and after 1952 appear to forget some of the horrible, barbaric, primitive acts committed in the course of European history.

How can one forget, for instance, what the Jacobins did during the French Revolution in France? How can one forget, while describing the Mau Mau methods and techniques, "The Reign of Terror" under Robespierre in the name of "Rights of Man?" There were "Jacobins" and other ultra-extremists in the Mau Mau Rebellion, as there were during the French Revolution and among the extreme revolutionaries during the Abbasid Revolution against the Umayyads in the Arabian Peninsula in A.D. 750!

Umayyad officials who were already dead had their graves dug out or opened so that their remains of bones could be punished.

Was Mau Mau a nationalist movement or a tribal organization? The answer is that Mau Mau was a nationalist movement. The grievances which leaders of the Mau Mau movement ventilated were: land alienation, racial discrimination in all walks of life, equal racial representation—only to mention a few. All had national implications in the entirety of Kenya. All these were practiced against all Africans of Kenya and not against the Kikuyu people alone.

On this question, Carl G. Rosberg, Jr., and John Nottingham write:

> Although oathing strengthened the Kikuyu organizational ability to challenge the colonial state, it nonetheless had the additional effect of limiting the institutional spread of the national movement to non–Kikuyu groups. This dilemma was not unrecognized by the Kikuyu leadership, for they envisaged the creation of other tribal oaths which would serve to mobilize and commit non–Kikuyu people to their style of militant nationalism. Lack of sufficient time and the administration's success in compartmentalizing and controlling African political activity were two important factors that prevented this from occurring in any extensive manner. Thus, the pattern of nationalism as it unfolded stemmed from a rationally conceived strategy in search of political power within a context of structured conditions which severely inhibited the growth of a country-wide national organizational movement.[3]

What Carl G. Rosberg, Jr., and John Nottingham write appears to be true, because Paul Ngei of Akamba was committed. Ochieng Oneko and Odede, both of the Luo people, were committed. As a matter of fact, Alexander Onyango Owino, who belonged to the Luo, was to be sent to Central Nyanza after a big meeting at Kandara, in Muranga, to start organizing and administering the Luo oath, which was binding according to the Luo tradition. Unfortunately, he was arrested in 1953, before he was ready to go to Kisumu from Nairobi. In addition, John O'Wachika, a Luhya of North Nyanza, was also committed. (Incidentally, Alexander Onyango Owino was nicknamed by the Kikuyu in Nairobi, "Wakirigu"— meaning the son of uncircumcised woman. He seems to have liked his nickname!)

Could there have been a Mau Mau movement without Kenyatta? While this may sound like a hypothetical question, one may ask: Could there have been an American Revolution without George Washington? In addition, could there have been a Glorious Revolution without individuals like the third Duke of Richmond, the third Duke of Crafton, Richard

Brinsley Sheridan, and Charles James Fox? The answer appears to be "yes" to all these questions. These revolutions were inevitable.

Was the Kenya African Union lacking as an instrument for political participation because it was an elitist organization of an isolated educated moderate African middle class, with little grass roots and without mass support?

It would be highly unfair to answer this question in the affirmative. Before the formation of the Kenya African Union, immediately after Mathu was nominated as the first African member of the Kenya Legislative Council, there was no political outlet for the Africans in Kenya. All political associations had been banned in 1940. Consequently, when the Kenya African Union emerged, it was as if there suddenly was "political fresh air" for the Kenyan Africans, so to speak.

It should also be remembered that political restrictions placed on the Kenya African Union and its leaders were extremely severe and inhibitive. Public meetings—which were absolutely necessary and were used as mass media in the absence of radio and television—were held under restricted circumstances.

Public meetings were also used as platforms for raising funds for the organization. Sometimes, the movement was financially embarrassed. In 1947–1949, after Mr. Mbiyu Koinange went to study at the London School of Economics and Political Science, Kenyatta was running both the Kenya African Union and the Teacher's College, Githunguri, simultaneously. Both were in dire need of money. Money had to be raised from the public at large. It was very difficult. There was no sizable African middle class which could have supported the Kenya African Union sufficiently alone without mass participation.

Raising money—necessary to support the movement in Kenya—was very difficult in the 1940s and the 1950s. There was no other way of raising the money except during the public meetings, which were held in Nairobi, Mombasa, and other towns and townships. A town like Nakuru was not, in those days, an ideal place for the Kenya African Union to hold a public meeting. The police commissioner at Nakuru was extremely hostile to the Kenya African Union. Nakuru was in the heartland of the White Highlands. It was regarded as an English country town. It was the home of an anti–African weekly paper, the *Kenya Weekly News*.

Were all Europeans in Kenya hostile to the African cause? As in the case of the Indians, the word "all" here would be unfair in its usage in a general statement. There were a few Europeans who were genuinely interested in the African cause. Some of those could be found among the European missionaries to start with. For example, when Sir Edward Northey, the first ex–military governor of Kenya after the World War of 1914–1918, authorized the Kenyan colonial government to direct African labor into the European farms, some influential missionaries were horrified. Dr. J. W. Arthur of the Church of Scotland Mission at Kikuyu, the Anglican Bishop of Mombasa and others formed an alliance, and sent a memorandum of protest to the Colonial Office in London.

It is not far-fetched to say that the missionary protest through their influential contact in England—by the name of J. H. Oldham, who was the head of International Missionary Council in London—had an indirect influence in the declaration of the White Paper of 1923. Other missionaries like Hooper of C.M.S. Kahuhia in Fort Hall (now Muranga), W.P. Knapp of G.M.S. Kambui, and Barlow of C.S.M. Tumutumu were also deeply interested in the African cause. In addition, there were European teachers and headmasters who were interested in African educational progress or advancement. Among these were: G. A. Grieve of the Alliance High School, C. Francis of Alliance High School, Edward Lindley, Principal of Kambui Primary School, who used to have lunches with the African teachers and socialize with them on equal basis regularly, the Rev. Bewes of C.M.S. Weithaga in Fort Hall (Muranga), and Dr. Leakey's family at C.M.S. Kabete.

Among the European settlers, one might give a rough guess that 95.5 percent of the population was hostile to the Africans. There were exceptions, but these were few and far between. From those very few, one could mention Sydney S. Carlin who had a huge farm south of Lumbwa Station on the way to Kericho. He was assisted by his relative C. R. Coulson to run the farm. He had many African squatters working on his farm, and he had allowed his African squatters to establish an elementary school for their children's education. There was also a church conducted by the African Christians who were working on the farm. Captain Carlin, as he was called, returned to England in 1937 and left the farm with C. R. Coulson.

When his former house servants learned about Captain Carlin's death in 1942, they were very sorrowful. In his will, he had authorized that 5,500 shillings in Kenyan money be given to his trusted house servant Karanja Njai Kamau, who was managing the entire household; 5,500 shillings be given to Kende, who was managing the cattle ranch; and £500 to be given as a pension to his trusted farm clerk, Nathaniel Arap Chumo. This was an astounding extension of goodwill, considering the attitudes of the majority of the European settlers toward their African workers. People of goodwill and kind hearts will always be remembered for their deeds, irrespective of their races, religions and nationalities. Good deeds and attitudes have no color.

Captain Carlin was eventually killed in Malta in 1942 during the Second World War. On Chepsion farm, which was left with C. R. Coulson, the policy of treating the African squatters well was continued. Mr. Coulson used to issue a huge supply of quinine for the African workers.

In Lumbwa, on the way to Kisumu, there was a European farmer who used to socialize with his African squatters very often. He would be found roasting goat meat with his African workers. He was nicknamed "Karia Mburi"—one who eats goat meat. To this, S. V. Cook should be added. He was one of the European representatives in the Kenya Legislative Council. He had a mind of his own, and sometimes sided with E. W. Mathu, the African representative in the Kenya Legislative Council. This was true especially during the debate on Colonial Paper 210 in 1947. There was also Mr. Smith who had a farm at Loudiani, and he had also allowed his African squatters to establish a school and a church, which were run by evangelical African Christians working on the farm. Above all, there was one Sir Derek Erskine, a European member of the Kenya Legislative Council, who also managed a very successful tools and farming equipment business in Nairobi. He fought valiantly for Kenyatta's release and bitterly opposed the Kipande system and racial discrimination.

These very few Europeans, even though they constituted about .5 percent, should not be forgotten. Individuals like these were like William Wiberforce, Mother Teresa or Pope Paul II, and they deserve a mention in history.

In conclusion, it must be mentioned that most African education was initially provided by the missionary schools. Indeed, most of the educated African leaders in 1920s, 1930s, 1940s and 1950s were products of the missionary schools. To omit this mention would be tantamount to committing an intellectual atrocity.

Comparatively speaking, the Britons who live or reside in the United Kingdom are highly civilized, generous, innovative, creative, determined, gentle and polite people, who are protective and possessive of their British Isles. Why did they send such abrasive, rude and inconsiderate members of their society abroad to establish their colonies? It was unfortunate.

Chapter Notes

INTRODUCTION

1. D. D. Rooney and E. Halladay, *The Building of Modern Africa* (London: George G. Harrap & Co. Ltd., 1966), p. 9.
2. *Ibid.*, p. 11.
3. *Ibid.*, p. 12.
4. George Bennett, *Kenya: A Political History* (London: Oxford University Press, 1963), p. 2.
5. B. A. Ogot and J. A. Kieran, *Zamani: A Survey of East African History* (Longmans of Kenya, 1968), p. 255.
6. *Ibid.*, p. 256.
7. *Ibid.*
8. *Ibid.*, p. 259.

CHAPTER 1

1. Report of the East African Commission 1953–1955, p. 180.
2. J. S. Mangat, *A History of the Asians in Africa* (London: Oxford University Press, 1969).
3. B. A. Ogot and J. A. Kieran, *Zamani: A Survey of East African History* (Longmans of Kenya, 1968), p. 263.

CHAPTER 2

1. Josiah Mwangi Kariuki, *Mau Mau Detainee* (London: Oxford University Press, 1963), p. xvi.

2. Roland Oliver, and Gervase Mathew, *History of East Africa, I* (London: Oxford University Press, 1963), p. 415.
3. George Delf, *Jomo Kenyatta* (London: Victor Gollancz, Ltd., 1961), p. 31.
4. *The Diaries of Lord Lugard*, edited by Margery Perham (London: Faber & Faber, 1959), pp. 318–319. See Ripharch K. P. Pankhurst, *Kenya: The History of Two Nations* (London: Independent Publishing Company, 1954), p. 19. See also Ewart S. Grogan and Arthur H. Sharp, *From the Cape of Cairo* (London, 1900), pp. 350–363.
5. *Op. cit.*, Oliver and Mathew, p. 397.
6. Lord Hailey, *An African Survey* (London: Oxford University Press, 1938), p. 742.
7. *Ibid.*, p. 730–731.
8. Lord Altrincham, *Kenya's Opportunity: Memories, Hopes and Ideas* (London: Faber and Faber, 1955), p. 26.
9. *Ibid.*
10. *Ibid.*
11. Z. A. Marsh and G. Kingsnorth, *An Introduction to the History of East Africa* (London: Cambridge University Press, 1957), p. 175.

CHAPTER 3

1. W. M. Ross, *Kenya From Within* (London: 1927), p. 44.
2. *Ibid.*

217

3. George Bennett, *Kenya: A Political History* (London: Oxford University Press, 1963), p. 9.

4. Article by Professor Donald Rothchild in *Transaction*, January 1972, p. 23.

5. Martin L. Kilson, *Journal of Negro History*, *XL*, #2 "Land of the Kikuyu: A Study of the Relationship Between Land and Kikuyu Political Movements" (Howard University: Washington, D.C.), April 1955, pp. 112–113.

6. R. L. Buell, *The Native Problem in Africa* (New York: 1928), p. 317.

7. *Op. cit.*, Bennett, p. 24–25.

8. *Op. cit.*, Rothchild, p. 23.

CHAPTER 4

1. Lord Hailey, *An African Survey* (London: Oxford University Press), 1938, p. 746.

2. *Ibid.*, p. 747. See also Judgment of the High Court in the case brought by the Masai Tribe against the Attorney General of the East African Protectorate and others, CMD. 6939 (1913).

3. George Bennett, *Kenya: A Political History* (London: Oxford University Press, 1963), p. 37.

CHAPTER 5

1. See *East Africa In the Nineteenth and Twentieth Centuries* Book 2, by Anderson, John D. (Heinemann Educational Books, 1972), p. 362.

2. Papers Relating to Native Disturbances in Kenya, CMD. 1691 (1922), p. 3f.

CHAPTER 6

1. See *Kenya Historical Biographies*, chapter by Kenneth King on Harry Thuku, p. 178.

CHAPTER 7

1. C. W. Hobley, *Kenya from Chartered Company to Crown Colony* (London, 1929), p. 235.

2. Margery Perham, *Lugard: The Years of Authority 1890-1945* (London: Collins, St. James' Place, 1960), p. 677.

3. *Ibid.*

4. Lord Altrincham, *Kenya's Opportunity:*

Memories, Hopes and Ideas (London: Faber and Faber Ltd., 1955), pp. 191–2.

5. *Ibid.*, p. 197.

6. Elspeth Huxley and Margery Perham, *Race and Politics in Kenya* (New & Revised Edition) (London: Faber and Faber, 1956), p. 185. For further discussion on closer union of Kenya, Uganda, and Tanganyika, see the following sources: Cmd. 2904, 1927; Cmd. 3378, 1929; Cmd. 3573 and 3574 of 1930, No. 184, 1931; No. 29, 1931; Col. No. 57, 1931; Cmd. 4141, 1932; Cmd. 4083, 1932; Cmd. 4182, 1932.

CHAPTER 8

1. Ruth Slade, *King Leopold's Congo* (London: Oxford University Press, 1962), p. 141.

2. J. B. Webster, *The African Churches Among the Yoruba 1888-1902* (New York: Oxford University Press, 1965), pp. 43–44.

3. Oliver Roland, *The Missionary Factor in East Africa* (London: Longmans, 1965), pp. 34–35.

4. H. B. Thomas and R. Scott, *Uganda* (London: Oxford University Press, 1935), p. 19.

5. David E. Apter, *The Political Kingdom of Uganda* (New Jersey: Princeton University Press, 1961), p. 70.

6. *Ibid.*, p. 71.

7. MacKay, *MacKay of Uganda*, biography by his sister (London: Hodder and Stoughtan, 1890), p. 470.

8. *Op. cit.*, Apter, p. 80.

9. *Ibid.*, p. 81.

10. Ruth Slade, *Catholics and Protestants in the Congo* (London: Oxford University Press, 1968), pp. 84–5.

11. *Op. cit.*, Slade, pp. 89–90.

12. Pope Pius XI, *Pie XI et la Medicine aux Missions* (Catholic Missions, 1928), p. 38.

13. *Op. cit.*, Slade, p. 30.

14. *Ibid.*, pp. 91–4.

CHAPTER 9

1. Report by the Financial Commission, 1932, Cd. 4093, pp. 26–7.

CHAPTER 10

1. George Bennett, *Kenya: A Political History* (London: Oxford University Press, 1963), p. 21.

CHAPTER 15

1. E. W. Mathu, addressing the Kenya Legislative Council in January, 1948.

CHAPTER 16

1. See *An Autobiography* by Harry Thuku (Nairobi: Oxford University Press, 1970), p. 71.

CHAPTER 17

1. C. T. Stoneham, *Mau Mau* (London: Museum Press, 1953), p. 23.
2. R. D. Corfield, *Historical Survey of the Origins and Growth of Mau Mau.*
3. The Jubilee Book of the Church of Scotland Mission, Kenya Colony, 1898–1948, p. 14.
4. Frank Kitson, *Gangs and Counter-Gangs* (London: Barrie and Rockliff, 1960), p. 79.
5. See an article, *"Mau Mau,"* by Johnstone Muthiora, *Africa Report*, October 1967 (Washington, D.C.).

CHAPTER 18

1. Josiah Mwangi Kariuki, *Mau Mau Detainee* (Oxford University Press, London, 1963), pp. 32–33.
2. See *We Fought For Freedom* by Cucu G. Gikonyo (East Africa Publishing House, Nairobi, 1979), p. 49.
3. Warahiu Itote (General China), *Mau Mau in Action* (Transafrica Book Distributors, Nairobi, 1979), p. 73.
4. See D. Mukaru Nganga, "Mau Mau Loyalists and Politics 1952–1970 in Muranga" Seminar Paper No. 75 (University of Nairobi Institute of African Studies, 1977), pp. 4–5.
5. Franz Fanon, *The Wretched of the Earth* (New York: Grove Press, 1963), Chapter I Passim.

CHAPTER 20

1. Fay Carter, a chapter in *Kenya Historical Biographies* (East African Publishing House, 1971), pp. 30–31.

CHAPTER 22

1. William Hance, *African Economic Development* (New York: Frederick A. Praeger, Publishers, 1967), p. 111.
2. *Ibid.*, p. 111.
3. *Ibid.*
4. International Bank for Reconstruction and Development, *Economic Development of Kenya* (Maryland: John Hopkins Press, 1967), p. 27.
5. Reginald H. Green, *Economic Cooperation in Africa—Retrospect and Prospect* (England: Oxford University Press, 1967), p. 114.
6. "Kenya," *Africa Report* (Washington D.C.: The African American Institute, 1967), p. 84.
7. Ricard Cox, *Kenyatta's Country* (New York: Frederick A. Praeger, Publishers, 1967), p. 217.
8. Dr. F. H. Karanja, "Kenya After Independence," *African Affairs* (England: Royal African Society & Oxford University Press, 1966), p. 293.
9. *Op. cit.*, Karanja, p. 293.
10. *Op. cit.*, Green, p. 116.
11. *Ibid.*
12. *Ibid.*
13. *Ibid.*
14. *Op. cit.*, Karanja, p. 294.
15. "Kenya," *World Book Encyclopedia of the Nations* (New York: World Mark Press, Inc., 1967), p. 360.
16. *Op. cit.*, "Kenya," *World Book*, p. 360.
17. *Op. cit.*, "Kenya," *African Report*, p. 91.
18. *Ibid.*
19. *Op. cit.*, "Kenya," *African Report*, p. 91.
20. *Ibid.*
21. *Op. cit.*, "Kenya," *World Book* (1963), p. 344.
22. *Ibid.* (1967), p. 361.
23. *Ibid.*
24. *Op. cit.*, "Kenya," *African Report*, p. 91.
25. *Ibid.*
26. Hans Rutenber, *African Agricultural Production Development Policy in Kenya 1952–1965* (Germany: Springer-Verlag, 1966), p. 213.
27. Edward W. Soya, *The Geography of Modernization in Kenya* (New York: World Mark Press, Inc., 1967), p. 187.
28. O. Coit, "Kenya," *World Book* (1967), p. 362.
29. *Ibid.*
30. *Ibid.*
31. *Op. cit.*, "Kenya" *World Book*, p. 362.
32. *Op. cit.*, Karanja, p. 296.

33. *Op. cit.*, Cox, p. 219.
34. *Ibid.*
35. *Ibid.*
36. Reginald H. Green and Ann Seidman, *Unity or Poverty* (Maryland: Penguin Books, Inc., 1968), p. 73.
37. Humphrey Slade, *The Parliament of Kenya* (Kenya: East African Publishing House, 1967), p. 53.
38. *Kenya's New Five Year Development Plan 1970-1974* (Washington D.C.: Embassy of the Republic of Kenya, 1969), p. 17.
39. *Ibid.*
40. *Ibid.*, p. 18.
41. *Ibid.*, p. 20.
42. *Ibid.*, p. 21.
43. *Ibid.*, p. 22.
44. "World Leaders in the News: Jomo Kenyatta," *Almanac of Current World Leaders* (California: 1969), p. 32.

CHAPTER 23

1. Peter Robson, *Economic Integration in Africa* (Northwestern University Press, Evanston, 1968), p. 104.
2. *Ibid.*, p. 98.

3. William A. Hance, *African Economic Development (Rev)* (New York: F. A. Praeger, Publishers, 1967), p. 195.
4. *Ibid.*, p. 196.
5. *Ibid.*, p. 199.
6. *Op. cit.*, Robson, pp. 98–100.
7. *Ibid.*, p. 112.
8. Arthur Hazelwood (editor), *African Integration and Disintegration* (London: Oxford University Press, 1967), p. 94.
9. *Op. cit.*, Robson, p. 153.
10. *Ibid.*, p. 154.
11. *Ibid.*, p. 163.
12. *Ibid.*, p. 164.

CHAPTER 24

1. B. A. Ogot and J. A. Kieran, eds. *Zamani* (Nairobi: East African Publishing House and Longman, 1968), p. 397.
2. Gucu G. Gikonyo, *We Fought for Freedom (Tulipigania Uhuru)* (Nairobi: East African Publishing House, 1979), p. 328.
3. Carl G. Rosberg, Jr., and John Nottingham, *The "Mau Mau" Myth: Nationalism in Kenya* (Meridian, New American Library, New York, 1970), p. 354.

Bibliography

OFFICIAL PUBLICATIONS

African Education: A Statement of Policy (1951).

African Education in Kenya: Report of the Committee Appointed to Inquire into the Scope, Content and Methods of African Education, Its Administration and Finance and to Make Recommendations (1949).

British Government, *Kenya Land Commission: Evidence and Memoranda*, 3 Vols. and Report (London, 1934).

British Information Services, *Kenya Progress and Problems* (New York, Reference Division I.D. 1293, April, 1958).

Carothers, Dr. J. C., M. B., D. P. M., *The Psychology of Mau Mau* (Nairobi, 1954).

Cmd. 309, Kenya, *Proposals for New Constitutional Arrangements* (Her Majesty's Stationery Office, London, November, 1957).

Cmd. 369, *Kenya Dispatch on the New Constitutional Arrangements* (London: H. M. S. O., February, 1958).

Cmd. 9103, *Kenya Proposals for a Reconstruction of the Government* (London: H. M. S. O., 1954).

Colony and Protectorate of Kenya, *Sessional Paper No. 39* (1955–56).

Colony Office Report on the *Colony and Protectorate of Kenya* for the year 1956 (H. M. S. O., London, 1957).

Command 778 (London: June, 1959).

Command 795 (London: July, 1959).

The Constitution of Kenya (Nairobi: The Government Printer, 1969).

Constitutional Progress in Kenya, C. O. I., British Information Services (New York) under heading: "Facts about Kenya" No. R. 3051, May 1955, Classification C. 2b.

Corfield, F. D. *Historical Survey of the Origins and Growth of Mau Mau* (Colonial Office: 1960), "Command 1030."

Coutts, W. F., *Report of the Commissioner Appointed to Enquire into Methods for the Selection of African Representatives to the Legislative Council* (Nairobi: Government Printer, 1955).

Report of the Education Commission of the East Africa Protectorate (1919).

East African Education Commission Evidence, 1919.

East African Law Reports, Civil Case 626/1921, Vol. IX.

East Africa Royal Commission Report (London: H. M. S. O., 1953–55), "Command 9475."

Education Department Annual Summary, 1955, Colony and Protectorate of Kenya.

Interterritorial Organisation in East Africa, Colonial Paper No. 191 (London: H. M. S. O., 1945).

Interterritorial Organisation in East Africa Rev. Proposals Colonial Paper No. 210 (London: H. M. S. O., March 5, 1947).

For further discussion on "Closer Union" of East Africa, the following sources are very important: Cmd. 2904, 1927; Cmd. 3378, 1929; 3573, 3574 of 1930. No. 184, 1931; No. 29, 1931; Col. No. 57, 1931; Cmd. 4141, 1932; Cmd. 4083, 1932; Cmd. 4182, 1932.

Kenya Education Annual Report, 1924.

Report of the Kenya Land Commission (1934), Cmd 4556.

Kenya Legislative Council Debates, April 16, 1947.

Official Gazette Supplement, Kenya, Vol. XLI, No. 9, Feb, 1939.

Parliamentary Debates (commands), July 14, 1933, Col. 1505.

The Report of the Social and Economic Progress of the People of Kenya Colony and Protectorate, 1938.

Report on Certain Questions in Kenya, Command 4093, 1932.

White Paper entitled "Indian in Kenya" Command No. 1922, 1923.

White Paper, Command 1509, 1921.

BOOKS

Altrincham, Lord. *Kenya's Opportunity: Memories, Hopes, and Ideas* (London: Faber & Faber, Ltd., 1955).

Anderson, J. E. *The Struggle for the Schools* (Nairobi: Longmans, 1970).

Anderson, John D. *East Africa in the Nineteenth and Twentieth Centuries* (London: Heinemann, 1972).

Apter, David E. *The Political Kingdom of Uganda* (New Jersey: Princeton Univ. Press, 1961).

Barnnet, D. L., and K. Njama. *Mau Mau from Within* (London: MacGibbon and Kee, 1966).

Bennett, George. *Kenya: A Political History—The Colonial Period* (London: Oxford University Press, 1963).

_____, and Carl Rosberg. *The Kenyatta Election: Kenya 1960–1961* (1961).

Blundell, Sir Michael. *So Rough a Wind* (London: Weidonfeld & Nicholson, 1964).

Bogonko, Sorobea N. *Kenya 1945–1963: A Study in African National Development* (Nairobi: Kenya Literature Bureau, 1980).

Brockway, Fenner. *African Journeys* (London: Victor Gollancz, 1955).

Buell, Raymond L. *Native Problem in Africa*, 2 Vols. (New York: Macmillan, 1928).

Cagnolo, Fr. C. *The Akikuyu* (Nyeri, Kenya: The Mission Printing School, 1933).

Campbell, Alexander. *The Heart of Africa* (New York: Alfred A. Knopf, 1954).

Carter, Gwendolen M., ed. *Politics in Africa: 7 Cases* (New York: Harcourt, Brace & World, 1966).

Church Harrison, R. J. *Modern Colonization* (London: Hutchinson's University Library, 1951).

Coupland, R. *East Africa and Its Invaders* (London: Oxford University Press, 1956).

Cox, Richard. *Kenyatta's Country* (New York: Frederick A. Praeger, 1965).

Crocker, W. R. *Self-Government for the Colonies* (London: Allen and Unwin, 1949).

Desai, Ram. *Christianity in Africa as Seen by Africans.* Article by Jomo Kenyatta (Denver: Alan Swallow, 1962).

Dilley, Marjorie Ruth. *British Policy in Kenya: A Colony* (New York: Barnes & Noble, 1966).

_____. *British Policy in Kenya Colony* (New York: Thomas Nelson & Sons, 1937).

_____. *British Policy in Kenya Colony* (New York: Barnes & Noble, 1968).

Eliot, Sir Charles. *The East Africa Protectorate* (London: Edward Arnold, 1906).

Fanon, Franz. *The Wretched of the Earth* (New York: Grove Press, 1968).

Farson, Negley. *Last Chance in Africa* (London, 1949).

Forrester, Marion W. *Kenya Today—Social Prerequisites for Economic Development* (Gravenhage: Mouton, 1962).

Furnivall, J. S. *Colonial Policy & Practice* (Cambridge University Press, 1948).

_____. *Netherlands India* (London, 1939).

Gatheru, R. Mugo. *Child of Two Worlds* (New York: Frederick A. Praeger, 1964).

Ghai, Dharam P. *Portrait of a Minority: Asians in East Africa* (Nairobi, 1965).

Gikonyo, Gucu G. *We Fought for Freedom* (Nairobi: East African Publishing House, 1979).

Gluckman, Max. *Custom and Conflict in Africa* (Oxford: Blackwell, 1955).

Green, Reginald H. *Economic Cooperation in Africa—Retrospect and Prospect* (London: Oxford, 1967).

_____, and Ann Seidman. *Unity or Poverty* (Baltimore: Penguin Books, 1968).

Gregory, J. W. *The Foundation of British East Africa* (London: H. Marshall, 1901).

Gunther, John. *Inside Africa* (New York: Harper and Brothers, 1955).

Hailey, Lord. *An African Survey* (London: Oxford University Press, 1938) (first edition).

_____. *An African Survey* (Rev. Ed.) (London: Oxford University Press, 1956).

_____. *Native Administration in the British African Territories* Part 1 (H.M.S.O., London Colonial Office, 1950).

Haines, C. Gove, ed. *Africa Today* (Baltimore: Johns Hopkins University Press, 1955).

Hance, William. *African Economic Development* (New York: Frederick A. Praeger, 1967).

Hazelwood, Arthur, ed. *African Integration and Disintegration* (London: Oxford University Press, 1967).

Henderson, Ian. *The Hunt for Kimathi* (London, 1958).

Hill, M. F. *The Dual Policy In Kenya* (Nakuru, Kenya Weekly News, 1944).

_____. *Permanent Way: The Story of the Kenya and Uganda Railway* (Nairobi: East African Railways and Harbours, 1950).

Hinden, Rita. *Local Government and the Colonies—A Report to the Fabian Colonial Bureau* (London: Allen & Unwin, 1950).

Hislop, F. D. *The Story of Kenya* (London: Oxford University Press, 1961).

Hobley, C. W. *Kenya: From Chartered Company to Crown Colony* (London: Witherby, 1929).

Hobson, J. A. *Imperialism* (New York: Macmillan, rev. ed., 1938).

Hodgkin, Thomas. *Nationalism in Colonial Africa* (London: Frederick Muller, 1956) (American Edition: New York University Press, 1957).

Huntingford, W. B. *The Southern Nilo-Hamites,* Part VIII (London: International African Institute, 1953).

Huxley, Elspeth. *A Thing to Love* (London, 1954).

_____. *White Man's Country: Lord Delamere and the Making of Kenya 1879–1931* (2 Vols.) (London: Chatto and Loindus, 1935).

_____, and Margery Perham. *Race and Politics in Kenya* (rev. ed.) (London: Faber & Faber, Ltd., 1956) (First Ed. 1943).

International Bank for Reconstruction and Development. *The Economic Development of Kenya* (Baltimore: John Hopkins Press, 1967).

Itote, Waruhiu (General China). *Mau Mau in Action* (Nairobi: Transafrica Book Distributors, 1979).

Jones, Carey N. S. *Anatomy of Uhuru* (New York: Frederick A. Praeger, 1966).

Karanja, Dr. F. H. "Kenya After Independence." *African Affairs* (London: Royal African Society & Oxford University Press, 1966).

Kariuki, Josiah Mwangi. *Mau Mau Detainee* (London: Oxford University Press, 1963).

Kenyatta, Jomo. *Facing Mount Kenya* (London: Secker & Warburg, 1938).

_____. *Harambee! The Prime Minister of Kenya's Speeches* (London: Oxford University Press, 1964).

_____. *Kenya—Land of Conflict* (Pan-African Series, Manchester & London, 1945).

King, K. J. Ph.d. thesis in the *Phelps Stokes Papers* (Edinburgh University, 1968).

King, Kenneth, and Ahmed Salim, eds. *Kenya Historical Biographies: Studies 2* (Nairobi: East African Publishing House, 1971).

Kipkorir, B. E., ed. *Biographical Essays on Imperialism and Collaboration in Colonial Kenya* (Nairobi: Kenya Literature Bureau, 1980).

Kirby, C. P. *East Africa* (London: Ernest Benn Ltd., Bouveris House, 1968).

Kitson, Major Frank, M.B.E., M.C. *Gangs and Counter-gangs* (London: Barrie and Rockliff, 1960).

Koinange, Mbiyu. *The People of Kenya Speak for Themselves* (Detroit: Kenya Public Fund, 1955).

Kraft, J. L. *Travels, Researches and Missionary Labours During an Eighteen Years' Residence in Eastern Africa* (London, 1860).

Leakey, L. S. B. *Defeating Mau Mau* (London, 1954).

_____. *Mau Mau and the Kikuyu* (London: Methuen, 1952).

Leys, Norman. *Colour Bar in British East Africa* (London: The Hogarth Press, 1941).

_____. *Kenya* (London: The Hogarth Press, 1924 and 1926).

_____. *A Last Chance in Kenya* (London: The Hogarth Press, 1931).

Lugard, Lord. *The Dual Mandate in British Tropical Africa* (London: Blackwood, 1929).

_____. *The Rise of Our East African Empires* (2 Vols.) (London: Frank Cass, 1893) (New Impression, 1968).

MacKay. *MacKay of Uganda—Biography by His Sister* (London: Hodder & Stoughton, 1890).

MacMillan, W. M. *Africa Emerges* (London: Penguin, 1949).

Maina, Paul. *Six Mau Mau Generals* (Nairobi: Gazelle Book Co., 1977).

Meinertzhagen, Colonel R. *Kenya Diary, 1901–1906* (London: Oliver and Boyd, 1957).

Mair, L. P. *Native Policies in Africa* (London: Routledge, 1936).

Mangat, J. S. *A History of the Asians in Africa* (Oxford University Press, 1969).

Marsh, Zoe, and C. W. Kingsworth. *An Introduction to the History of East Africa* (Cambridge University Press, 1957).

Mason, Mike. *Development and Disorder: A History of the Third World Since 1945* (Hanover and London: University of New England Press, 1997).

Maxon, Robert M. *Struggle for Kenya: The Loss and Reassertion of Imperial Initiative, 1912–1923* (New Jersey: Dickinson University Press, 1993).

Mboya, Tom. *Freedom and After* (London: Andre Deutsch, 1963).

_____. *The Kenya Question: An African Answer* (London: Fabian Colonial Bureau, 1956).

_____. *Tradition and Transition in East Africa* (ed. by P. H. Gulliver) (Berkeley & Los Angeles: University of California Press, 1969).

McDermott, P. *British East Africa, or IBEA: A History of the Formation and Work of the Imperial British East Africa Company* (London: Chapman & Hall, 1893).

McIntosh, B. G., ed. *Ngano: Nairobi Historical Studies* (Study I) (Nairobi: East African Publishing House, 1969).

Mitchell, Sir Philip. *African Afterthoughts* (London: Hutchinson, 1954).

Mungeam, G. H. *British Rule in Kenya, 1895–1912: The Establishment of Administration in the East Africa Protectorate* (London: Oxford University Press, 1966).

Muriuki, Godfrey. *A History of the Kikuyu, 1500–1900* (London & Nairobi: Oxford University Press, 1974).

Ngugi, James. *Cry Not, Child* (London: Heinemann, 1964).

Nyerere, Julius. *Freedom and Unity* (London: Oxford University Press, 1967).

Odinga, Oginga. *Not Yet Uhuru* (London: Heinemann, 1967).

Ogot, Bethwell A., ed. *Hadith 2* (Nairobi, East African Publishing House, 1970).

_____, ed. *Hadith 3* (Nairobi: East African Publishing House, 1971).

Ogot, B.A., and J. A. Kieran. *Zamani—A Survey of East Africa History* (London: East African Publishing House and Longmans, Green & Co., 1968).

_____, and William Ochieng. *Decolonization and Independence in Kenya: 1940–1988* (Athens: Ohio University Press, 1995).

Oldham, J. H. *New Hope in Africa* (London: Longmans, 1955).

Oliver, Roland C. *The Missionary Factor in East Africa* (London: Longmans Green, 1952 and 1965).

Ominde, S. H. *Land and Population Movements in Kenya* (Evanston, Ohio: Northwestern University Press, 1968).

Padmore, George. *Africa: Britain's Third Empire* (London: Dennis Dobson, 1948).

Parker, Dr. Mary, ed. *How Kenya Is Governed* (East African Literature Bureau, rev. ed., 1955).

Perham, Margery. *Colonial Governments* (London: Oxford University Press, 1950) (For Nuffield College).

_____, ed. *The Diaries of Lord Lugard* (London: Faber & Faber, 1959).

Peristiany, J. G. *The Social Institutions of the Kipsigis* (London: George Routledge & Sons, Ltd., 1939).

Pope Pius XI. *Pie XI et la Medicine aux Missions* (Catholic Missions, 1928).

Pratt, Professor. *America's Colonial Experiment* (New York: Prentice Hall, 1950).

Reusch, Richard. *History of East Africa* (Germany: Stuttgart, Evang. Missionsverlag Gmbh, 1954).

Robson, Peter. *Economic Integration in East Africa* (Evanston: Northwestern University Press, 1968).

Rooney, D. D., and E. Halladay. *The Building of Modern Africa* (London: George G. Harrap & Co., 1966).

Rosberg, Carl G., Jr., and John Nottingham. *The Myth of the "Mau Mau": Nationalism in Kenya* (New York: Frederick A. Praeger, 1966).

Ross, McGregor W. *Kenya from Within* (London: George Allen & Unwin, Ltd., 1927).

Rothchild, Donald, ed. *Politics of Integration* (Nairobi: East African Publishing House, 1968).

Routledge, S. K. *With a Prehistoric People: The Akikuyu of British East Africa* (London: Edward Arnold, Pub. to the Indian Office, 1910).

Sandgren, David P. *Christianity and the Kikuyu* (New York: Peter Lang Publishing, 1989).

Sigmund, Paul E. *The Ideologies of Developing Nations* (New York: F. A. Praeger, 1967).

Slade, Humphrey. *The Parliament of Kenya* (Nairobi: East African Pub. House, 1967).

Slade, Ruth. *Catholics and Protestants in the Congo* (London: Oxford University Press, 1968).

_____. *King Leopold's Congo* (London: Oxford University Press, 1962).

Smith, J. Stephen. *The History of the Alliance High School* (Nairobi: Heinemann Educational Books, 1973).

Stillman, Calvin W., ed. *Africa in the Modern World* (Chicago: University of Chicago Press, 1955).

Thomas, H. B., and R. Scott. *Uganda* (London: Oxford University Press, 1962).

Townsend, Mary Evelyn. *European Colonial Expansion Since 1871* (Chicago, Philadelphia, New York: J. B. Lippincott, 1941).

Wachanga, H. K. *The Swords of Kirinyaga*, edited by Robert Whittier (Nairobi, Kenya Literature Bureau, 1975).

Walker, Eric A. *Colonies* (Cambridge University Press, 1944).

Wamweya, J. *Freedom Fighter* (Nairobi: East African Publishing House, 1971).

Ward, W. E. F., and L. W. White. *East Africa: A Century of Change: 1870-1970* (New York: Africana Publishing Corporation, 1971).

Webster, J. B. *The African Churches Among the Yoruba, 1888-1902* (New York: Oxford University Press, 1965).

Welbourn, G. B. *East African Rebels* (London: SCM Press, 1961).

Wieschhoff, H. A. *Colonial Policies in Africa.* "African Handbook No. 5" (Philadelphia: University of Pennsylvania Press, 1944).

Wright, Martin. *The Development of the Legislative Council: Studies in Colonial Legislatures No. 1* (London: Faber & Faber, 1946).

JOURNALS

The Africa Bureau, *Reflections on the Report of the Royal Commission on East Africa 1953-1955* (London: Published under the auspices of the Africa Bureau, 65 Denison House, Vauxhall Bridge Road, S.W.1, 1956), pp. 7–9.

Africa Digest, May-June, 1957, Vol. IV, No. 6 (London).

Africa Digest, July-August, 1958, Vol. VI, No. 1 (London).

Africa Special Report, March 29, 1957, Vol. 2, No. 3 (Washington D.C.: African-American Institute, Inc.).

Africa Weekly, "Will Britain Help Build a Democracy in Kenya?" August 28, 1957, Vol. 11, No. 1 (New York).

African Affairs, Vol. 45, 1946 (London).

African Forum, Cooley, John K. "From Mau Mau to Missiles," 1966, Vol. 2, No. 1. (New York: American Society for African Culture).

American Political Science Review, Young, R., and Liebenow, J. G., Jr., "Survey of Background Material for the Study of Government in East Africa," March, 1954, Vol. 48, No. 1, pp. 187–203.

American Political Science Review, "Nationalism in Tropical Africa," June, 1954, Vol. 47, No. 2, pp. 404–426.

Christianity Today, Staples, John, "The Church's Need in Africa," Jan. 7, 1968.

Church Missionary Review, McGregor, A. W., "Kikuyu and Its People," Vol. 60, 1909, pp. 30–36.

East Africa and Rhodesia, Dec. 1945, Vol. 22, No. 1109 (London).

East Africa and Rhodesia, Jan. 1946, Vol. 22, No. 1111 (London), p. 451.

East Africa and Rhodesia, Jan. 24, 1946, Vol. 22, No. 1114 (London), pp. 523, 527.

East Africa and Rhodesia, Jan. 31, 1946, Vol. 22, No. 1115 (London), pp. 547–549.

East Africa and Rhodesia, Feb. 1946, Vol. 22, No. 1116 (London), pp. 571–577.

East Africa and Rhodesia, Feb. 1946, Vol. 22, No. 1118 (London), pp. 619–624.

East Africa and Rhodesia, Feb. 1946, Vol. 22, No. 1119 (London), p. 658.

East Africa and Rhodesia, March 14, 1946, Vol. 22, No. 1121 (London), pp. 691–697.
East Africa and Rhodesia, April 4, 1946, Vol. 22, No. 1124 (London), p. 778.
East Africa and Rhodesia, April 25, 1946, Vol. 22, No. 1127 (London), p. 846.
East Africa and Rhodesia, May 30, 1946, Vol. 22, No. 1132 (London), pp. 963–970.
East Africa and Rhodesia, June 20, 1946, Vol. 22, No. 1135 (London), p. 1062.
East Africa and Rhodesia, June 27, 1946, Vol. 22, No. 1136 (London), pp. 1074, 1084.
East Africa and Rhodesia, August 1, 1946, Vol. 22, No. 1141 (London), p. 1212.
East Africa and Rhodesia, March 13, 1947, Vol. 23, No. 1171 (London).
East Africa and Rhodesia, April 24, 1947, Vol. 23, No. 1177 (London), p. 851.
East Africa and Rhodesia, May 8, 1947, Vol. 23, No. 1179 (London), p. 902.
East Africa and Rhodesia, June 26, 1947, Vol. 23, No. 1186 (London), pp. 1010–1079.
Geographical Journal, Crawshay, R., "Kikuyu: Notes on the Country, People, Fauna and Flora," Vol. 20, 1902, pp. 24–49.
International African Institute, "Social Implications of Industrialization and Urbanization in Africa South of the Sahara." Prepared under the auspices of UNESCO (Paris, 1956).
Kenya Comment July 18, 1958, Vol. XIII, No. 29 (Nairobi), p. 14.
"Kenya's New Five Year Development Plan (1970–1974)" (Washington, D.C.: Embassy of the Republic of Kenya, 1970).
The Political Quarterly, Mair, Lucy, "East Africa," July-Sept., 1958, Vol. 29, No. 3 (London), pp. 279–288.
The Saturday Review of Literature, Kiano, Gikonyo Wa, "Mau Mau, An African View" May 2, 1953 (New York), p. 19.
Time, "Africanization or Exile" Feb. 17, 1967.
Transaction, "Social Science and Modern Society" 1972, No. 3.
Western Political Quarterly, "Coleman, James S., "Problem of Political Integration in Emergent Africa," March, 1955, Vol. 8, No. 1, pp. 44–57.

NEWSPAPERS

Africa Report (Washington, D.C.), October, 1967.
The Daily Mail (London), January 23, 1960.
East African Chronicle, 1922.
The East African Standard (Nairobi), January 11, 1919.
The East African Standard (Nairobi), November 20, 1920.
The East African Standard (Nairobi), May 27, 1921.
The East African Standard (Nairobi), June 7, 1921.
The East African Standard (Nairobi), June 10, 1921.
The East African Standard (Nairobi), July 22, 1921.
The East African Standard (Nairobi), December 15, 1921.
The East African Standard (Nairobi), June 2, 1923.
The East African Standard (Nairobi), December 14, 1945.
The East African Standard (Nairobi), August 8, 1947.
The Guardian (London), January 23, 1960.
Kenya Weekly News (Nakuru), Vol. XX, No. 1, 1946.
Kenya Weekly News (Nakuru), Vol. XXII, No. 14, 1948.
Kenya Weekly News (Nakuru), No. 1198, 1950.
The Leader (Nairobi), January 14, 1921.
The Leader (Nairobi), July 7, 1921.
The Leader (Nairobi), July 13, 1921.

The Leader (Nairobi), January 14, 1922.
The Leader (Nairobi), January 22, 1922.
The Leader (Nairobi), March 17, 1922.
The Leader (Nairobi), March 25, 1922.
The New York Times, Gordon, W. E. "Conditions in Kenya," a letter to the editor, May 6, 1954.
The Observer (London), January 24, 1960.
The Times (London), December 28, 1935.
The Times (London), January 19, 1960.
The Times (London), January 22, 1960.
The Times (London), January 24, 1960.
The Times (London), February 22, 1960.

PAMPHLETS

Askwith, Tom. "The Story of Kenya's Progress" (Nairobi: Eagle Press, 1953).
Newman, J. R. "The Ukamba Members Association Transafrica Historical Papers No. 3 (Nairobi: Transafrica Publishers, 1974).

MONOGRAPHS

Racial and Communal Tensions in East Africa (Nairobi: East Africa Publishing House, 1966).

Index